Lovecraft and Egypt:
A Closer Examination

Duncan Norris

That the works of Howard Phillips Lovecraft should intersect with the land, culture, and history of Egypt is a seemingly natural convergence. One of the oldest civilizations on Earth, Egypt is filled with ruined cities, sand-covered temples, and forgotten tombs, easily lending itself to an atmosphere tailor-made to a serious horror writer having an historical inclination. Likewise, the Egyptians' strong cultural fascination with the dead and the afterlife fits in perfectly with Lovecraft's leitmotifs of immortality and survival beyond death. Yet with the notable exception of "Under the Pyramids," famously ghostwritten for Harry Houdini and thus with its setting being outside Lovecraft's control, no lengthy part of any story takes place in Egypt. Neither are Lovecraft's usages tied to standard Egyptian tropes, such as the vengeful mummy or the tomb curse. This is hardly surprising, as Lovecraft deliberately avoided the use of the stereotypical conventions of the horror genre, even whilst deftly subverting them when they appear. Yet Lovecraft's literary connections to the land of Egypt are present in a variety of forms throughout the entire corpus of his work. This connection stretches from his very earliest writings as a pre-teen preparing a version of Egyptian myths for small children, sadly non-extant (Joshi, *I Am Providence* 41), to his final literary works. This minor but persistent connection to Egypt ultimately adds an interesting substratum to Lovecraft's writings, and the following survey will examine them.

Before beginning this analysis a few relevant facts about Egyptian history and cultural practices are in order. Egyptian history is divided successively by modern historians into the Predynastic and

Early Dynastic (or Archaic) Periods, followed by the Old, Middle, and New Kingdoms, with each Kingdom block followed sequentially by the appropriate First, Second, and Third Intermediate Period. These broad divisions are further broken down into various sequentially numbered Dynasties. The Archaic Period and Old Kingdom were the era of unification of the country under a single ruler, the time of the building of the Sphinx and the Great Pyramids, whilst the Middle Kingdom was the classical age of language and literature. The New Kingdom is the greatest epoch of Egyptian civilization, filled with still familiar names such Ramesses and Tut-Ankh-Amen. It also saw the creation of the Valley of the Kings mortuary complex, while many of the most famous temples date from this time. The Intermediate Periods were eras of unstable and fractured rule, generally with weak central government and foreign incursions common.

The Archaic Period, Three Kingdoms, and Intermediate Periods overall broadly constitute the era of classical Egyptian civilization. The Third Intermediate Period was followed by an Egyptian resurgence and then an immediate and continuing age of decline and increasing foreign rule, encompassed under the banner of the Late Period, which leads ultimately into the Greco-Roman Period. This final era was under the rulership of the Greek descendants of Alexander the Great's general Ptolemy (commonly called the Ptolemaic Period) until the defeat of Anthony and Cleopatra at Actium in 31 B.C.E., when the victorious Octavian (soon to be the Emperor Augustus) annexed the country into the Roman Empire as a province under his direct control.[1] Yet whilst almost all modern scholars use this model for dating in ancient Egypt, there is legitimate ongoing debating as to more specific dates prior to the Late Period, ranging from a few years' difference to almost a century between events in some chronologies. Equally there is a remarkable disunity of opinion concerning the boundaries between the broad divisions of the pre-Greco-Roman period, as for example, which dynasties belong in the Middle Kingdom rather than

---

1. This is not to imply that Egyptian history concluded with the Roman conquest. Rather, this admittedly arbitrary demarcation reflects the fact that the later Christian and Muslim eras make almost no impact, outside a single glancing reference in a revision work, upon HPL's writings.

THE LOVECRAFT ANNUAL

Edited by S. T. Joshi   No. 10 (2016)

Contents

Abbreviations used in the text and notes:

AT   *The Ancient Track* (Hippocampus Press, 2013)
CE   *Collected Essays* (Hippocampus Press, 2004–06; 5 vols.)
CF   *Collected Fiction* (Hippocampus Press; 2015–16; 4 vols.)
LL   *Lovecraft's Library: A Catalogue*, 3rd rev. ed. (Hippocampus Press, 2012)
SL   *Selected Letters* (Arkham House, 1965–76; 5 vols.)

Copyright © 2016 by Hippocampus Press

Published by Hippocampus Press, P.O. Box 641, New York, NY 10156
http://www.hippocampuspress.com

Cover illustration by Allen Koszowski. Hippocampus Press logo designed by Anastasia Damianakos. Cover design by Barbara Briggs Silbert.

Lovecraft material is used by permission of The Estate of H. P. Lovecraft; Lovecraft Holdings, LLC. The text and images in "Postcards to Jonathan E. Hoag" are used by permission of the John Hay Library, Brown University, Providence, R.I.

Lovecraft Annual is published once a year, in Fall. Articles and letters should be sent to the editor, S. T. Joshi, % Hippocampus Press, and must be accompanied by a self-addressed stamped envelope if return is desired. All reviews are assigned. Literary rights for articles and reviews will reside with *Lovecraft Annual* for one year after publication, whereupon they will revert to their respective authors. Payment is in contributor's copies.

ISSN 1935-6102
ISBN 978-1-61498-180-0

the Second Intermediate Period. So whilst overall there is a remarkable degree of continuity in Egyptian civilization and practises, there is scholarly disagreement about many particulars, and the sheer quantity of time involved means that many practices evolved, changed, and were adapted over many centuries. For example, the famed New Kingdom *Book of the Dead*, a document important to whoever could afford it for its invaluable help in the afterlife, grew out of the *Coffin Texts* of the nobility of the Middle Kingdom. These in turn evolved from the *Pyramid Texts*, exclusive to the royal family in the Old Kingdom. Hence there is a very wide scope in ascribing dates and religious and cultural practices to the ancient Egyptians.

The other important factor for the purpose of this examination is names, of both people and places. To give an idea of the complexities involved, at least as early as the Middle Kingdom Dynasties pharaohs had at least five separate names: a Horus Name, *Nebty* ("two ladies") Name referring to the two patron goddess of Upper and Lower Egypt, a Golden Horus Name, a Throne Name, and a Birth Name. For example, Tjemaa, Semenkh tawy, Iri meret netjeru, Kheper ka Ra, and Nakhtnebef are all names of the same Pharaoh, and there are no fewer than twenty-two variations on the hieroglyphic depictions of these five names. Yet modern historians commonly know him by his Hellenized name of Nectanebo I. Thus to this native plethora of names for Egyptian people, places, and gods come to us the alternative names given to them by foreigners (the quintessential Egyptian deity of Aset is actually most widely known by the Greek version of her name, Isis), or after being transliterated into other languages. Nor is such nomenclature uncommon, such as the case of Soris for Snefru, Ozymandias for Ramesses the Great (Ramesses II), or Rhampsinitos for Ramesses III. To add to the obfuscation, modern interpretations often have variant spellings of these names dependent on tradition, scholarly exactness, and the latest linguistic understanding. Further contributing to this confusion is that the ancient Egyptians used three different scripts (hieroglyphic, hieratic, and demotic) to express the same written language.

Places and monuments likewise have undergone numerous name changes. The modern city of Luxor was the New Kingdom capital of Thebes, but was titled Waset ("City of the *was*," the *was* being a specific type of scepter associated with authority and power), among a host of other designations, in Egyptian writings. The iconic Sphinx is known only by its Greek name: what the ancient Egyptians generally called it and sculptures like it is unknown, although the phrase *shesep ankh* ("living image") sometimes appears in conjunction with them. Even more confusingly, gods and goddesses from the Egyptian pantheon often have dozens of titles, appearances, and aspects, sometimes contradictory and often overlapping. For the purposes of consistency this examination shall use the names as written in Lovecraft's stories, and add appropriate details so as to clarify any important factors. As a final point, for the ancient Egyptians, being oriented to the flowing of the Nile to the Mediterranean Sea, Lower Egypt is in the north and Upper Egypt is in the south.

In terms of focus, this monograph is not seeking, in the main, to dig for underlying influences and solely thematic connections to Egypt, such as might be extrapolated from the hieroglyphic tombs of the extinct beings of "The Nameless City." Likewise, the carven face of Ngranek, described as having "long narrow eyes and long-lobed ears . . . [and] thin nose and pointed chin" (*CF* 2.129) in *The Dream-Quest of Unknown Kadath*, accurately mirrors a description of images of the heretic Pharaoh Akhenaton. Hence whilst these Egyptian underpinnings are certainly present, they are not the objective of this work. Neither are historical references to Egypt in works not intended for publication as literary pieces, such as letters, although these sources will be utilized to supplement the stories as appropriate. Rather, this examination is seeking for more concrete connections in terms of names, places, and more tangible and demonstrable links inside the stories and Lovecraftian mythopoeia themselves, in order to understand how Lovecraft used the reality and perception of Egyptian myth and history to add to his own creations.

There are many aspects of Lovecraft's stories that can be broadly linked to Egyptian themes, but for specific references beyond the simple mentioning of a name the first true usage occurs in the fairytale-like "The Cats of Ulthar" (1920). This tale, centering upon the dangerous aspects of the mystic nature of cats and the solution the villagers of Ulthar came up with to deal with the implicit threat, describes cats in the third sentence as "the soul of antique Aegyptus" (CF 1.151). Aegyptus is of course the Roman name of Egypt. It seems likely that Lovecraft is using this variant, in addition to his own love of both the Romans and of non-standard spelling, to emphasize the idea of Egypt being considered ancient even in the time of the Romans, not just from his own twentieth-century perspective. Mentioned in the same sentence is Meroë, a city on the Nile now in modern Sudan, but which was at various times part of Egypt. Meroë was particularly important to the Twenty-Fifth Dynasty, the final dynasts of the Third Intermediate Period and a general era that will reappear in Lovecraft's later work. The reference to the quintessentially Egyptian icon of the Sphinx (by which Lovecraft almost undeniably means the Great Sphinx at Gizeh;[2] we shall examine the famous statue in greater details in the section on "Under the Pyramids"), and of the cat antedating it unambiguously uses the idea of Egypt as a signpost for great age that will be utilized over and again in Lovecraft's work. This motif can be found as early as the poem "Nemesis" ("I was old when the Pharaohs first mounted / The jewel-deck'd throne by the Nile" [AT 47]), written nearly three years earlier on 1 November 1917, and was expressed again in a simple form in "Beyond the Wall of Sleep" (1919), the possessive entity declaring: "Next year I may be dwelling in the dark Egypt which you call ancient" (CF 1.83). In a nonfictional context, but clearly to the same point, Lovecraft's short essay concerning the Great War, "At the Root," comments on the innate savagery of human nature in that "the instincts that governed the Egyptians and Assyrians of old govern us as well" (CE 5.29).

The eponymous animals of "The Cats of Ulthar" were famously strongly revered in pharaonic Egypt, and cat mummies as votive offerings are found in hundreds of thousands of caches. The cat-headed goddess Bastet (or Bast) had a strong worship in Lower Egypt and had a particularly virile cult located at the city named in her honor, Bubastis.[3] Lovecraft invokes this city by name, and

---

2. Giza in modern usage.

3. Bubastis is the Greek name for the city. It was Per-Bast to the Egyptians and is

the temples to Bast by direct implication, in *The Dream-Quest of Unknown Kadath*. Indeed, the entire law that "no man may kill a cat" that bookends "The Cats of Ulthar" is reflected in Egyptian cultural practice as recorded by the Greek historian Diodorus Siculus. The author of the *Bibliotheca Historica* ("Historical Library") claimed that the sacredness of cats was so integral to Egyptian culture that, after a Roman soldier who accidentally killed a cat was murdered at the insistence of an angry mob of outraged locals, the mob went unpunished in deference to local custom and sensibilities (1.83).

The "caravan of strange wanderers" (*CF* 1.152) who appear in the third paragraph of "The Cats of Ulthar" are strongly implied to be the ancestors of the ancient Egyptians. The human-bodied, animal-headed images on their wagons are the classic theriocephalic depiction of Egyptians deities. All the individual animal-headed figures mentioned ("cats, hawks, rams, and lions" [*CF* 1.152]) have a correlation with known Egyptian gods and goddesses, although Egyptian deities are generally worshipped and displayed as triads or multiples thereof, with the noted exceptions of in more functional usages, such as the Four Sons of Horus who were the guardian gods of the four canopic jars that held a mummy's internal organs. Most likely the lion- and cat-headed figures correspond respectively to Sekhmet and Bastet, and although there are numerous other leonine Egyptian deities (such as Shesemtet, Tefnut, or Maahes), they are far more obscure than the two goddesses first named. More significantly, Lovecraft will eventually invoke Sekhmet and Bastet together by name in an amusing piece of doggerel composed in 1934 as the anthem for his Kappa Alpha Tau cat collective (Joshi, *I Am Providence* 887).

Paradoxically, this pairing of goddesses accidentally undermines the idea of the caravan of wanderers being the ancestral progenitors of the Egyptians, from a factual historic standpoint. To vastly simplify a complex situation, Bast and Sekhmet were originally both lion-headed protective regional goddesses, correspondingly worshipped separately in Lower and Upper Egypt. After Egyptian unification, rather than an amalgamation or syncretism as hap-

Tell-Basta in modern Arabic.

pened with many other Egyptian deities, Sekhmet largely retained her iconography whilst Bast instead evolved after 1000 B.C.E. in depictions as the cat goddess Bastet, probably reflecting the increasingly important role of domestic cats in reducing food-despoiling vermin as urban pest control. Thus Bastet and Sekhmet would in all probability never have appeared together prior to the unification of Egypt under a single ruler. Of the other figures on the wagons, Amon-Ra and Khnum both had depictions using a ram's head, whilst the ubiquitous deity Horus, usually depicted as a falcon, was also sometimes depicted as a hawk. This hawk depiction was also typically true of Nephthys, a goddess associated with the dead, to whom we will return later. Likewise in the story the caravan leader "wore a head-dress with two horns and a curious disc betwixt the horns" (CF 1.152), which corresponds precisely with the headdress in depictions of the goddess Hathor. Both Horus and Hathor, or deities related to them and their aspects, appear on the famed Narmer Palette.

The Narmer Palette seems like an object unearthed in a Lovecraft story, depicting as it does central motifs of a king in the act of a ritual killing on one side and a hybrid monster on the reverse. Over five millennia old and yet in pristine condition, it was unearthed by archaeologists in the very late nineteenth century. It is commonly interpreted to depict the crucial moment of the unification of Upper and Lower Egypt under the king Narmer, and this singular and arresting image of Narmer defeating his foes was to be copied by Pharaohs throughout Egyptian history. The importance of the Narmer Palate to Lovecraft becomes apparent with the naming of the orphan boy of the strange wanderers in "The Cats of Ulthar" as Menes, the character who goes on to be the protagonist of the story. Menes is the traditional name for the Pharaoh who united Egypt and founded the First Dynasty, and most scholars agree that Narmer and Menes are likely the same individual. The prayer of the young boy Menes as "he stretched out his arms toward the sun" (CF 1.153) likewise connects directly with Egyptian veneration of the solar disk and its rays.

However, it must be noted that there is an alternative explanation concerning the use of the name Menes. The works of Lord Dunsany heavily influence "The Cats of Ulthar." This is immediately notable in such Dunsanian signatures as its short length, combination of real-world and fantastical imagery (what ancient fairytale village has a notary and coroner?), and ambiguous moral and didactic tones. Indeed, the story would not sit amiss betwixt "The Horde of the Gibbelins" and "How Nuth Would Have Practised His Art upon the Gnoles" in Dunsany's *The Book of Wonder* (1912). Thus it is possible that the name Menes was suggested to Lovecraft by the central figure of Lord Dunsany's *King Argimēnēs and the Unknown Warrior*, published as part of *Five Plays* in 1914. This short play, about the uprising of the enslaved King Argimenes of Ithara against the tyrant King Darniak, is deliberately riffing on names familiar to anyone who has read the classical works and history of the ancient Mediterranean. These include such connections as King Darius of Persia, Ithaca, home of Odysseus, Argives (a poetical term for Greeks), and, of course, Menes. Furthermore, a succinct summary of the Osirian myth of his betrayal and return is offered in the lines "Once an enemy cast Illuriel into the river and overthrew the dynasty, but a fisherman found him again and set him up, and the enemy was driven out and the dynasty returned" (Dunsany, *Five Plays* 73).

Dunsany was certainly a huge influence on Lovecraft in this period of his writing, by his own admission (*SL* 2.277): as but one example it is tempting to see a connection between the "dark-green idol" of Illuriel (*Five Plays* 77, 83) in the play and the "sea-green stone idol" of Bokrug in "The Doom That Came to Sarnath." Yet ultimately all this remains speculative concerning the crucial usage of the name of the orphan boy and his small black kitten. Anyone who has made even a cursory study of Egyptian history, and we know Lovecraft was rewriting their myths as a very young child, will almost certainly come across the name Menes. If Lovecraft was prompted to remembrance or imitation by this Dunsany play, it seems that Dunsany was himself deliberately invoking this famous name. So in either case the Egyptian connection seems to be a valid one, and the chances of Lovecraft choosing the name from the Dunsany story coincidentally rather than knowingly, given the other patent Egyptian motifs in the short tale, seem remote. Overall this mixture of blatant and subtle Egyptological lore and references in "The Cats of Ulthar" gives the short and suitably mysterious tale a more superior depth than its brevity might otherwise warrant, and is a great foreshadowing of Lovecraft's use of this technique in his later masterworks.

The mention of Atlantis in "The Temple" (1920), the fabled lost land whose existence Plato ascribes to information coming to him (via several intervening parties) from an Egyptian priest (Plato, *Timaeus* 21–25), could be seen as a reference to Egypt. However, the entire character of the story is rather patent in its Hellenic undertones as explanation, and the ruined submerged city "imparts an impression of terrible antiquity, as though it were the remotest rather than the immediate ancestor of Greek art" (*CF* 1.165). Yet Egyptian civilization is again used tangentially to ascribe the city a fabulous age, given that it existed according to the narrator at a time when "the Nile flowed unwatched to the sea" (*CF* 1.166). Egypt has a demonstrably unique and developed culture as early as the fourth millennium B.C.E. and knew human habitation from the Paleolithic Era. As mentioned earlier, this usage of ancient Egypt to give a reference point to prehistoric ruins of great age is a motif that Lovecraft will return to on multiple occasions.

The lesser-known "Poetry and the Gods," written in the same year as "The Temple" and in collaboration with Anna Helen Crofts, is a true Lovecraftian oddity, being his only genuine piece of romantic fiction. Whilst the story drips, possibly even drowns, in Greek mythology and literary allusions, Egypt does gain a tantalizing mention in this context, with the author proclaiming "there came a sound in the wind blowing from far Egypt, where at night Aurora mourns by the Nile for her slain son Memnon" (*CF* 4.29). Aurora was the Roman name for the personification of the dawn whom the Greeks called Eos, although Lovecraft is almost certainly mixing the mythologies in this particular story due to Aurora's noted associations with erotic poetry. Incidentally, this myth Lovecraft refers to is not as obscure as the average person might assume. The head of a man in the lap of a woman in Greek artistic usage in indicative of his being dead, and the image of the goddess of dawn cradling her dead son on her lap is the archetypal image that informed the later Christian *Pietà*. However, other than the detail of locale the mythology behind this story is purely Greek, although we will examine Memnon again in greater detail in "The Nameless City."

Nyarlathotep, first appearing in the story/dream transcription of the same name, deserves an especial consideration. Lovecraft recorded in his correspondence to Rheinhart Kleiner on 14 December 1920 a vivid dream in which the name occurred. In this dream his friend Samuel Loveman wrote the name Nyarlathotep in a letter and strongly advised Lovecraft to see this person (*SL* 1.160–62). The name Nyarlathotep, like that of Abdul Alhazred, is etymologically false for the culture from which it is supposed to originate, yet close enough in aspects to invoke them. The letter *l*, for example, was introduced to the Egyptian alphabet by the Greeks relatively late in its development. Lovecraft was fond of this type of pseudo-etymological indulgence, and in a fake genealogy in a 1927 letter gives one his own ancestors as an Egyptian priest with the very recognizable name of Ra-ankh-Khamses (*SL* 2.204). Robert M. Price has speculated, with distinct plausibility, that Lovecraft subconsciously created the word Nyarlathotep in his dream out of the names of Alhireth-Hotep and Mynarthitep from the works of Lord Dunsany (Price, "Lovecraft's 'Artificial Mythology'" 252). However, it is equally likely that there are other sources of inspiration in Egyptian history, such as one of the first authors in human history, Ptahhotep ("peace of Ptah" or "Ptah is pleased, happy, satisfied"), or the far better-known Imhotep ("he who comes in peace, is at peace"). The latter is still justly famous as a physician and the architect of the original pyramid at Sakkarah[4] and, to modern horror fans, as the titular animate mummy in both the 1930s and 1999/2000s film series.

Hotep (technically *htp*, as Egyptian writings omit the vowels) is a frequently appearing Egyptian word in both in general writing and in names. Commonly it is given a meaning of "peace," "offerings," or "satisfaction." It appears as a hieroglyph in the form of an altar/offering table.

htp as a hieroglyph

4. Saqqara in modern usage.

However, these translation renderings do not properly convey the ideas of usage to the modern reader. English is an unusual language in the large number of synonyms it includes. Most other languages, including ancient Egyptian, utilize the reverse principle of a single word having a multitude of meanings. *Htp* appears literally dozens of times in words and situations associated with offerings connected with the dead, who played such an important part in ancient Egyptian thought and practice. The peace and satisfaction interpretations of *htp* all commonly align toward this idea of offering, such as in *dbht htp* ("funerary meal, altar, offering table, food needs"), *sxt-htp* ("food box [in the Hereafter]"), or *htp-dj-nswt* ("funerary offerings"). There is less certain evidence that the word evolved from an earlier meaning of "to hunt, to slaughter" and further back from a root word for "cut, slice, and burn." Its later understanding as sacrifice and offering certainly give validity to these assertions. Overall it is uncertain if, as well as extremely unlikely that, Lovecraft knew enough serious Egyptology to craft such a name in a dream as laden with meaning as Nyarlathotep, but it is an interesting happenstance whatever the cause.

That Lovecraft recognized the powerful literary value of the name Nyarlathotep, sometimes divorced from its Egyptian origins and other times explicitly reconnected, can be judged by the fact that Nyarlathotep is the most widely reoccurring character in his work. As a result, this monograph will not espouse every mention of Nyarlathotep as an Egyptian reference but will largely confine itself to references wherein they are explicitly connected. An argument could be made that, for example, the alien Mi-Go in "The Whisperer in Darkness" who invoke his name do so because Nyarlathotep is best known in our terrestrial sphere in this incarnation. However, this speculation, while interesting, is largely abstruse and conjectural and thus is not relevant to central premise of Lovecraft and Egypt.

As to the story "Nyarlathotep," the eponymous figure's actual connection to the land of the pyramids is surprisingly scant, in term of verbiage, although in typical Lovecraftian fashion deep in implication. We are told that he "came out of Egypt" and "was of the old native blood and looked like a Pharaoh" (*CF* 1.203). Lovecraft uses the term *fellahin* in the next line and, although at base it is simply a Middle Eastern term for peasant/farmer/agricultural worker, it was noted by scholars as a class in Egypt that they have a distinct continuity with the practices and beliefs of their distant ancestors. Whilst historically the leaders of Egypt frequently and commonly changed and were eventually from extra-Egyptians sources, the peasantry remained largely native. Significantly, the *fellahin* are the ones who knelt when they saw Nyarlathotep "yet could not say why" (*CF* 1.203).

In his final connection to Egypt in the story Lovecraft writes that Nyarlathotep "had risen out of the blackness of twenty-seven centuries" (*CF* 1.203). Doing a simple count of the numbers of centuries would thus seem to place Nyarlathotep in the seventh century B.C.E., from around the time of the Twenty-Sixth Dynasty at the start of the Late Period. Known to modern historians as the Saites from their new capital of Sais, this was the last great native Pharaonic dynasty to rule Egypt. A more mathematical approach (the current date at time of writing, 1920, minus 2700 years) places Nyarlathotep approximately a century earlier in the late portion of the Third Intermediate Period. However, these Third Intermediate Period dynasties were largely composed of foreigners and, as such, given Nyarlathotep's physical description, the Saite Dynasty seems a more likely origin. In either case this is roughly the era when Egyptian history becomes able to be dated with a far greater exactness not possible with earlier times, the last period in which speculations can be applied without historians being more readily able to swing against them the hammer of scholarly certainty. However, in the tale nothing about Nyarlathotep's behaviors and belief system connects him to Egypt. He is very much an evil of his own making. Lovecraft would later effectively distill and rewrite "Nyarlathotep" as sonnet XXI of his poem *Fungi from Yuggoth* almost a decade later, but add nothing more in that piece to the Egyptian aspect of this character.

There is a brief but tantalizing, obscure, and possibly irrelevant Egyptian reference in "The Picture in the House" (1920). The "catacombs of Ptolemais" mentioned as hunted by "searchers after horror" (*CF* 1.206) (a particular large and viable group in the Lovecraftian universe, one must assume) are most likely an homage to Edgar Allan Poe's usage of the same term in his lesser-known short tale "Shadow—A Parable." The passage whence the term emerges is certainly a dark one: "And the shadow answered, 'I am SHADOW, and my dwelling is near to the Catacombs of Ptolemais, and hard by those dim plains of Helusion which border upon the foul Charonian canal'" (191). Certainly it is well suited thematically to the dark hints of murderous anthropophagy as a means to immortality, which form a central focus of the tale. Lovecraft's writings at this time still exhibited a particularly strong influence from Poe. In the nesting doll of influences it appears that Poe in turn took his description from Jacob Bryant's *New System: or an Analysis of Antient Mythology* (see Poe 191n9).

It is less likely that the passage in the Lovecraft story refers directly to one of the historical cities named for the Ptolemaic Pharaohs of Egypt, of which there are no fewer than five different locations sharing the appellation, as none of these are noted for their catacombs. Eminent Lovecraft scholar S. T. Joshi proffers the Ptolemais in modern Libya as the referred-to locale, observing that although it has no catacombs it does have a "huge Hellenistic tower-tomb" (Lovecraft, *Call of Cthulhu* 34n1). In a dissenting opinion Leslie S. Klinger considers the phrase to be referring to Ptolemais Euergetis in the Faiyum Oasis (Lovecraft, *New Annotated H. P. Lovecraft* 35–36n2). This ancient city has undergone many name changes: it was originally known to the Egyptians as Shedyt and as Crocodilopolis to the pre-Ptolemaic Greeks. It is distinguished for its once-huge mortuary temple, incorrectly called a labyrinth by Herodotus (2.148), although this edifice was largely pillaged to destruction in Ptolemaic times. The region does contain an archaeologically significant necropolis, but necropoleis are hardly a rare feature in Egypt.

It is worth noting in passing that native Egyptian civilization never really developed catacombs in the commonly understood sense of a shared subterranean cemetery along the model so famous in Rome. The sacred dead of Egypt, whilst certainly grouped together and often clustered near a central royal tomb complex, were inhumed in sepulchers along the lines of differentiated hypogea[5] and have distinct individual or family tombs. It is animal

---

5. A Greek term from the combination of hypo ("under") and Gaia ("Mother

necropoleis, such as the animal mummies of the Ibis Galleries and Serapeum at Sakkarah wherein the bodies of the Apis bulls were interred, that are more truly fitting of the catacomb descriptor. However, this conflation with catacombs is partially misleading, as the Apis bull was buried only with others of its kind, held a unique divine position, and was only replaced after its death by a perceived identical (and possibly reincarnated, although this is a controversial theory) successor, thus making the Serapeum to some extent the tomb of a single being. Likewise, the Ibis Galleries and their ilk are of votive offerings, rather than burials *per se.*

Yet in the second century C.E., during the Roman period, an underground communal tomb and temple complex was created under the port city of Alexandria, known today as the Catacombs of Kom el Shoqafa ("Mound of Shards"). The name refers to the broken pottery found at the site. In ancient times mourners would go and hold feast with the dead on special occasions, and the cutlery and dishware used on such occasional was generally discarded afterwards. In these catacombs the fusion of Pharaonic, Greek, and Imperial Roman influences, such as a figure of the god Anubis in Greek garb and posed next to a Roman style statue, is certainly very eerie and striking. Although it stretches credulity to assert definitively that Lovecraft meant to refer to these catacombs, rediscovered some twenty years before the story was written, it is certainly possible. As Alexandria was founded by the most famous of Greeks whose name it bears and was the chief city of the Ptolemaic Dynasty, it may be a conflation of these ideas of these catacombs in the chief city of the Ptolemies and Ptolemais that underlies the sort of imagery Lovecraft had in mind when using the term "catacombs of Ptolemais" in such a context. He utilized a similar metaphoric usage in the closing passage of his essay "Supernatural Horror in Literature," declaring: "Who shall declare the dark theme a positive handicap? Radiant with beauty, the Cup of the Ptolemies was carven of onyx" (*CE* 2.125). Lovecraft will mention catacombs as a haunt of ghouls in another more specific Egyptian context again in "The Outsider" (1921), as the location of

Earth"), literally meaning "underground" but used in modern context for underground tombs or temples. The singular is variously spelt hypogaeum or hypogenum.

Egypt's "dead and abysmal pharaonic heart" (*CF* 1.435) in "Under the Pyramids," and claimed in a letter to Clark Ashton Smith commenting on his memory aid document, which was later published as the "History of the 'Necronomicon,'" that Abdul Alhazred had spent time in "Memphis's catacombs"(*SL* 2.201), although the subsequent published document reads only as amidst the "subterranean secrets of Memphis" (*CF* 2.405).

Egypt comes up equally tangentially in "The Nameless City," used in the same manner as in "The Temple" to establish a baseline for the great age of another ruin. The oddly eponymous yet nameless city is described as "this great-grandmother of the eldest pyramid," a ruin "before the first stones of Memphis were laid," and which "had seemingly risen to a higher order than those immeasurably later civilizations of Egypt and Chaldaea,"[6] and was a "place too old for Egypt and Meroë to remember" (*CF* 1.232). Memphis, located approximately twenty kilometers south of modern Cairo, was the capital of Egypt during the Old Kingdom and founded according to legend by Menes, whom we have already encountered.

A further Egyptian reference is to a sound greeting the sun "as Memnon hails it from the banks of the Nile" (*CF* 1.232). "The Nameless City" is one of a minority of stories in which Lovecraft repeated sentences inside the narrative precisely to give especial emphasis, deserves further explanation. Memnon refers to the Colossi of Memnon, two huge but badly disfigured statues still extant outside the city of Thebes.[7] Despite the name, they are actually twin statues of Amenhotep III and originally stood at the entrance of his mortuary temple. When constructed this edifice, or rather related edifices, were bigger than the famed temple complex at Karnak, which in time grew to be the largest of its kind on Earth down to the present day. The Colossi were given their current appellation by the later arriving Greeks, who named them after the legendary figure of the Trojan War, Memnon. This designation of the Colossi was likely due to the connections of

---

6. Commonly spelt Chaldea but known to the Assyrians as Kaldu, as Babylonian Kasdu, and Kasddim in Hebrew.

7. Modern Luxor as previously noted.

Memnon in post-Homeric traditions to Ethiopia (to the Greeks this vague geographic term could be construed as the Upper Nile as well as any Sub-Saharan African location) and the well-attested tales of the northern statue having taken to emitting sounds around the dawn. Significantly, Memnon was the son of Tithonus and Eos, goddess of the dawn mentioned in "Poetry and the Gods" under her Roman name, making him the "son of the Dawn." These mysterious sounds apparently uttered by the statues drew many pilgrims, including the Roman Emperors Hadrian and Septimius Severus, and were believed to be a particularly efficacious oracle. This oracular noise appears to have been caused by expansion and contraction of the rock, or the moisture or cool air trapped inside it, with temperature changes at sunrise. These noises, described by Pausanias as like "that of a harp or lyre when a string has been broken" (*Description of Greece* 1.42.3) and Strabo as "as of a slight blow" (*Geography* 17.1.46), began after the statue was damaged in an earthquake, and later disappeared in antiquity after repair work was undertaken. It is to this sound that Lovecraft is making allusions in his tale.

"The Outsider," Lovecraft's great homage to Poe, is also the first to deal with Egypt as a location, rather than as a reference to things of, and places in, Egypt. The fleeing and disillusioned protagonist of the tale (it is difficult to call a ghoul a hero, no matter the literal literary meaning), unable to make his way back to his originating lair, finds his way to this ancient land of tombs as a substitute. He spends his time "by day amongst the catacombs of Nephren-Ka in the sealed and unknown valley of Hadoth by the Nile. I know that light is not for me, save that of the moon over the rock tombs of Neb, nor any gaiety save the unnamed feasts of Nitokris[8] beneath the Great Pyramid" (*CF* 1.272). This is a classic Lovecraftian mix of truth and fiction that makes his work so vibrant with plausibility. First we shall attend to the factual aspects of the passage, although the Great Pyramid, while surely needing no introduction, will be dealt with at length in "Under the Pyramids." Nitokris in an interesting figure, and the original account of her in Herodotus (2.100) is worth quoting in full:

---

8. Also commonly spelled Nitocris.

. . . and the name of the woman who reigned was the same as that of the Babylonian queen, namely Nitocris. Of her they said that desiring to take vengeance for her brother, whom the Egyptians had slain when he was their king and then, after having slain him, had given his kingdom to her,—desiring, I say, to take vengeance for him, she destroyed by craft many of the Egyptians. For she caused to be constructed a very large chamber under ground, and making as though she would handsel it but in her mind devising other things, she invited those of the Egyptians whom she knew to have had most part in the murder, and gave a great banquet. Then while they were feasting, she let in the river upon them by a secret conduit of large size. Of her they told no more than this, except that, when this had been accomplished, she threw herself into a room full of embers, in order that she might escape vengeance.

Even a person only casually familiar with Egyptian practices might wonder at the ease with which a woman had assumed the position of Pharaoh. There was an almost insurmountable bias toward male rulership in Egypt. Despite this, there are several occurrences of women ascending to power, such as Sobeknerferu and Nefertiti, though the most famous and successful was probably Hatshepsut, whose restored mortuary temple is directly outside the entrance to the Valley of the Kings. However, this unusual turn toward matriarchal rule hardly seems likely to be tolerated and encouraged by people who had just murdered a male Pharaoh they disapproved of. Likewise the idea of Nitokris immolating herself alive, which would destroy her corpse and thus her chances at the afterlife, seems far-fetched behavior for any Egyptian. The only other sources for Nitokris, absent any inscriptions or statues, are the *Aegyptiaca* ("History of Egypt") by Manetho written in the third century B.C.E., and the *Turin King List*, which dates from the reign of Ramesses the Great. Manetho's claims that Nitokris was the builder of the Third Pyramid at Gizeh cast serious doubts upon his accuracy (it was actually built by the Fourth-Dynasty Pharaoh Menkaure), whilst the previous corroborating section of the *Turin King List* was recently shown to have been mistakenly added to the wrong section in reconstructing the papyrus. Thus it will come as no surprise that modern scholars consider Nitokris entirely mythical, the result of scribal misunderstandings and copying errors, although she was considered to be historical until well after the time of Lovecraft's death.

Whilst there are other genuine figures named Nitokris in later Egyptian history, there is no doubt that Lovecraft is referring here to the queen so rudely dethroned by historians. The reference to the "unnamed feasts" solidifies the connection, although it seems likely that Lovecraft was brought to a greater awareness of her by attending a reading of a play entitled *The Queen's Enemies* (*SL* 1.91–92). Its author, Lord Dunsany, who as noted was a favorite of Lovecraft, was publicly touring and reading his own work, and the experience cannot have failed to make a great impression upon his American admirer. This short play is a dramatization of the events related anecdotally by Herodotus, and the double meaning of the feast is the sacrifice of the heroine's enemies to an anthropomorphized Nile. As expressed in such lines such as "for it is not the meat of beasts only. I have slaves for you and princes and a King" (Dunsany, *Queen's Enemies* 38), the very river takes on an aura of cannibal intent. This influence can be seen in the unnamed feast of ghouls Lovecraft hints at here and which he will develop more fully in "Under the Pyramids."

Neb presents us with a curious dilemma. It is entirely possible that it is simply a complete Lovecraft invention, but this seems unlikely for a number of reasons. It is a proper Egyptian word, conveying a similar idea to the English word *lord*, but with dual meanings connecting with obedience and prostration before a god or ruler or of unity under the same. It was in common use as part of Egyptian names such as Nebnefer, who was priest of Sobek from the reign of the aforementioned Amenhotep III. Lovecraft himself owned an art and history book entitled *The Tomb of Perneb* (*LL* 646). The book is actually an accompaniment to the eponymous exhibition of the entire structure, which was dismantled and reconstructed inside the Metropolitan Museum of New York. The tomb is (unsurprisingly) that of the titular Perneb, a court official from the Fifth Dynasty. It was rediscovered in 1907 and eventually purchased for the museum from the Egyptian authorities by philanthropist Edward Harkness in 1913. Knowing all this, Lovecraft may simply have chosen the second syllable from Perneb for an Egyptian effect. However, it is worth noting that the name of the previously mentioned goddess Nephthys, who was associated with death and funerary aspects, is the Greek version of her name: the Egyptians knew her as Nebthet. As the wife of the infamous Set and mother to Anubis, the god of embalming with his (to a modern reader) eerie jackal-headed representation, it seems at least possible that the Neb mentioned in a line concerning rock tombs refers obliquely to her.

Nephren-Ka is another imitation Egyptian coinage by Lovecraft. Unlike Nyarlathotep, it is more etymologically sound but ultimately nonsensical, unless we accept that Nephren-Ka is female. This is not as incongruous as it might seem. At least one female ruler in Egypt, Hatshepsut, did so in the aspect of a male Pharaoh, much as Jadwiga of Poland was a female king elected in that nation in the fourteenth century, and official images show Hatshepsut wearing the traditional symbolic beard of the pharaoh. *Neph* means something akin to "mistress" or "lady" in the sense of being a female in charge, whilst *ren* is approximately understood as one's true name as the foundation of the individual, one of the five parts of the soul as envisioned by Egyptian religious thought. The *ka* is another very Egyptian concept that has no analogue in modern theological thinking, although for completeness it should be noted that it is also the name of a legendary pre-dynastic Egyptian ruler. One's *ka* is a spiritual and immortal part of oneself that advised and guided the living person and took care of the *ba*, more analogous to the modern Western conception of the soul, after death. It is the *ka* that returns to the tomb to inhabit the mummy or the replica *ka* statue, and it gains nourishment by ingesting the spiritual portion of food offerings made to it. If a *ka* was not so nourished it could make limited ventures forth from the tomb by night to seek provender itself, commonly in the unlovely form of excrement, although there are implications that it could drink the blood of the living. To the unquestionably fictional Hadoth there is little that can be noted, save that its aspect as "a sealed and unknown valley by the Nile" conjures parallels with the Valley of the Kings that are probably intentional.

"The Hound" (1922), a story that like "Herbert West—Reanimator" is overwritten to the edge of parody, describes the grave-robbed amulet connected with the monster of the title as an "oddly conventionalised figure of a crouching winged hound, or sphinx with a semi-canine face, and was exquisitely carved in antique Oriental fashion from a small piece of green jade" (CF 1.343). However, despite the mention of the Sphinx, there is no definitive connection to Egypt. The sphinx was actually a mythological monster of the Greeks, and unlike the Egyptians whose statuary's naming rights they arrogated to themselves, the Hellenes gave the creature wings. The decidedly un-Egyptian material of jade gives it a further distance, as does the reference to the Orient, where sphinxes are still present in temples in the modern day.

"The Rats in the Walls" (1923), whilst an excellent story steeped in historical reference, has but glancing references to Egypt. The protagonist describes his infamously named cat racing past "like a winged Egyptian god" (CF 1.395). This metaphor seems oddly out of place, given that most Egyptian gods do not have wings, those that do are most often female, and none of these deities are particularly associated with speed. It is possible, however, that Lovecraft subtly seeks to evoke Egypt before reintroducing the otherwise under-described "mad faceless god" (CF 1.395) Nyarlathotep, who at the time of writing had only appeared in his eponymous prose-poem in which he was directly connected with Egypt. The ancient land of the Nile again gets a glancing reference to evoke an idea of great epochs of time in "The Festival" with the beautifully cadenced line "It was the Yuletide, that men call Christmas though they know in their hearts it is older than Bethlehem and Babylon, older than Memphis and mankind" (CF 1.406). It is tempting to see a connection with Egypt as portrayed in "Under the Pyramids" in the passage from the *Necronomicon* about "the nethermost caverns" (CF 1.417) that closes the tale, but such an assertion both lacks proof and is far too open to alternative interpretation for any absolute scholarly credibility. As concerns "Under the Pyramids," it must be noted that, geographically, Gizeh and the Lovecraftian catacomb-warrened Memphis are certainly part of the same area, or even the same overarching site, depending on how one chooses to define the boundaries, and therefore it is this tale that will be examined next.

In a curious confluence of characters, Lovecraft's (paradoxically) most celebrated piece of ghostwriting, "Under the Pyramids," was done for the famed escapologist Harry Houdini. It is also Lovecraft's only sustained piece set in Egypt, and as such deserves particularly thorough attention. Commissioned by *Weird Tales* owner J. C. Henneberger for a pre-publication $100 payment ("ONE HUNDRED BERRIES! No spoofin'" [*SL* 1.313]), it was based upon an allegedly true story told by Houdini, as related internally in the narrative. "Allegedly" here is used advisedly. Lovecraft himself wrote in letters to Frank Belknap Long that he had natural doubts as to the authenticity of the narrative, specifically stating, "I judge that the magician tries to pass off these Munchausens as real adventures" (*SL* 1.312), and following up in another letter that "my Egyptian research at the library proved indubitably that Houdini's story is *all* a fake" (*SL* 1.317; emphasis in original). Initially conceived as a shared-author byline, Lovecraft's name was cut as potentially confusing in a first-person narrative, and the story was originally published as the cover story for the first anniversary edition of *Weird Tales* published in May–June–July 1924 under the title "Imprisoned with the Pharaohs."

However, "Imprisoned with the Pharaohs" was not the original title. Lovecraft lost the typescript of the story en route to New York and placed an advertisement in the *Providence Journal*, vainly as it transpired, to see if anyone had found the typescript, titled "Under the Pyramids." He retyped the entire story following his wedding and on his honeymoon, a patent presage that this marriage was to be neither a typical nor a happy one. "Under the Pyramids" itself is both enjoyable and rather simplistic, dealing with Houdini's sinister trials of his 'magic' against the olden magic of Egypt, as arranged by the seemingly immortal Pharaoh Khephren.[9] Lovecraft doesn't appear to have initially held Houdini in too high a regard, as he writes of him in a playful yet derogatory manner in his letters, once calling him both a "bimbo" and "boob" within five words of each other (*SL* 1.312). This may explain why the Houdini in the story has a Lovecraft protagonist record total of three unmanly faints. However, Lovecraft, after later meeting Houdini in person and eventually undertaking talks about a book collabora-

---

9. Known variously as Khafra, Khafre, Khefren, and Chephren.

tion to have been entitled *The Cancer of Superstition,*[10] seems to have mellowed in his opinion of the famous escapologist and wrote to him warmly. Thus it is but another note of sadness that Houdini's untimely death in 1926 forestalled any further developments in both of these areas.

The exact reason for Lovecraft's initial dislike of Houdini is unknown. It may have resulted from Lovecraft's low opinion of the other work published under Houdini's name in *Weird Tales*, Houdini's easy assumption of cover privileges, the magician's boastful showman's air so at odds with Lovecraft's ideal of the behavior of a proper gentleman, or simply Houdini's clearly false tale of adventure, which was to be represented as truth. Curiously Houdini had, many years earlier, a far less pleasant encounter with another noted writer of weird fiction, William Hope Hodgson. In 1902, whilst Houdini was performing in Blackburn, England, with his regular challenge that he could escape all regulation irons used by the police on pain of £25, Hodgson approached Houdini with six sets he had altered deliberately to make escape impossible. Hodgson ran the local Physical Culture School, which helped train local policemen, and was perhaps acting for their part: the police were apparently smarting over Houdini's easy escape from their jail earlier and looking to gain revenge. The resulting performance was an ugly scene all around and did little credit to Hodgson, who had maliciously plugged the locks, although Houdini eventually managed to escape after an excruciating ordeal. Yet this incident with Hodgson does seem to have informed the text of "Under the Pyramids." The article from the *Blackburn Star* reproduced in the anonymous *The Adventurous Life of a Versatile Artist: Houdini* notes the escapologist had "been subjected to such brutality as that to which his bleeding arms and wrists gave witness" and that he was noted as coming out after escaping "with torn clothing and bleeding arms" (25). These latter lines find a distinct analogy in the expression such as of "pains not formerly felt were racking my arms and legs" and "my legs, blood-encrusted beneath my shredded trousers" (*CF* 1.441, 442) in "Under the Pyramids." What, if anything, Lovecraft knew of these reasonably obscure events, which occurred in another country

---

10. The original notes to which were recently uncovered and auctioned in April 2016.

when he was twelve, is unknown, but the entire incident was published in the aforementioned book on Houdini in 1922 and thus at least theoretically available for him to discover. However, Lovecraft's connection to Hodgson, other than their mutual love of judicious quoting from imaginary grimoires and writing the speech of ill-educated rustics phonetically, occurred long after writing "Under the Pyramids," and the introduction to Hodgson's novels that caused Lovecraft to write so favorably of him in a late revision of his essay "Supernatural Horror in Literature" came only in 1934.

Another, far stronger influence on the story is the historical romance by Théophile Gautier, "Une Nuit de Cléopâtre" ("One of Cleopatra's Nights"), of which Lovecraft owned the 1882 translation by Lafcadio Hearn (*LL* 344). Unlike the largely speculative connections with Hodgson, we have a more definitive proof of the impact of the Gautier story from Lovecraft himself. He praises Gautier generally, and this story specifically, in "Supernatural Horror in Literature." In truth he effectively almost commits a self-plagiarism in "Under the Pyramids" that deeply reflects the connection between "One of Cleopatra's Nights" and his own creation. In his literary essay Lovecraft writes:

> Gautier captured the inmost soul of aeon-weighted Egypt, with its cryptic life and Cyclopean architecture, and uttered once and for all the eternal horror of its nether world of catacombs, where to the end of time millions of stiff, spiced corpses will stare up in the blackness with glassy eyes, awaiting some awesome and unrelatable summons. (*CE* 2.98)

The influence betwixt the Gautier tale and "Under the Pyramids" can be easily seen, both thematically and otherwise, via a (by no means exhaustive) selection of quotations from *One of Cleopatra's Nights* from Hearn's translation:

> . . . it is only a vast covering for a tomb—the dome of a necropolis; a sky dead and dried up like the mummies it hangs over. . . . And, moreover, this land is truly an awful land; all things in it are gloomy, enigmatic, incomprehensible. Imagination has produced in it only monstrous chimeras and monuments immeasurable; this architecture and this art fill me with fear . . . (16–17)

Of what invisible flock are those huge sphinxes the guardians, crouching like dogs on the watch, that they never close their eyelids, and forever extend their claws in readiness to seize? Why are their stony eyes so obstinately fixed upon eternity and infinity? What weird secret do their firmly locked lips retain within their breasts? On the right hand, on the left, whithersoever one turns, only frightful monsters are visible—dogs with the heads of men; men with the heads of dogs; chimeras begotten of hideous couplings in the shadowy depths of the labyrinths . . . (17–18)

. . . each city stands upon twenty layers of necropoli [sic]; each generation which passes away leaves a population of mummies to a shadowy city. (20)

. . . upon this land, which was never aught else than a vast tomb, and in which the living appeared to be solely occupied in the work of burying the dead . . . (6)

The last quotation is actually almost paraphrased by Lovecraft in his story's condemnation of the perceived Egyptian obsession that "all these people thought of was death and the dead" (CF 1.438). Yet ultimately Gautier's dramatic outpourings are the observations of a bored potentate, and the story itself has no horrors save those thoughts oppressing of the mind of the queen. Lovecraft melded these in far stranger forms still.

The nucleus of "Under the Pyramids," as related by Houdini, with the treacherous guide, staged fight atop the Great Pyramid, and the lowering by rope into a underground prison to test his 'magical' skills, are all in the final version of the tale, although Lovecraft removed the action from Campbell's Tomb as had been in the magician's draft proposal. Houdini's conception was that he was to have been "shaken to the core with some hideous experience" in his exit, and it was Lovecraft's job "to invent the incident" (SL 1.312). The idea of the immortal Khephren as sinister guide seems to have occurred to Lovecraft at a late date in the creative process, as he writes to James F. Morton on 19 February 1924 of floating an idea of having "them guides dress up as mummies to scare the bound Houdini" and when he returns with the police finding them strangled *"with marks of claws on their throats . . . which could not by any stretch of the imagination belong either to their own hands or to the hands of Houdini!!!"* (*SL* 1.313; italics and exclamation points in original).

It would be tedious to list all the references to Egypt, its history, and its mythology in "Under the Pyramids." It would also be redundant, as much of the information is given explanation in the tale itself. Lovecraft clearly chose to sprinkle the tale liberally with little didactic moments, probably to create atmosphere, add plausibility, and no doubt prove to his commissioner he had done his homework. He states in one letter the difficulty of adding fictional locales for the action whilst "at the same time adhering to the literal verisimilitude on which Henneberger insists" (*SL* 1.317). This concludes in odd moments in the tale such as when, through the supposed voice of Harry Houdini, the protagonist lectures his audience on pyramid dimensions and the different names for the same person who built them. It also achieves the desired outcome of a great addition of credibility to aspects of the story. For example, after a long and accurate lesson on the actual history of the pyramids after Houdini's arrival there in the story, Lovecraft throws out the line about the appearance of the Sphinx having "a face probably altered to form a colossal portrait of Khephren" (*CF* 1.424), setting up the question of the real identity of the Sphinx that will be the dénouement at the end of the story. In addition to the needs of the plot, it is possible Lovecraft was sourcing the works of noted Egyptologist E. A. Wallis Budge, whose translation of *The Book of the Dead* he later owned (*SL* 5.208). Budge, a scholar from the British Museum, specifically put forth this re-carving idea as valid in other of his publications, and the academic debate still continues, although the majority consensus is that Khephren was the original sculptor. It should be noted that the re-carving of monuments and inscriptions was in truth a common Egyptian practice. Ramesses the Great was a particularly egregious offender in this department and is sometimes on this account facetiously referred to as the Great Chiseller by Egyptologists.

The diorite statue of Khephren[11] mentioned as "before which I stood in awe" (*CF* 1.425) still retains its central position in room 42 on the ground floor of the Museum of Egyptian Antiquities in

---

11. Commonly known today as Khafre Enthroned.

Cairo, and it is both an artistic and technical wonder. A *ka* statue, viewed from the front it is simply an impressive image of Khephren. Yet invisible except from the rear or side is carved an image of Horus as a falcon, protecting the head of the Pharaoh with his wings. Interestingly, considering the choice of villain protagonist, Khephren did in fact have a lingering tradition of a bad reputation, which was still extant when Herodotus wrote his *Histories*. However, the truth of Khephren's character cannot be easily determined as the preservers of his memory in writing, the priesthood and scribes, had a reason to be universally hostile if stories that he had closed the temples, presumably to gather the income and manpower needed for his building works, are in fact true.

The ominous mention of Thutmosis IV and his dream is a genuine piece of history as recorded in the internally mentioned Dream Stele, but far less sinister than Lovecraft cunningly implies. Thutmosis IV merely claimed he dreamed that if he uncovered the Sphinx from the covering sands he would be made Pharaoh, and some scholars think it was a piece of royal propaganda designed to support his ascension despite not being the designated crown prince. It is also clear that Lovecraft drew heavily from his copy of *The Tomb of Perneb* in his research for this story. The tomb is even name-checked twice in the tale itself. Lovecraft had visited the exhibition to which the book is connected as early as 1922 and speaks of going "delving into antique Aegyptus at the Met.[tropolitan] Mus.[eum]" (*SL* 1.326) in connection with writing the story.

The mention of the bodies of the Egyptian mummies which "for thousands of years those bodies rested gorgeously encased and staring glassily upward" (*CF* 1.439) is distinctly reminiscent of Harley Warren's preoccupation with "his theory, *why certain corpses never decay, but rest firm and fat in their tombs for a thousand years*" (*CF* 1.133-34) in "The Statement of Randolph Carter." In combination with the multitude of books in Arabic in that short 1919 tale, this confluence of ideas concerning the enduring dead is certainly highly suggestive of an Egyptian connection and may reflect Lovecraft calling back to his earlier work deliberately, but this cannot be ascertained textually. In fact, to the contrary the later Randolph Carter tale "The Silver Key" alludes to these events with Harley Warren but makes connections specifically with India and Arabia rather than Egypt.

Lovecraft's mixture of the poetic and the scholarly sometimes has odd results. For example, the sentence "the deeper mysteries of primal Egypt—the black Khem of Re and Amen" (*CF* 1.423) reads well and uses the old name of Egypt, Khem, to emphasize temporal distance. However, Khem actually means "the Black Land," creating a hidden tautology. The black actually refers to the rich black alluvial soils deposited by the Nile, rather than any more ominous implications. Incidentally, Khem forms, via a curious series of linguistic contortions, the base of the word alchemy and ultimately that medieval vocation's offspring, both linguistically and scientifically, of chemistry.

Another poetical/scholarly confusion occurs over the Thomas Moore quotation. The original poem from which it derives, *Alciphron*, deals with the eponymous man's journey to Egypt in search of immortality and secret rites in a huge temple under the pyramids, and thus its relevance and deliberate homaging is obvious. Lovecraft had previously quoted from it in "The Nameless City," having it spoken aloud by the narrator during the latter's descent into the subterranean depths of the temple in the titular metropolis. Here Lovecraft takes an effective creative license in turning Moore's Memphian boatmen who "tells such wondrous tales" (Moore, *Alciphron* 46) into more sinister mutterings. Furthermore, in his associating of the "lady of the Pyramid" with Nitokris for the named "fair Rhodope" (*Alciphron* 46) of the poem, Lovecraft is perpetuating a confabulation of names made in antiquity that associated the historical *hetaera* Rhodopis with Nitokris as the builder of the Third Pyramid at Gizeh. This confusion was further promulgated by syncretism with the tale of a distinctly less historically attested Rhodope (or Rhodopis), alleged to have married the Pharaoh Psammetichus. The latter was said to have tracked Rhodope down after her shoe was dropped into his lap by an eagle, in the first known recording of the Cinderella tale. In this error, though, Lovecraft is in good company. In addition to Thomas Moore, both Strabo (*Geography* 17.1.33) and Pliny the Elder (*Natural History* 36.17) report the mythical Rhodope, although Herodotus had disproved the matter centuries before (2.143.1).

A few notes on non-human mummies are probably worthwhile at this juncture. In addition to their own dead, the Egyptians mummified a variety of other animals, including most commonly all those named by Lovecraft in the text. Whilst animal mummification was practiced from Pre-Dynastic times, it was increasingly more common from the late New Kingdom and began to accelerate in production from around 800 B.C.E. down into the Roman period. The extensiveness of this practice cannot be overlooked, with total animal mummies in Egypt by some estimates amounting to perhaps 70 million. However, all the different categories of animal mummies are not of the same purpose and intention, and need to be understood in the proper context.

Sacred animal mummies were those of sacrosanct animals who died of natural causes (the best known being the Apis Bull, although other equally specific kine were worshiped at Mnevis and Buchis), and were treated as reverently as deceased Pharaohs and viewed as divine. This category of special animals also includes cherished pets, which were sometimes mummified to go with their owners to the afterlife. A second type of animal mummy, often referred to as victual mummies, were those designed to be food for the occupant of a tomb or to the gods. The tomb of Tut-Ankh-Amen, for example, held forty-eight boxes of such victual mummies.[12] A third, and most numerically common, category are votive mummies, which are those given as offering to the deity to whom they were sacred. They were often bred and killed for this purpose, being sold to pilgrims and worshippers as desired and commonly placed in a pottery jar, although more elaborate receptacles were sometimes created.

The ancients were not above some shysterism in regard to these offerings. Animal "mummies" have been unearthed that are merely fakes created around cores of various substances designed to deceive the trusting devotee. Recent computed tomography (CT) analysis of some 800 animal mummies by the University of Manchester and Manchester Museum showed only about a third of animal mummies containing the remains of a full animal, although it must be noted that the exact reasons for this are still be-

---

12. For the record they were various cuts of beef, four geese, nine ducks and a variety of small birds.

ing debated. Nor is the noting of this phenomenon a recent occurrence. In *The Archive of Hor*,[13] a glorious name for a collection of discarded potsherds used as writing drafts by a minor priest of Isis after whom the collection is named, Hor mentions his concern about such forgeries and wanted there to be, in his own wonderful phrase, "a god in every pot."

Whilst in the tale itself many of the references are self-evident, specific instances of Egyptological note are worthy of examination in greater detail. In Lovecraft's mention of Tut-Ankh-Amen, it must be recalled that this Pharaoh's tomb was only discovered in late 1922 and that the excavation was ongoing, breaking news when Lovecraft was writing his tale in February and March of 1924. The granite lid of Tut-Ankh-Amen's sarcophagus was only removed by Howard Carter in his excavation on 12 February 1924, thus Lovecraft's allusion to the "Theban rock valley where Tut-Ankh-Amen sleeps" (*CF* 1.427) was still factually accurate at the time of writing, although of course the story is set fourteen years prior to the publication date, and Houdini could not have known of the location of Tut-Ankh-Amen when he was in Egypt. In fact, it was commonly believed by many scholars that the minor tomb KV54,[14] discovered in 1909 and which contained Tut-Ankh-Amen's embalming cache, was actually Tut-Ankh-Amen's tomb. Indeed, Tut-Ankh-Amen would probably have remained an obscure and unimportant Pharaoh save for the happy chance that his tomb remained the only one discovered to date that was largely unlooted.

The reappearance of Nitokris begins with an epitome of Herodotus' account of her in the tale, followed immediately but the curious (yet plot-crucial) deviation that she was buried alive. Contrary to horror films' constant assertions to the contrary, this was never Egyptian practice, although there is one historically attested case that might conceivably fit the scenario of a person deliberately embalmed and inhumed alive. This concerns the mummy known as Unknown Man E (Exhibit No. 61098), currently locat-

---

13. Hor is the Egyptian name for the god rendered as Horus by the Greeks.
14. All tombs in the Valley of the Kings are given K(ings)V(alley) numerical designations. Tut-Ankh-Amen's actual tomb is KV62.

ed in the Museum of Egyptian Antiquities in Cairo. This mummy was discovered tightly wrapped and with preservative natron and resin packed about the body, but was in an undecorated, ill-fitting coffin and had not undergone any of the customary forms of evisceration. His facial expression is undeniably reminiscent of a person in great pain, and it is this probably chance circumstance that initiated the early conjectures about his being embalmed alive by the archaeologists who first looked upon him. However, Unknown Man E was significantly buried with a sheepskin wrap. The Middle Kingdom *Tale of Sinhue*, concerning an exile's adventures and return to Egypt for restoration to Pharaoh's grace and ultimately a proper burial, specifically states that *"Thou shalt not be placed in a sheep-skin,"* implying it as a terrible fate. This, in combination with the lack of evisceration and "screaming" facial expression, has led to speculation that this unfortunate man was embalmed alive as a punishment, although an equally plausible theory is that he was simply embalmed in great haste without time for the accustomed procedures. It has been speculated that the reason for the sloppy techniques is that the embalming was performed by inexperienced or possibly even non-Egyptian embalmers on an Egyptian native requiring repatriation after death in a foreign land, and that these embalmers, who were unsure as to certain procedures, resorted to local practices to fill in gaps in knowledge.

Similarly, it was once thought possible that the person was an Asiatic visitor to Egypt who died and had certain aspects of his native customs performed for him. The sheepskins dreaded by the people of the Nile were commonly used in certain of the funerary rites of Egypt's neighbors. However, to the punishment hypothesis a disputed identification, recently bolstered by genetic analysis, of Unknown Man E contends that he was Pentaware, a prince of the Twentieth Dynasty and son of Ramesses III. Pentaware is known to have been involved in an unsuccessful harem conspiracy to gain the throne, and it is conjectured that the inconsistent aspects of the mortuary protocols were due to his body being embalmed with great urgency to ensure that his body did not undergo a worse indignity and suffer a truncated or absent afterlife.

In our final observations on Nitokris as seen by Lovecraft, it is notable that he twice refers to her as a "ghoul-queen" (CF 1.440,

446). This statement is ambiguous as to whether she is merely mistress of ghouls or a ghoul herself, but the latter is certainly implied given that "half of her face was eaten away by rats or other ghouls" (CF 1.448). Curiously, her appearance corresponds in many ways with that of the Norse goddess of the inglorious dead, the malefic Hel, although Lovecraft's intent with this, if deliberate, is decidedly unclear and may be largely coincidental.

The charges that Lovecraft makes about a decadent priestcraft creating composite animal/human hybrid mummies have no basis in fact, although it is certainly true that there were different levels of embalming available, depending on what one could afford, and that embalming changed in numerous ways over the millennia the Egyptians practiced it. Mistakes were also made at times, such as in the case of Nesperennub. A priest from approximately the ninth century B.C.E., Nesperennub appears to accidentally have had the unfired clay resin bowl used in embalming stuck to his head, with the error literally covered up in the expectation that no one would ever discover it. The closest analogies to Lovecraft's composite mummies are a few examples, exclusively from the Greco-Roman period, with supernumerary or lacking limbs, again apparently the result of sloppy embalming practices.

Likewise, in conjunction with his slander of Egyptian priests, Lovecraft's painting of Osiris as a baleful leader of "stiff legions of the dead" (CF 1.439) does the god a grave disservice. Whilst modern conceptions of gods of the dead tend to be negative, Osiris was the lord of the afterlife and resurrection, a decidedly positive deity in the eyes of ancient Egyptians; and even Lovecraft acknowledges that the resurrection "was to have been a glorious rebirth" (CF 1.439). Lovecraft's perception of Egyptian beliefs about the afterlife may have been filtered through the lens of the works of the French natural historian Benoît de Maillet (1656–1738), whose 1735 *Description of Egypt* concerning the dead is worth quoting:

> The priests and sages of Egypt taught their fellow citizens that, after a certain number of ages, which they made to amount to thirty or forty thousand years, and at which they fixed the epoch of the great revolution when the earth would return to the point at which it commenced its existence, their souls would return to the

same bodies which they formerly inhabited. But, in order to ar-
rive, after death, to this wished for resurrection, two things were
absolutely necessary; first, that the bodies should be absolutely
carefully preserved from corruption, in order that the souls might
re-inhabit them; secondly, that the penance submitted to during
this long period of years, that the numerous sacrifices founded by
the dead, or those offered to their manes[15] by their relations or
their friends, should expiate the crimes they had committed during the time of their first habitation on earth. With these conditions exactly observed, these souls, separated from their bodies,
should be permitted to re-enter at the arrival of this grand revolution which they anticipated. (Cited in Gannal 9–10)

Although there is no definitive proof that Lovecraft read de Maillet or others following on from his work, this inaccurate and out-
moded understanding and description of Egyptian beliefs certainly
dovetails rather well with Egyptian funerary practices as discussed
and referred to in "Under the Pyramids."

When Lovecraft mentions that "statues of the Pharaoh were
found in curious juxtaposition to the statues of baboons" (CF
1.425), he may be hinting obliquely at the spatial relationship between a pair of dog and baboon mummies found in tomb KV50.
In this tomb, discovered and excavated by Theodore M. Davis in
1906, the two animals were placed nose to nose, and it has been
suggested that this uncharacteristic positioning may have been a
grim jest made by the original tomb robbers. Baboons held a special place in Egyptian mythology. The Tomb of Tut-Ankh-Amen,
for example, has twelve baboons painted on its west wall, each
baboon representing an hour of the night, guiding Tut-Ankh-
Amen's solar boat through the darkness as escort into the afterlife.
Baboons were also the greeters of the sun, itself a facet of various
deities, this being a reflection of the behavior of actual baboons
who commonly make noise at daybreak. As an aspect of Thoth a
baboon was commonly depicted standing upon the middle of the
scales that weighed the heart of the deceased at the final judgment
against the feather of *Ma'at* ("truth/order"), who was simultane-

---

15. A Roman term corresponding roughly to what modern persons would think
of as the souls of the dead.

ously an incarnated goddess and a central conception of Egyptian theological thought. Some depictions have monstrous baboons as the eaters of the souls judged unworthy, which is unsurprising given that the baboon species most often depicted in Egyptian images is the aggressive *Papio hamadryas*. The baboon-headed Hapi, one of the four sons of Horus, was depicted on, and protector of, the canopic jar that held a mummy's lungs.

As has curiously often happened with further developments in the world of knowledge since Lovecraft wrote his stories, the changes have been largely providential. His general understanding of Egyptian funerary practices and beliefs as displayed in the story remains broadly accurate, if turned to uniformly sinister motives. Khephren's mummy has still not been located, whilst the possibility that historians may have redacted Nitokris from the record curiously adds to the conspiratorial idea put forth that the authorities in Cairo know about the dangers but are keeping it suppressed. The exact dating, and even the possible re-carving, of the Great Sphinx remains a continuous and contentious issue among serious scholars, whilst the popular fringe science notions of this monolithic statue having suffered immersion in water seems as if it could have been an alternative aspect of Lovecraft's tale come to life. Likewise the reference to Tut-Ankh-Amen's location remains accurate. The body of the young Pharaoh is not in a museum but rather is on display in his own tomb, under the logic that, because it is an undisturbed burial site, the beliefs of the interred should be respected.

After the heavy immersion of Egypt inside "Under the Pyramids," the next literary reference in which Lovecraft utilized the Land of the Pharaohs was extremely minimal. "Cool Air" (1926), the last of the New York stories, has the dead Doctor Muñoz developing "strange caprices, acquiring a fondness for exotic spices and Egyptian incense till his room smelled like the vault of a sepulchred Pharaoh in the Valley of Kings" (*CF* 2.16). This use of Egyptian tombs as a simile, the hints of embalmed mummies in the use of the interlocked terms "spices and incense," and the "tightly bandaged" (*CF* 2.18) doctor here all deliberately foreshadow the dénouement at the end of the tale, but overall "Cool Air" is largely connected to Egypt only by allusion.

"The Call of Cthulhu" (1926) makes another tangential reference to Egypt. In the familiar manner of expressing gulfs of distance, Lovecraft has Wilcox make a statement concerning the bas-relief he fashioned from his dreams, commenting, "dreams are older than brooding Tyre, or the contemplative Sphinx, or garden-girdled Babylon" (CF 2.25). In an amusing aside from our topic, it is interesting to note the narrator in the story, Francis Wayland Thurston, speaks about Wilcox as "of a type, at once slightly affected and slightly ill-mannered, which I could never like" (CF 2.43). Lovecraft originally conceived the Sphinx line "precisely" in a 1920 dream, in which he himself had been both the artist and the utterer of the line (SL 1.114). Curiously, in the original dream Lovecraft describes the carving that would become the Cthulhu bas-relief as follows: "its design was that of a procession of Egyptian priests" (SL 1.115).

The Dream-Quest of Unknown Kadath (1926–27), set in the ill-delineated dreamlands, could be argued as having no connection to Egypt by virtue of its very location. However, as noted earlier, Bubastis is invoked directly whilst one of the cat breeds mentioned as part of the military assault on the moon is Egyptian (Egyptian Mau, to give it its proper name according to the Cat Fanciers' Association, Mau being derived from the Middle Egyptian mw, meaning cat and charmingly onomatopoeic). The Temple of the Cats at Ulthar, seemingly distinct from the Temple of the Elder Ones, seems to have been a temple for cats rather than for Bast, but as The Dream-Quest of Unknown Kadath never underwent a true final draft, such details remain unclear. The names of the two priests Nasht and Kaman-Thah definitely have an Egyptian cadence, and are decidedly similar to actual names such as Nascht-Amen ("strength of Amen"). Both are described as wearing "pshent-bearing heads" (CF 2.100). The pshent is the name of the Double Crown of Ancient Egypt, which signified the union of Upper and Lower Egypt, and is mentioned a number of times in the story as a synonym for crown. This includes the one upon the head of Nyarlathotep, who is again described as looking like an "antique Pharaoh" (CF 2.204), although nothing else of his description or behavior hints particularly at Egypt.

The Case of Charles Dexter Ward (1927), concerning the resurrection of a dead necromancer through the unwitting actions of his descendant, returns to Lovecraft's own Egyptian mythos. By this time accuracy in Lovecraft's writings on Egyptian mythology has almost entirely been replaced by his own allusions to the subject in previous stories. In an early letter recovered by the luckless Charles Dexter Ward and dating from late 1770 or early 1771, Jedediah Orne mentions having trouble with "ye VII. Booke of ye Necronomicon" (*CF* 2.251) in relation to their necromantic undertakings. The same Jedediah, known under the name of his 'son' Simon, writes in a letter of 11 February 1928 that he received a scar seventy-five years ago from a "Thing" originating in "Aegypt" (*CF* 2.320). In the 7 March 1928 letter send to Joseph Curwen by his compatriot in evil, Edward Hutchinson, there is a mention of "that Darke Thing belowe Memphis" (*CF* 2.324), continuing the themes of evils in Egyptian catacombs. All this connects tantalizingly with Abdul Alhazred's relation to that location as laid out in Lovecraft's "History of the 'Necronomicon,'" and his subsequent letter to Clark Ashton Smith about it (*SL* 2.201), both written in the same year as *The Case of Charles Dexter Ward*. The mention in the Hutchinson letter of "ye Legions from Underneath" (*CF* 2.324) corresponds in many respects to the horrors of "Under the Pyramids," wherein Lovecraft (erroneously) states that Osiris will "lead forth the stiff legions of the dead from the sunken houses of sleep" (*CF* 1.439), as Egyptian myth is a foreshadowing of the real subterranean nightmares encountered in their unhallowed worship.

To sign off in one of his letters Hutchinson significantly uses the expression "Nephren-Ka nai Hadoth" (*CF* 2.324). Clearly this refers to Nephren-Ka, allowing for linguistic shifts over the centuries as perceived by Lovecraft. For example the twentieth-century "Yog-Sothoth" is rendered as "Yogge-Sothothe" in Joseph Curwen's original seventeenth-century jottings. Hadoth is certainly the unknown vale of Hadoth that we have encountered previously, although no specific new information is thus presented. "Nai" is likely the transliterated Greek meaning "yes, certainly, even so," and given the context from other letters the signing off may be an affirmation of Nephren-Ka's status as a resident or ruler in Hadoth, or perhaps an allegiance to him akin to a Christian believer completing a letter "yours in Christ."

Egyptian mummies also play a minor but important part in this tale. A British customs schooner seeking contraband accidentally intercepts a cargo of mummies from Cairo, and although not proven to be intended for Curwen in the tale, few even in his own time had doubts that he was their ultimate destination. Curiously, Curwen's defense of this unspoken accusation of importation of the ancient dead, as he speaks of the chemical value of balsams used in mummies, is historically accurate. Mummia, being parts of a mummy, were once commonly believed to have curative properties and were sold pharmacologically to this effect. The demand was so great that fake Egyptian mummies became a trade in themselves, and European doctors started to produce new mummies so as to ensure their perceived efficacy by a known provenance. As a side note the mummy creation instructions of the alchemist Crollius (1563?–1609), whilst sadly too long to quote here, includes—in a reflection worthy of Curwen himself—a note that if you could get the flesh from a living man for your mummy preparation it would be "still the better" (Gannal, *History of Embalming* 17).

Egypt remains largely absent from Lovecraft's stories from this point onward, although references do frequently occur in his collaborations and ghostwritten tales. There is a passing reference to scrolls of "Ægyptus" in the dream-transcription "The Very Old Folk" (*CF* 3.498), but this is once more used to capitalize on the idea of Egypt's antiquity, even as viewed by the Romans of the story. "The Last Test," a revision piece commissioned by Adolphe de Castro, has the heroine mention that the villainous Surama looks like "a Pharaoh's mummy, if miraculously brought to life" (*CF* 4.63). Despite several other moments hinting at a dark origin of this skeletal man, it is ultimately left up to the reader to decide if this is a poetical allusion or an accurate intuition, although the latter seems highly probable. Yet even if the idea of Surama being resurrected is literal, it seems more likely from the internal evidences of the story that his ultimate cultural origin would have been from the Atlanteans or another, non-human race. "The Mound," a story ghostwritten for Zealia Bishop, utilizes Lovecraft's now familiar idea of Egypt and distance in time in a curiously novel way, with the narrator comparing the gulfs between himself and the author of the missive he is reading as nothing compared to the gulfs separating them both from the mystery of the mound, and that it would be the same it were "Cheops[16] and I" (*CF* 4.183). Cheops was the Pharaoh who built the Great Pyramid and a very early figure in human history, and thus the gap of roughly 4500 years between the narrator and Cheops emphasizes the truly "dizzying gulfs that yawned between all men of the known earth and the primal mysteries it represented" (*CF* 4.183).

Another revision piece for the same author, "Medusa's Coil," makes a tangential reference to "the group of mystics Marsh ran with" being connected with "some cult of prehistoric Egyptian and Carthaginian magic" (*CF* 4.254), whilst the femme fatale of the tale called herself "Tanit-Isis" in Paris. Tanit was the main female deity of Carthage and is roughly equivalent to the Egyptian Isis, although unlike the benign Isis, Tanit has persistent stories of child sacrifices attributed to her that continue to be a subject of scholarly debate as to their authenticity over being Roman blood-libel propaganda. The legend of the origins of the *Coma Berenices* ("Berenice's Hair") constellation epitomized in the tale as the "Ptolemaic myth of Berenice, who offered up her hair to save her husband-brother, and had it set in the sky" (*CF* 4.254) is a genuine legend about the real Egyptian queen Bernice II, wife of Ptolemy III Euergretes ("the Benefactor"). The demonic painting in the tale is described using another interesting Lovecraft variation on Egypt as a signpost to great age, in the description of figures in it "dancing in a pattern that Egypt's priests knew and called accursed!" (*CF* 4.287).

At the Mountains of Madness has a passing reference by way of analogy to the totemic aspect of the scarabaeus in Egypt, while the wing of mummies inside the Cabot Museum in the ghostwritten "Out of the Aeons" contained "typical examples of Egyptian embalming from the earliest Sakkarah specimens to the last Coptic attempts of the eighth century" (*CF* 4.405). Sakkarah is a reference to the site of the original Step Pyramid burial site of Djoser of the First Dynasty, whilst the Copts are the Egyptian descendants of the original Christian converts, who still form a distinct religious minority in Egypt to this day. Early Coptic gravestones include traditional images from older Egyptian mythology, most

---

16. Also known as Khufu, Khêops and Súphis.

notably the ankh. It is in "Out of the Aeons" that we hear of von Junzt having presented evidence in his *Black Book* that the cult of Ghatanothoa had penetrated Egypt, although whether it was active in later ages is open to doubt according to this authority.

Whilst definitely a lesser work, the revision/collaboration with Duane W. Rimel, "The Tree on the Hill," foreshadows the far better use of an unnatural gem, intrusion of a hostile and horribly alien presence of indistinguishable form, and Egyptian priests in "The Haunter of the Dark" (1935). The wonderfully named character of Constantine Theunis "was writing a treatise on Egyptian mythology," and the author of his copy of the *Chronicle of Nath* apparently "borrowed some of his lore from Hermes Trismegistus, the ancient Egyptian sorcerer" (CF 4.464). This tome, apparently designed to be Rimel's *Necronomicon*, mentions a "Ka-Nefer the High-Priest" (CF 4.465) who kept a sacred gem as against the nebulous alien shadow that is the threat in the story, and that said gem was lost with Phrenes "who braved the horror and was never seen more" (CF 4.___). Hermes Trismegistus is a topic of much scholarly dispute; and although tradition has him as a single individual sorcerer, he is far more likely a syncretic fusion of Egyptian and Greek gods, in particular Thoth and Hermes, during the Ptolemaic period, and the works attributed to him the accumulation of a multitude of different writers and traditions. Ka-Nefer is an actual Egyptian name, known to be have been used separately by both a prince and a priest of Ptah in the Old Kingdom, with the familiar *ka* combined with the common Egyptian term *nefer*, the latter as will by now be obvious being frequently used in names and roughly translating as "beautiful." However, these historical figures are both highly obscure, and the name may have been a modern creation utilizing Egyptian words that happened to be a valid combination. This supposition is given weight by the fact that no ancient Egyptian names begin with *phr*, and it seems probable that Phrenes is a combination derived of Menes and Khephren.

There is, however, a return to the land of the Nile in the final two of Lovecraft's great short stories, "The Shadow out of Time" (1934–35) and "The Haunter of the Dark." These two tales' Egyptian connections are so intertwined that it is best to examine them together rather than separately. Nathaniel Wingate Peaslee of

"The Shadow out of Time," whose mind was swapped out with a member of the Great Race of Yith, meets a similar sojourner named "Khephnes, an Egyptian of the 14th Dynasty who told me the hideous secret of Nyarlathotep" (CF 3.399). Like Phrenes, the name Khephnes is likely derived from a portmanteau of Khephren and Menes. The attribution to the Fourteenth Dynasty is well chosen. These rulers are from the Second Intermediate Period and are particularly badly attested in the historic record. The secret of Nyarlathotep is probably connected with the events noted in Lovecraft's final great story.

"The Haunter of the Dark" deals with the accidental summoning of the eponymous creature by an unlucky writer, and was actually written as a sequel of sorts to Robert Bloch's "The Shambler from the Stars." In that story the author, a young man still decades away from wider fame as the author of *Psycho*, gruesomely kills a thinly veiled Lovecraft stand-in. Lovecraft repays the favor with interest in the doom of "Robert Blake" in his literary reply. (For the sake of completeness it is to be noted that Bloch wrote a third story in this unusual trilogy, "The Shadow from the Steeple," but this does not concern the present topic.) Curiously, in Lovecraft's extremely rare use of his own poetry in a story for which it was not particularly written and which appears as an epigraph, he chose a section of "Nemesis," which we noted earlier for its slight Egyptian connection. Many of the dramatic scenes in "The Haunter of the Dark" are set inside the old Federal Hill Church, which was given over to the strange cult of Starry Wisdom after the return of Enoch Bowen from excavations in Egypt in May of 1844. Even the nominally Christian altar "resembled the primordial ankh or crux ansata of shadowy Egypt" (CF 3.460). This is hardly surprising, given what is in the notes of the deceased reporter Edwin M. Lillibridge, whose body has remained in the church undisturbed for decades:

> 7 disappearances 1848—stories of blood sacrifice begin . . . Fr. O'Malley tells of devil-worship with box found in great Egyptian ruins—says they call up something that can't exist in light. Flees a little light, and banished by strong light. Then has to be summoned again. Probably got this from deathbed confession of Francis X. Feeney, who had joined Starry Wisdom in '49. These

people say the Shining Trapezohedron shews them heaven & other worlds, & that the Haunter of the Dark tells them secrets in
some way. (CF 3.463–64)

Likely this incarnated devil-worship and human sacrifice is the secret of Nyarlathotep, which was told to the mind-swapped Nathaniel Wingate Peaslee by Khephnes. It is important to note
specific aspects of Egyptian mythology that bear on these matters
at this juncture. The ankh, a quintessentially Egyptian symbol, resembles a Christian cross with a loop above the transverse bar. It
is ubiquitous in depictions of Egyptian deities and is most commonly interpreted as meaning "eternal life." In funerary depictions
it is this symbol that bestows life upon the mummy of the deceased. There is a further elaboration later in the text detailing the
history of the Shining Trapezohedron, which informs us (via
Blake's further researches) that it was purchased by

> swarthy merchants from nighted Khem. The Pharaoh Nephren-
> Ka built around it a temple with a windowless crypt, and did that
> which caused his name to be stricken from all monuments and
> records. Then it slept in the ruins of that evil fane which the
> priests and the new Pharaoh destroyed, till the delver's spade once
> more brought it forth to curse mankind. (CF 3.467)

Thus is finally revealed the status of Nephren-Ka as a Pharaoh accursed. His[17] perfidy is thus tied back to all his previous shadowy
appearances, and it seems likely that the "sealed and unknown valley of Hadoth" (CF 1.272) is the location of his temple. Although it
is not absolutely proven, it is a reasonable conjecture that the previously mentioned Khephnes is a priest. This is to be extrapolated
as the Great Race only took minds intellectually suitable to their
purposes (the educated elite of Egypt were the priests), and how
else could Khephnes know of a person and events that had been
stricken from the record? If one accepts this premise as plausible,
it is possible, even probable, that Khephnes himself participated
in the eradication. This nexus of dark events is given a certain authenticity as Peaslee in "The Shadow out of Time" speculates that

---

17. Or, as noted earlier, "Her". For the sake of simplicity a single male gender will
be utilised in reference to this character, but it should not be read as definitive.

certain events and locales create "a peculiar vulnerability as regards such shadows" (CF 3.364) that are conducive to individuals' being taken by the Great Race as a vehicle, although this is purely speculative.

Taking this as an accurate reading of events, it is therefore a reasonable conclusion to place Nephren-Ka sometime in the Fourteenth Dynasty. Interestingly, this period was marked by a prolonged famine, which one could interpret as being the cause of, or reaction to, Nephren-Ka's deeds, although how much Lovecraft knew of this or intended it to be thus understood is unrecoverable. However, it is certainly possible that Khephnes alludes to another horror altogether. The Haunter of the Dark is explicitly stated to be "an avatar of Nyarlathotep, who in antique and shadowy Khem even took the form of man" (CF 3.476), and it may be to this infamy to which Khephnes is referring, rather than the inhabitant of the evil fane noted above. Yet for a number of reasons this seems most unlikely. The Nyarlathotep in human guise in his eponymous tale could be as much as a thousand years separated from the Fourteenth Dynasty. Given the close proximity in the writing of the two final tales less than eight months apart with no non-collaboration fictional material created between them, and given that Lovecraft frequently added elements from a previous story directly into latter ones, that there is an unquestionably "hideous" aspect to human ritual sacrifices, and that there is a clear focus on the Haunter of the Dark in the titular tale, it is a reasonable, although not absolute, supposition that Khephnes' "hideous secret" refers to Nyarlathotep in this aspect.

As noted, it is unfortunately an historical reality that the striking of names from monuments and records is frustratingly common in ancient Egypt, and was frequently done specifically in response to perceived heresies. This idea of heresy was a concept with a broad range of application in a culture viewing their ruler as a literal god. Ironic on a number of levels, not the least to the modern anti-polytheistic theological perspective, the most infamous of these heretics was the Pharaoh, arch-apostate, and first ruling monotheist in history, Akhenaton. To the ancient Egyptians the removal of names was believed ultimately to be effecting the actually destruction of the person, as the name was part of the reality of the person it represented. To any standard of the ancient Egyptians the actions of Nephren-Ka would most certainly have been seen as violently heretical, as the sun as deity and deities as aspects of the sun were central motifs of Egyptian religious thought. Whilst the inner sanctuaries of temples were kept in darkness to emphasize their sacred nature, the holy items in them were brought out for worship. A lightless crypt as a place of divine veneration would have stood in stark contrast to their entire belief structure. Truly was Nephren-Ka worthy of being stricken from history.

Overall, an examination of Egypt in Lovecraft shows several common threads. His usage of the historical Egypt as a signpost for antiquity, antediluvian ages, and tangents to the historical realities of Khem gradually gave way to a Egyptian mythos that is very much of his own creation yet strengthened immeasurably by the realities besides and upon which it rests. One of the advantages of drawing upon objects, names, and ideas of great antiquity is that they lend a natural depth to the subject, having inherently a backstory of their own. Even if all this backstory is not entirely known to the writer, if done with skill it will still add to the levels for the reader as they bring their own knowledge to bear upon the subject in question. Lovecraft certainly applied that skill, and his widespread usage of Egypt as fascinating subject, subtext, and shadowy holder of secrets adds an extra dimension to his entire body of work, making it as ever more than the sum of its parts.

Works Cited

Anonymous. *The Adventurous Life of a Versatile Artist: Houdini.* n.p.: Wilson, 1920.

Diodorus Siculus. *Diodorus of Sicily in Twelve Volumes.* Tr. C. H. Oldfather. Cambridge, MA: Harvard University Press, 1989.

Dunsany, Lord. *Five Plays.* New York: Mitchell Kennerley, 1914.

———. *The Queen's Enemies.* London: G. P. Putnam's Sons, 1918.

Gannal, J. N. *History of Embalming.* Tr. R. Harlan. Philadelphia: Judah Dobson, 1840.

Gardiner, Alan H. *Notes on the Story of Sinuhe.* Paris: Librairie Honoré Champion, 1916.

Gautier, Théophile. *One of Cleopatra's Nights and Other Fantastic Romances*. Tr. Lafcadio Hearn. New York: Brenano's, 1906.

Herodotus. *The Histories*. Tr. A. D. Godley Cambridge, MA: Harvard University Press, 1920.

Joshi, S. T. *I Am Providence: The Life and Times of H. P. Lovecraft*. New York: Hippocampus Press, 2010.

————. *Lovecraft's Library: A Catalogue*. New York: Hippocampus Press, 3rd ed. 2012.

Lovecraft, H. P. *The New Annotated H. P. Lovecraft*. Ed. Leslie S. Klinger, New York: Liveright, 2014.

————. *The Call of Cthulhu and Other Weird Stories*. Ed. S. T. Joshi. New York: Penguin, 1999.

Maillet, Benoît de. *Description of Egypt*. 1735.

Moore, Thomas. *Alciphron: A Poem*. Philadelphia: Carey & Hart, 1840.

Pausanias. *Description of Greece*. Tr. W. H. S. Jones. Cambridge, MA: Harvard University Press, 1918.

Plato. *Plato in Twelve Volumes: Volume 9*. Tr. W. R. M. Lamb. Cambridge, MA: Harvard University Press, 1925.

Pliny the Elder. *The Natural History of Pliny*. Tr. John Bostock and H. T. Riley, London: George Bell & Sons, 1893.

Poe, Edgar Allan. *The Collected Works of Edgar Allan Poe: Volume II, Tales and Sketches*. Ed. Thomas Ollive Mabbott. Cambridge, MA: Cambridge University Press, 1978.

Price, Robert M. "Lovecraft's 'Artificial Mythology.'" In *An Epicure in the Terrible: A Centennial Anthology of Essays in Honor of H. P. Lovecraft*, ed. David. E. Schultz and S. T. Joshi. Rutherford, NJ: Fairleigh Dickinson University Press, 1991.

Ray, J. D. *The Archive of Hor*. London: Egypt Exploration Society, 1976.

Strabo. *The Geography of Strabo*. Tr. H. C. Hamilton and W. Falconer. London: George Bell & Sons, 1903.

Forgotten Influence: A. Merritt's "The Face in the Abyss" and H. P. Lovecraft's "The Mound"

Peter Levi

Following the publication of S. T. Joshi's definitive *I Am Providence* (2010) and the unlikelihood of discoveries like the autograph draft of "The Shadow out of Time" (discovered in 1994 and published seven years later [*SOT* 27]), there are meager pickings in the world of Lovecraft studies these days. Fans can only look forward to collections of letters (most of whose critical material has long been available) and various articles wherein stories are tackled by whatever method is current in literary criticism (Donald R. Burleson is still busy deconstructing texts, for example). There is value to be had in the aforementioned, but the meaty content of yesteryear seems passé. That being said, I believe there is at least one cause whose merit has not yet seeped into the collective consciousness of Lovecraft studies. I wrote a rushed pass at it ten years ago, which appeared in *Lovecraft Annual* (2007), but a full treatment is needed to establish that A. Merritt's "The Face in the Abyss" had a profound impact on Lovecraft's "The Mound."

Before getting into the particulars of my comparison, let us establish the basic groundwork. We know (both from Lovecraft himself and subsequent studies) that Lovecraft's revisions for Zealia Bishop were essentially original work. As R. H. Barlow noted about "The Mound" (*IAP* 754), Bishop's contribution to the tale was this: "There is an Indian mound near here, which is haunted by a headless ghost. Sometimes it is a woman." This trivial suggestion gave Lovecraft an enormous amount of freedom to do as he wished with a substantial and challenging story. I bring this up to illustrate that the points discussed below come from Lovecraft and not from the nominal author. In terms of chronology, the story was written from late 1929 to early 1930.

Our second point of interest is A. Merritt himself. We know Lovecraft admired Merritt's work ("The Moon Pool" in particular [see *IAP* 639]; see also *SL* 4.342), and that he was familiar both with "The Face in the Abyss" in its *Argosy* appearance in 1923 (see *ES* 545) as well as its subsequent novelization as *The Snake Mother* in 1930 (he owned the book version, titled *The Face in the Abyss* [*LL* 603]). Here is what Lovecraft said to August Derleth about it in 1933 after re-reading the tale (citation above): "Merritt *could* be a marvellous atmospheric creator . . ." And (*ES* 547): "Yes—'The Face in the Abyss' is by no means bad. Merritt has an incipient magic all is [*sic*] own, which might have produced wonders had commercialism not intervened."

So we have established that the substance of "The Mound" has not been dictated by Zealia Bishop, and that Lovecraft was familiar with Merritt's work and saw good things amidst the commercial dreck (amusingly enough, Lovecraft mentions both works in the same paragraph, *OFF* 144, but alas with no internal reflections).

The plot of "The Mound" is well known, and S. T. Joshi summarizes it brilliantly (*IAP* 745):

> "The Mound" concerns a member of Coronado's 1541 expedition, Panfilo de Zamacona y Nuñez, who leaves the main group and conducts a solitary expedition to the mound region of what is now Oklahoma. There he hears tales of an underground realm of fabulous antiquity and, more to his interest, great wealth, and finds an Indian who will lead him to one of the few remaining entrances to this realm, although the Indian refuses to accompany him on the actual journey. Zamacona comes upon the civilisation of Xinaian (which he prounces "K'n-yan"), established by quasi-human creatures who (implausibly) came from outer space. These inhabitants have developed remarkable mental abilities, including telepathy and the power of dematerialisation—the process of dissolving themselves and selected objects around them to their component atoms and recombining them at some other location. Zamacona initially expresses wonder at this civilisation, but gradually finds that it has declined both intellectually and morally from a much higher level and has now become corrupt and decadent. He attempts to

escape, but suffers a horrible fate. A manuscript that he had written of his adventures is unearthed in modern times by an archaeologist, who paraphrases his incredible tale.

It is worth noting that Joshi proposes no specific literary influences on "The Mound" in his seminal volume. The tale predates the much more refined civilizations found in *At the Mountains of Madness* (1931) and "The Shadow out of Time" (1934–35)—indeed, *all* the substantial civilizations Lovecraft creates follow in the footsteps of "The Mound" (cf. Joshi, *World in Transition* 122, where the tale is first in the chronology of Joshi's explorations).

The plot of "The Face in the Abyss" can be summarized much more easily. An American mining engineer, Nicholas Graydon, while searching for lost Inca treasure in South America, encounters Suarra, handmaiden to the Snake Mother of Yu-Atlanchi. She leads Graydon to an abyss where Nimir, the Lord of Evil, is imprisoned in a face of gold. While Graydon's companions are transformed by the face into globules of gold on account of their greed, he is saved by Suarra and the Snake Mother, whom he plans to aid in their struggle against Nimir.

There are a large number of similarities between the two stories that are not very apparent from the above summaries, so let us tackle them one at a time:

Each story is told by unnamed, intermediary narrators: in Merritt, the vacationing narrator encounters the hero Graydon (*FFM* 22), while in Lovecraft an unnamed archaeologist finds the records of Panfilo de Zamacona y Nuñez (*CF* 4.180). The nature of Lovecraft's story does not require this particular method of telling Zamacona's story (an anonymous narrator discovering the first-person account), although it is not an unusual choice (cf. "The Call of Cthulhu"). This is the first of many similarities between the two stories.

Both Zamacona (*CF* 4.185) and Graydon (*FFM* 24) are seeking treasure. In both cases the protagonists are looking for legendary Native treasures (Incan gold in Merritt, a treasure more potent than Coronado's in Lovecraft).[1] The fact that Lovecraft has chosen

---

1. Franciso Vázquez de Coronado was the governor of the Kingdom of New Galicia (an autonomous kingdom within the viceroyalty of New Spain). He launched

the same plot device for his protagonist to pursue suggests he was influenced by Merritt (Lovecraft seems to have used the Coronado expedition based on its antiquity in relation to his setting; cf. *SL* 3.88).

The protagonists are both led by Native guides (*CF* 4.185) or followers (*FFM* 25) who know something of the horror ahead. In each case, the prior narrative choices dictate this similarity, so there is not much to conclude from it, other than a cumulative weight we will get to later.

Zamacona (*CF* 4.186–87) and Graydon (*FFM* 25) are going to regions known to be haunted, and each dismisses the haunting as superstition (*CF* 4.188; *FFM* 28). The former decision (the haunting) has been made for Lovecraft by Bishop's plot germ, although the choice to be dismissive about the supernatural is something typical of Lovecraft.

Each of the regions explored—the Oklahoma mound and the Cordillera de Carabaya—are found to be the home of an ancient race who are the ancestors of modern humanity (*CF* 4.187; *FFM* 73), and in both cases, anomalously white. This similarity is much more difficult to explain. For Lovecraft, there is no driving need in the narrative for this racial choice (perhaps it made the pseudo-romance in the story more palatable for him, but removing that decision would do little to diminish the horror of the tale—there is no effort to have miscegenation form the climax of the narrative). This parallel in particular is where we start to see the influence Merritt has had on Lovecraft.

Let us look at the kind of race each author discovers. Merritt's Yu-Atlanchi are ancient immortal beings, living in a near-impossible-to-find region cut off from the outside world and ruled by a snake-like god (*FFM* 73). The inhabitants of Lovecraft's Xinaian (usually called K'n-yan; *CF* 4.203) are ancient immortal beings, having come from the stars and begot mankind, from whom they eventually sundered themselves (*CF* 4.186). The people of K'n-yan live in isolation underground, the doors to their

---

his expedition after Friar Marcos de Niza told him that he had found a golden city called Cibola in the area now known as New Mexico. Coronado spent two years fruitlessly searching for riches, bankrupting himself in the process.

realm shut, worshipping Yig (the Father of Snakes), as well as Tu-lu (a.k.a. Cthulhu; *CF* 4.188). The snake-parallel could be a coincidence (given that Lovecraft's revision of "The Curse of Yig" precedes "The Mound"), but it is an interesting parallel that we have the Mother and Father of Snakes represented respectively and it requires an a stronger defense than simply the chronology of Lovecraft's compositions. There is no narrative requirement for Lovecraft to have the K'n-yan people cut off from the world—their splendid isolation and decay could be achieved in other ways and is another indication of Merritt's influence. The immortality is also not required of Lovecraft (e.g., the Elder Things in *At the Mountains of Madness* are not immortal and yet achieve similar ends).

The Yu-Atlanchi use dinosaurs called Xinli (*FFM* 30) and have part-human, part-insect creatures as servants and hunting for sport (*FFM* 60). Similarly, the K'n-yan people use half-human, half-animal servants (called gyaa-yothn [*CF* 4.213], who are also sometimes food), their animated dead, and a subhuman slave class to run their society. Invisible birdlike beings help defend the Yu-Atlanchi from interlopers (*FFM* 69), while the K'n-yan people are themselves capable of becoming immaterial (*CF* 4.205) and use that state for both defense and pleasure. These parallels require an explanation beyond coincidence—the Xinli and gyaa-yothn in particular are both hybrid creatures serving similar functions, and to my mind the latter *must* have been born from Merritt's tale.

Finally, Graydon learns a great deal from his love interest, Suarra of the Yu-Atlanchi. She tells him that the Yu-Atlanchi are the most ancient people, living in Cordillera de Carabaya due to tectonic shifts of land over time, but also enjoying their isolation (*FFM* 73–74):

> "[T]hey let the years stream by while they dream—the most of them. For they have conquered dream. Through dream they create their own worlds; do therein as they will; live life upon life as they will it. . . . Why should they go out into this one world when they can create myriads of their own at will? . . . Why should they mate with their kind, these women and men who have lived so long that they have grown weary of all their kind can give them? Why should they mate with their kind when they can create new lovers in dream, new loves and hates! Yea, new emotions, and

forms utterly unknown to earth, each as he or she may will. And so they are—barren. Not alone the doors of death, but the doors of life are closed to them, the dream makers!"

Like Graydon, Zamacona develops a local love interest (T'la-yub, CF 4.227) who also helps him attempt to escape the hidden country. The people of K'n-yan, like the Yu-Atlanchi, spend their time trying to amuse themselves: "He [Zamacona] felt the people of Tsath were a lost and dangerous race—more dangerous to themselves than they knew—and that their growing frenzy of monotony-warfare and novelty-quest was leading them rapidly toward a precipice of disintegration and utter horror" (CF 4.223).

In each case the advanced race has fallen into decadence despite their obvious powers, and both protagonists have a romantic partner to further the plot. While the latter is certainly a pulp norm for Merritt, it is *not* a device Lovecraft typically used, and to have it tied to a fallen race is unique (for example, *At the Mountain of Madness* and "The Shadow out of Time" use much different methods). Admittedly, Lovecraft's protagonist has quite different feelings toward his partner than Merritt's Graydon does (CF 4.228):

> T'la-yub he would perhaps allow to share his fortunes, for she was by no means unattractive; though possibly he would arrange for her sojourn amongst the plains Indians, since he was not overanxious to preserve links with the manner of life in Tsath. For a wife, of course, he would choose a lady of Spain—or at worst, an Indian princess of normal outer-world descent and a regular and approved past. But for the present T'la-yub must be used as a guide.

There are, by my count, ten specific points of similarity between the stories. While it may be tempting to dismiss these points in isolation in an attempt to credit Lovecraft with complete originality (or deny the influence of a pulp author like Merritt), the crucial similarity of so many basic elements of the story (decadent fallen race; hybrid slaves; romantic interest; hidden location; immortality) cannot be dismissed so readily. The plot and character parallels clearly demonstrate Merritt's influence on "The Mound."

None of the above is meant to suggest that the literary merits or goals of the stories are the same (much as H. B. Drake's *The Shadowy Thing* influenced "The Thing on the Doorstep" [*IAP* 863]): Lovecraft isn't simply rehashing "The Face in the Abyss." Merritt's tale contains no social critique other than very simplistic moralizing about greed (*FFM* 86), nor does "The Mound" contain a generic pulp romance or a *deus ex machina* to save the protagonist (*FFM* 82). Merritt's tale ends without resolution, while Lovecraft's protagonist suffers a horrible fate (*CF* 4.243). S. T. Joshi is able to spend two full pages (*IAP* 745–76) describing the depth of plot of Lovecraft's story, and that substance is what separates the two tales (there is nothing even remotely similar to Lovecraft's "narrative within a narrative within a narrative" [Joshi, *World in Transition* 270]). What the above establishes is a clear and significant influence of "The Face in the Abyss" on "The Mound."

Works Cited

Joshi, S. T. *I Am Providence: The Life and Times of H. P. Lovecraft.* New York: Hippocampus Press, 2010. 2 vols. (numbered consecutively). [*IAP*]

———. *Lovecraft and a World in Transition: Collected Essays on H. P. Lovecraft.* New York: Hippocampus Press, 2014.

———. *Lovecraft's Library: A Catalogue.* 3rd ed. New York: Hippocampus Press, 2012. [*LL*]

Lovecraft, H. P. *O Fortunate Floridian: H. P. Lovecraft's Letters to R. H. Barlow.* Ed. S. T. Joshi and David E. Schultz. Tampa: University of Florida Press, 2007.

———. *The Shadow out of Time.* Ed. S. T. Joshi and David E. Schultz. New York: Hippocampus Press, 2001. [*SOT*]

Lovecraft, H. P., and August Derleth. *Essential Solitude: The Letters of H. P. Lovecraft and August Derleth.* Ed. David E. Schultz and S. T. Joshi. New York: Hippocampus Press, 2008. 2 vols. (numbered consecutively). [*ES*]

Merritt, A. "The Face in the Abyss" (1923). In *Famous Fantastic Mysteries*, ed. Stefan R. Dziemianowicz, Robert Weinberg, and Martin H. Greenberg. New York: Gramercy Books, 1991. [*FFM*]

Essential Saltes: Lovecraft's Witchcraft

John Salonia

Sorcery—H. P. Lovecraft's work is drenched with the stuff. Not only through the "witchery of words" (to borrow Fritz Leiber's fine phrase) but as a lifelong fictional expression of his philosophy of scientific materialism. This is not the paradox it appears to be.

"Howard Phillips Lovecraft was the Copernicus of the horror story. He shifted the focus of supernatural dread from man and his little world and his gods to the stars and the black and unplumbed gulfs of intergalactic space. To do this effectively, he created a new kind of horror story and new methods for telling it."

So wrote Leiber in his perceptive and invaluable essay "A Literary Copernicus" (282). As Leiber correctly points out, one aspect of Lovecraft's new approach to traditional horror fiction was his transformation of both subject and treatment into science-fictional terms. He discovered science-fiction equivalents for conventional terror themes, making them intellectually resonant in our technological society and thus increasing their emotional and aesthetic effectiveness. However, I do not think Leiber went far enough. I wish to amplify his statement by pointing out some previously overlooked examples.

Lovecraft converted the ancient spectral themes of the Faustian bargain, necromancy, and demonic/dybbuk possession into forms more congruent with our mechanized modern culture. He accomplished this by imagining superhumanly powerful alien beings, which were misinterpreted by primitive humans as gods and demons, as the ultimate sources of "magical" power. Instead of deals with the devil, misguided wizards form pacts with alien horrors that have sinister agendas of their own. Instead of conjuring up a vaporous swirl of ectoplasm, the dead are physically reconstituted from powder prepared by special chemical (possibly alchemical) treatment, via the assistance of an extradimensional alien "god" who interpenetrates our consensual space-time reality at all points and thus can exert some measure of control over it—and the objects in it, such as these specially prepared corpses—in ways beyond human power.

Lovecraft updated the dybbuk—a disembodied human spirit that takes possession of a living person's body—by transforming it into forcible mind exchange, accomplished either through physical instrumentality, as in "The Shadow out of Time" (1934–35) and re-used in the round-robin tale "The Challenge from Beyond" (1935), or through the steely will of a human magician forcibly displacing the mind of a weaker-willed individual in "The Thing on the Doorstep" (1933). One can thus view "The Shadow out of Time" as a hyperphysical[1] reworking of "The Thing on the Doorstep."

In either case the substitution of the materialistic concept of "mind" (defined as the complex total gestalt of brain activity) for the metaphysical concept of "spirit" or "soul" provides us with a rational hook on which to suspend our disbelief, thus greatly buttressing the stories' effectiveness. From the point of view of Nathaniel Wingate Peaslee, the victim of a usurping alien mind from the prehistoric Great Race of Yith, he certainly suffers an attack by an entity long dead in his time-period and which may provisionally be classified as a dybbuk. Or, if one prefers, this case can be considered the science fiction analogue of demonic possession. And Edward Pickman Derby certainly is the victim of a literal dybbuk—as is his wife Asenath (whose name is varying translated as "She who is consecrated to Neith," "Gift of the sun-god," and, appropriately enough in this context, "She belongs to her father").

Magic is a complex subject. It embraces the sum total of human history, dating back to Neolithic cave paintings (and possibly to prehuman times, as evidenced by the ritual burials practiced by Neanderthal people) and extending to modern world leaders. An infamous example is President Ronald Reagan, who cleared his national policy decisions with professional astrologer Joan Quigley—

---

1. "Hyperphysics" is used throughout this paper as a catchall term to denote physical aspects of the universe not yet discovered, explicated, or experimentally verified by current scientific disciplines.

a situation sardonically prefigured in Robert A. Heinlein's 1961 novel *Stranger in a Strange Land*.

Billions of human beings throughout the world, in advanced technological cultures as well as so-called primitive peoples, still believe in and practice various forms of magic. Countless Americans place phone calls with professional psychics, who then read back information gathered via the Internet to their clients as "proof" of their psychic powers. This primitive streak has not been eradicated despite generations who have grown up with a *soi-disant* rational education.

If this is not a complete indictment of modern education, then perhaps magical thinking can arguably be classified as an instinctual conception of the human mind. That we tacitly accept this about ourselves is seen in the popular film *Forbidden Planet* (which owes more to Stevenson's *The Strange Case of Dr. Jekyll and Mr. Hyde* than to its putative source, Shakespeare's *The Tempest*), in which even the incredibly advanced Krel civilization is eradicated "overnight" by "monsters from the Id" and "the mindless primitive." This concept strikes a nerve, and for good reason. Knowing ourselves, we immediately accept the fate of the Krel as a harbinger of our own doom.

This type of non-rational, poetic-logic thinking is the taproot of all religions, which posit a spiritual world in addition to the material world of everyday consensual reality. This spiritual world is neither matter nor energy but an imponderable thing of a third category; a different essence not subject to the laws of nature we observe in the physical cosmos.

Magic is the desire to render the chaos of existence into an ordered, comprehensible, and controllable form, thus satisfying a basic psychological need for security; and its practice unsurprisingly continues to this day throughout the world, from American magazine and newspaper horoscopes and psychic hotlines to Japanese businessmen using ancient divination techniques before closing deals.

Chapter 9 of Michael Edwardes's *The Dark Side of History* is titled "The Raising of the Pentagon," meaning both the magical symbol formed at the nexus of a pentacle's intersecting lines and the Pentagon Building in Washington, D.C. An extract will illustrate the book's main argument:

Magic was important in ancient, medieval, and Renaissance culture. The heritage of Greece and Rome . . . is saturated with magical beliefs. The best minds of the Middle Ages drew on this rich mine . . .They may have disapproved of some magical practices . . . but they did not deny the effectiveness, the reality or the importance of magic.

Magic involved not just witchcraft and pacts with the Devil, but also a whole concept of the world and man's relation to it. Thinkers such as St. Albertus Magnus, St. Thomas Aquinas, and Dante believed in sympathetic bonds linking all reality, in the existence of occult qualities, astral influences, and the actions of good and bad demons as described in the books of magic compiled by lesser men. Most historians, particularly those of science, have chosen to ignore this.

The Renaissance carried on without a break this traditional belief in magic. In fact, there was a direct continuity of magical traditions from the Middle Ages right down to the seventeenth century. In the Renaissance, for all its humanist pretensions, magic was considered to be even more important than it had been in medieval times. It was part of the intellectual baggage of any man of culture, whether he was painter or pope, ruler or revolutionary.

By the end of the seventeenth century, it appeared that the new science of such men as Sir Isaac Newton[2] had banished magic . . . In the eighteenth century, the philosophers of the Age of Reason convinced themselves that magic was dead. The technicians of the first Industrial Revolution did not think about magic at all, and the Victorian empire builder . . . viewed it as something objectionable practiced by inferior races.[3] In our own century, magic . . . has been regarded as the concern of the bored, the affluent, the psychotic, and the cultural anthropologist, all of them peripheral to the mainstream of life.

. . . Under the onslaught of reason and science, the occult went underground—but not very far. It reappears, in a manner distaste-

---

2. Paradoxically, Newton retained a lifelong belief in alchemy. See White, who lists 31 index entries under "alchemy."

3. This fits neatly into HPL's concept of degenerate cultists, such as those figuring in "The Call of Cthulhu" and "The Shadow over Innsmouth." The idea of alien-assisting cultists also appears in "The Shadow out of Time," "The Whisperer in Darkness," and "The Haunter of the Dark."

ful to the orthodox liberal historian, in radical and revolutionary political and social theories; in anti-colonialism; in popular education; in efforts to conserve the environment.

The explanation of the persistence of the occult tradition is simple enough. Reason, rationalism, scientific ideas have never been capable of containing either human aspiration or human suffering. Religion for the majority has never been more than a tranquilizer—accept, wait, and on the other side, if you have been good, you will find paradise. Magic, on the other hand, has always been activist, a statement of faith in the capacity of man rather than the compassion of God. (3–4)

Magic has played an important role in literature equally as long as its role in history. As far back as Homer's *Odyssey* we have a necromantic ritual designed to attract the spirits of the dead and empower communication with them via a blood sacrifice, which temporarily grants these ghosts the power to speak intelligibly to the living. It is no wonder that Lovecraft, with his innate love of order and tradition and his philosophical conviction of an ordered mechanistic universe, should have made fictional use of magic throughout his life. To him, sorcery was both a means of controlling the cosmos and an ironic method of imaginative escape from the binding strictures of time and space.

Lovecraft's fictional interest in magic is therefore not only understandable but also actually inevitable. As he was philosophically incapable of believing in magic as a literal physical reality, sorcery became for him an essential mode of imaginative escape and release; a way of realizing, if only subjectively, the sensation of "adventurous expectancy" that was one of his lifelong emotional goals—a favorite phrase expressed many times throughout his voluminous correspondence.

Magic has been many things to many people. Lovecraft derided much of it even as a source of aesthetic satisfaction. Intellectually, of course, he rightly considered the supernatural a blatant impossibility, but some forms of it appealed to him as a means of crystallizing aesthetic impressions, even while scoffing at puerile wish-fulfillment worldviews that accepted magic as an actual operative force in consensual reality. (Aleister Crowley and C. G. Jung are both extreme examples of how even persons of a high order of intelligence can be insidiously seduced by their own imaginative creations, embracing their models of alleged "reality" under the all-forgiving aegis of: "I believe the universe to be this way because I want the universe to be this way.")

Roughly, sorcery can be divided into High Magic and Low Magic. High Magic is ritual or ceremonial magic: spirit invocations and evocations, and the summoning and binding of demons to the magician's will. A subset is the Faustian pact with demonic creatures (whether actual devils in the theological sense or alien beings perceived and explicated as demons by superstitious human beings is immaterial), exemplified by "The Dunwich Horror" (1928) and "The Shadow over Innsmouth" (1931).

Low Magic concerns such things as *maleficia* and *veneficia*, using spells and poisons to raise storms, blast cattle, plague personal enemies with illness and misfortune, and inflict death-curses via image magic; and love-magic to attract love or arouse sexual desire.

Lovecraft had no use for such banal concepts love-philters or magically induced impotence by tying knots in a "witch's ladder." Fictionally, he concerned himself primarily with High Magic, although George Gammell Angell's death via a suspected poison-needle administered by a Cthulhu cultist could be considered a rare instance of *veneficia* in his stories.

I have found no evidence that Lovecraft ever read Christopher Marlowe, but I believe that parts of Faustus' famous soliloquy would have resonated with him:

> These metaphysics of magicians
> And necromantic books are heavenly;
> Lines, circles, letters, characters:
> Ay, these are those that Faustus most desires . . .
> But his dominion that exceeds in this
> Stretcheth as far as doth the mind of man . . . (Marlowe 9)

Other subsets of High Magic are magic as a form of worship, as in "The Call of Cthulhu" and "The Dreams in the Witch House"; and magic as natural philosophy, a common eighteenth-century conceit[4] and thus attractive to Lovecraft, with his well-

---

4. This renaming was basically a dodge by students of the occult to avoid prosecution for sorcery or heresy.

documented attachment to the Georgian period. In this view, magic is a form of as-yet-unexplained science, i.e., the use of natural laws and forces not yet discovered by formally recognized scientific disciplines, as portrayed in *The Case of Charles Dexter Ward* (1927), for which see below.

Somewhere in between these extremes lies "The Dunwich Horror," with its Faustian bargain between the degenerate Old Whateley and the extracosmic entity Yog-Sothoth, who rewards Old Whateley with antique gold coins for prostituting his half-witted daughter Lavinia for the conception of an earthly spawn of Yog-Sothoth capable of opening the interdimensional gates to the Old Ones. Like Faustus, Old Whateley supplicates superhuman powers to gain an earthly advantage—the debased and petty advantage of being guided to hidden buried treasure, a common means by which demons, fairies, and other supernatural creatures grant wealth to mortals in both folktales and fiction (e.g., Washington Irving's "The Devil and Tom Walker").

By harnessing these folktales to the Old Ones who dwell in a dimensional structure that interpenetrates our own, making them extracosmic aliens instead of theological demons, Lovecraft ingeniously subverts all folktales of sorcerers' pacts with devils as superstition-garbled accounts of an ongoing traffic between human beings and the Old Ones throughout human existence. This lends a feigned historicity to his fiction and thereby buttresses its convincingness. It is one of the tale's many clever and inventive touches.

Such supplication implies a degree of worship, or at least veneration, in the sense of acknowledging the superiority of the supplicated being, which must be placated and cajoled by an offering of the sorcerer's soul or some other form of human sacrifice; in this case Lavinia Whateley. Marlowe makes this same point both explicitly and implicitly at several points, depicting Faustus as an unwilling worshipper of Mephistophilis, Lucifer, and Beelzebub. He placates these infernal deities through fear of their reprisals. Possibly Old Whateley fears the Old Ones; primitive veneration is born of fear.

"The Dunwich Horror" has been characterized as a simple good-vs.-evil story, but it has its complexities. Both the good (Dr. Armitage) and the evil (Old Whateley) are embodied solely in human beings and human perceptions. Like his father Yog-Sothoth, Wilbur Whateley is indifferent to such human moral considerations and works only to further the Old Ones' desired reclamation of the earth.

However, it is perfectly valid from the human perspective to view the Old Ones' intentions toward us as malevolent. This dramatically demonstrates that morality is purely a matter of viewpoint, since the Old Ones could conceivably claim that the earth is actually theirs by right of prior possession, and that they are simply exercising a form of pest control by exterminating all terrestrial life. Such an affirmation that morality is purely a selfish and limited human concern fits in well with Lovecraft's bleak materialistic cosmos, in which anthropocentric values have no objective worth.

This point demands a slight digression. Much has been written in recent scholarship rebutting August Derleth's pseudo-Catholic misrepresentation of Lovecraft's fictional pantheon. Repeatedly it is pointed out that Lovecraft's aliens are beyond anthropocentric concepts of good and evil. While this is undeniably true, it has been unduly stressed, to the point where these creatures' unfailingly malign intentions toward humanity are downplayed or ignored outright. Many commentators describe Lovecraft's monsters as "indifferent" to humanity.

Fritz Leiber pointed out as early as 1945: "I believe that the entities . . . employed by Lovecraft are predominantly malevolent, or, at best, cruelly indifferent to mankind" (277). However, Leiber's vital point of malevolence has become somewhat obscured in recent years, and I think it useful to reemphasize this aspect of Lovecraft's stories.

Lovecraft wrote tales of horror, in which he intended to crystallize fear. To do so, he had to populate them with creatures inimical to mankind. That this artistic stance is both philosophically and aesthetically valid—as well as scientifically accurate—is proved by the fact that the vast majority of cosmic phenomena are actively hostile to human life. Vacuum, extremes of temperature and radiation, atmospheric and gravitational conditions on most alien worlds—why, we cannot even inhabit nearly 71 percent of our own planet! Dramatizing this staggeringly enormous environmental hostility as hostile alien monsters is perfectly valid—indeed, inevitable. It is, quite simply, "good theater."

That Lovecraft's alien "gods" have no interest in human moral terminology and have no concern with anthropocentric religious views does not negate their abiding desire to use and abuse us for their own sinister purposes and to achieve their own horrific goals. Even the least malevolent of Lovecraft's aliens—the star-headed crinoid beings of *At the Mountains of Madness*, who fully merit Leiber's characterization as "cruelly indifferent"—have no hesitation in curiously dissecting and then feeding on the unknown mammalian bipeds (the unfortunate Lake and his party) among whom they awaken after their long hibernation. Additional examples can be adduced from many of Lovecraft's stories as proof of this contention, but to avoid beating the point to death, I will mention only a few salient instances.

"The Shadow over Innsmouth": the Deep Ones desire to mate with human beings, thereby creating a degenerate hybrid stock with allegiance to the underwater breed and opposed to normal human beings. Their ultimate aim seems to be the complete removal of a purely human race and civilization in favor of this hybrid stock (which might possibly serve as a slave class to the purebred Deep Ones). They have already established a secretive beachhead in Innsmouth for this insidious ongoing infiltration, and they ruthlessly extirpate any normal humans who stumble on their secret.

"The Colour out of Space": the alien vapor actively preys on the Gardner family to nourish itself.

"The Shadow out of Time": the Great Race of Yith bypasses the human race in their mass migration of minds into their future, but that is only because the Blind Beings they fear still survive during the lifespan of our species. This is pure pragmatism at best. If the Blind Beings had become extinct before humanity evolved, the Great Race might well have ruthlessly invaded *us* instead of the coleopterous species that will succeed us in Lovecraft's imagined future. Such a geologically earlier invasion would in fact better suit the Great Race's plans, since it would increase their span of occupancy of the earth before planetary cooling forces them to invade worlds nearer the sun.

"From Beyond": the extradimensional, interpenetrating amoeboid beings that fill all space disintegrate the servants of Crawford Tillinghast. Whether they do so from hunger, curiosity, malice, or mere accident matters little to the victims. But these examples will suffice.

"The Call of Cthulhu" and "The Dreams in the Witch House" depict pseudoscientific magic as the truth behind mystery cults and witchcraft (the two terms overlap somewhat). In *Charles Dexter Ward* there appears a form of actual (i.e., nonfictional) sorcery quoted from the works of Petrus Borellus in the 1702 first edition of Cotton Mather's *Magnalia Christi Americana*, a copy of which Lovecraft owned. Barton Levi St. Armand pointed out the source of the Borellus quotation in *Nyctalops*.[5] And Lovecraft typically adopted it into his ongoing hyperphysical reinterpretation of magic.

The Borellus quotation is used as a headpiece to *Charles Dexter Ward*:

> The essential Saltes of Animals may be so prepared and preserved, that an ingenious Man may have the whole Ark of Noah in his own Studie, and raise the fine Shape of an Animal out of its Ashes at his Pleasure; and by the lyke Method from the essential Saltes of humane Dust, a Philosopher may, without any criminal Necromancy, call up the Shape of any dead Ancestour from the Dust whereinto his Bodie has been incinerated. (CF 2.214)

Petrus Borellus was Pierre Borel (1620?–1671), a French polymath who was a physician and botanist as well as a chemist. Significantly, he was rumored to be an alchemist as well. Borel also studied optics, ancient history, philology, and bibliography. He is the author of *Historiarium et observationum medico-physicarum centuria IV* (1653) and *Biblioteca chimica* (1654), either of which may have served as the source of the passage Mather quoted.

An interestingly similar process can be found in Vallemont's *La Physique occulte*, published in Amsterdam in 1693:

> Salt, heat and motion is the whole secret of the vampire,[6] accord-

5. I am indebted to S. T. Joshi for supplying this information.

6. Parenthetically, the immaterial life-sucking alien entity in "The Colour out of Space" (1927) can be viewed as an aesthetic perfection of the vaporous manifes-

ing to the Abbé de Vallemont, Pierre de Lorraine (1649–1721). Anything which has been, can appear again . . . The dead can return, just as plants and animals can be revived, at least temporarily. Take a flask and put into it the vital essence of the seed of a beautiful rose. Burn this to ashes, imbue it with the morning's dew, collecting enough for a modest distillation. Extract the salt from the ashes and mix it with the distilled dew; seal the bottle with pounded glass and borax. Lay the vessel on fresh horse manure [a source of steady warmth as it decays, often employed in alchemy] and leave it there for a month. Then expose it alternately to the sunlight and to the moonlight. When the gelatinous matter at the bottom of the vessel swells, this shows the experiment has been a success. Now, each time you expose your bottle to the sunlight, the spectre of the rose will appear . . . this process can be repeated indefinitely. (Seligmann 305)

Both Borellus and Vallemont use natural if hitherto unknown physical processes to recall the dead in material or semi-material form. In other words, necromancy is being subsumed by natural philosophy (science).[7] This would have greatly appealed to Lovecraft's scientific bent as well as suiting his fictional needs.

However, portraying Joseph Curwen as a benevolent natural philosopher hardly suited Lovecraft's purpose. He thus added Yog-Sothoth to the mix, prefiguring that entity's reappearance a year later in "The Dunwich Horror." Possibly Lovecraft was still working out Yog-Sothoth's exact nature (as an alien being that interpenetrates our four-dimensional plenum) in *Charles Dexter Ward*. Vallemont's formula requires only sunlight as an operative power, and not the invocation of a sinister extradimensional alien. Yog-Sothoth's presence in the story certainly underlines Joseph Curwen's baleful aspirations, for—despite Borellus' disingenuous assertion—Curwen is certainly guilty of "criminal Necromancy."

Both young Ward and his ancestor exemplify another of the High Magician's choicest desiderata: the gaining of arcane and oc-

---

tations of the buried vampire in "The Shunned House" (1924).

7. Shades of the DNA cloning of long-dead animals in Michael Crichton's *Jurassic Park* (1990) and its little-known predecessor, Harry Adam Knight's *Carnosaur* (1984). One might poetically describe DNA as the "essential saltes" of a living creature.

cult knowledge; i.e., a better understanding of the nature of reality. This is no ignoble goal, and one with obvious appeal to Lovecraft's boundless intellectual curiosity. Dr. Faustus spends a significant portion of his time in Marlowe's play in questioning Mephistophilis about the hidden secrets of nature and metaphysics, just as Curwen questions (sometimes forcibly, as hinted by his collection of torture-chamber equipment) his resurrected wizards and savants.

Similarly, Lovecraft's fictional Starry Wisdom cult worships the Haunter of the Dark in order to obtain cosmic knowledge from the monstrous entity evoked via the Shining Trapezohedron. Discovering the true nature of reality is one of the dominant themes of Lovecraft's entire fictional output, spilling over into his more interesting poetry as well (*Fungi from Yuggoth*, "The Poe-et's Nightmare," "The Nightmare Lake," etc.). One might facetiously summarize this relentless pursuit of ultimate understanding at all costs as "Curiosity killed the cat—but the cat had no choice; it *had* to know."

In "The Dunwich Horror," Old Whateley sells out the human race for money, whereas the more intellectually sophisticated Professor Enoch Bowen does so for occult knowledge in "The Haunter of the Dark." Both men traffic with superhuman alien entities, and the end result is the same: the invasion of the earth by malefic forces from beyond.

This equivalent end result sardonically couples the highest and lowest types of human endeavor: the quest for knowledge and the desire for material self-aggrandizement. This coupling echoes Lovecraft's philosophical conviction of the ultimate pettiness of the human species and all its concerns. No matter how nobly or ignobly we behave, we are still insects from the cosmic viewpoint—and, like insects, we will end up squashed by greater beings if we get in their way.

One of Lovecraft's most interesting tales from the perspective of his hyperphysical predilection is "The Dreams in the Witch House." It is a continuation of his paradigm shift from "magic" (in the purely supernatural sense) to hyperphysics as both plot-mechanism and worldview.

Lovecraft continued to employ traditional forms of magic such as crystal-gazing ("The Haunter of the Dark") and mind projection (a pseudoscientific variant of astral projection, or spirit journeys), but he used them in new ways that furthered his scientific-materialistic views. This is not a paradox; the magic in these tales is unexplained science that allows contact between human beings and entities existing either in the remote past or in alien dimensional planes. It is clearly not the same sort of magic employed by supernatural-universe fantasy fiction characters such as Gandalf the Grey, Elric of Melniboné, or Albaric Corwen.

Lovecraft's usage of this so-called magic can be viewed as mechanism-assisted forms of psionic powers: the Shining Trapezohedron and the strange device used to force a re-exchange between the usurping psyche of a Great Race member and Nathaniel Wingate Peaslee's mind are both forms of instrumentality—with an emphasis on the mentality. Without such tools, these powers cannot be utilized; one does not simply draw a magic circle, light some human-fat candles, wave a wand, and recite the magic words. One may conjecture that the very shape of the Shining Trapezohedron—which, being a crystal, it embodies right down to the molecular or even the atomic level, depending on whether it is composed of a compound or an element[8]—allows the bridging of the dimensional barriers between our cosmos and the realm in which the Haunter exists.

"The Dreams in the Witch House" posits witchcraft as a form of hyperphysics utilized by a sinister cult that worships Nyarlathotep, who embodies himself in the form of the traditional Black Man of the covens. The story also cleverly postulates that the latest advances in human knowledge (quantum mechanics, universes based on non-Euclidean geometries, etc.) are science's ironic first feeble fumbling steps toward rediscovering this ancient lore bestowed by Nyarlathotep on his primitive worshippers and preserved through their immemorial esoteric tradition. (And, since learning a small scrap of this ancient lore proves so dire for Walter Gilman, what will science's continued progress in this field do to the rest of us?)

---

8. Thus bringing us whole orders of magnitude closer to the subatomic world of quantum uncertainty—a chaotic realm in which contact with an entity like the Haunter of the Dark seems somehow more plausible.

"The Dreams in the Witch House" is a highly detailed example of what came to be known as Clarke's Law: "Any sufficiently advanced technology is indistinguishable from magic." Arthur C. Clarke formulated it in a 1973 revision of his essay "Hazards of Prophecy: The Failure of Imagination," which first appeared in 1962 in *Profiles of the Future*. Possibly Lovecraft (or his influence on the fantasy field) helped inspire Clarke's observation.

As Lovecraft aged, his fiction gradually substituted more openly rationalistic science for the more romantic concepts of forbidden lore and black magic, but his fictional sorcery had always smacked of science—magic viewed through the lens of Clarke's Law. It was more a shift of terminology than of viewpoint.

This treatment of sorcery was echoed in the 1942 use of "Witchcraft to the ignorant . . . simple science to the learned" (Brackett 39) and serves as the basis of the planet-wide techno-theocratic future totalitarianism in Fritz Leiber's 1943 novel *Gather, Darkness!* Since Lovecraft was already moving in this fictional direction, a passage in H. Rider Haggard's *She* quite possibly spurred him along: "Have I not told thee that there is no such thing as magic, though there is such a thing as understanding and applying the forces which are in Nature?" (191). In a letter to August Derleth dated October 31, 1926, Lovecraft notes having recently read the novel. Very likely it reinforced his bent toward hyperphysics.

The theme of "sorcery as unknown science" was a popular one among Victorian writers of fantasy. In addition to Haggard, Arthur Machen and Bulwer-Lytton also employed the idea. Bram Stoker touched on it fleetingly in *Dracula* as a possible explanation for the Count's longevity, and much more extensively in *The Jewel of Seven Stars* as a rationale for Queen Tera's impending resurrection.

But none of these earlier writers tied the idea of magic to technological science as explicitly and consistently as did Lovecraft. None of them exploited hard science in the tale of terror as fully as he did, always refining and extending the concept. These previous writers took hyperphysics as a given, sometimes dreaming up elaborate examples, but these were always colorful one-shots. Lovecraft seriously developed the idea throughout his writing career.

The ectoplasm-disintegrating vibrations of the Crookes tube in "The Shunned House" ironically prove ineffective, since the life-sucking mist (Lovecraft's adroit pseudoscientific restatement of the ability of Count Dracula and his vampiric brides to manifest themselves as a cloud of dissociated particles of "elemental dust"[9]) is actually some hellish amalgamation of both the material and the ethereal, which the Crookes waves cannot dissipate.

Yet the tube's matter-of-fact inclusion in Dr. Whipple's arsenal along with the more traditional occult weapon of purifying fire (the flame-throwers intended to burn out the vampire's heart, as in the famous Exeter case) is a telling touch. The occult may be the unknown, but in Lovecraft's fictional canon science trumps it: simple chemistry has the ultimate victory when carboys of sulfuric acid destroy the physically inert vampire, ending its centuries-long haunting of the shunned house.

Even in his description of the monster's corporeal state Lovecraft respects the laws of science: since matter and energy can neither be created nor destroyed but only transformed, the victims' stolen life-energy is accounted for by the monstrous growth of the vampire's buried body.

In the early years of the twentieth century Algernon Blackwood and William Hope Hodgson often dropped pseudoscientific references (e.g., Carnacki's "Electric Pentacle") into their tales, but neither of them systematically employed the concept in their fiction, especially in any form of linear development. Other fantasists such as Seabury Quinn picked up the gimmick (e.g., Jules de Grandin electrocuting a ghost with an energized copper window screen).

However, none of these writers made this an ongoing and vital expression of their work. Lovecraft is the first to develop and extend the concept of "hyperphysical magic" not only for fictional purposes, but also as a statement of a personal credo. He did it in an almost systematic fashion, constantly mining plot-ideas and incidents from earlier stories and reformulating them along increasingly rational (i.e., science-fictional) lines. I specify "almost systematic" because I do not believe Lovecraft was developing this theme along the lines of any *conscious* plan, but rather on a catch-as-catch-can basis, feeling his way along as inspiration struck sparks from his prevailing worldview.

---

9. This phrase irresistibly reminds me of "essential saltes."

Lovecraft utilized hyperphysical sorcery ten years before Brackett in "The Dreams in the Witch House." Certainly there was a widespread twentieth-century fictional promulgation (particularly among the pulps) of this conception of sorcery as an ancient, superstition-encrusted form of scientific knowledge surpassing our own and lost and/or suppressed by ecclesiastical proclamation over the ages, although preserved by an esoteric tradition of *soi-disant* supernatural wisdom.

Lovecraft's growing fame among weird fiction aficionados probably has a great deal to do with this proliferation. Obviously the idea had been in the air since the previous century. However, Lovecraft's tireless dedication to making his weird fiction convincing and his undoubted success at accomplishing this made the attractive concept even more popular. (We may disregard Lovecraft's disparaging and despairing dismissal of his own work for failing fully to capture all the exquisite facets of the glittering dark jewels that blossomed like night-black nenuphars in his fertile brain, for they certainly glitter sufficiently for *us*.[10] We cannot read his mind, only his texts.)

Lovecraft long favored the ideas Margaret Murray expressed in *The Witch-Cult in Western Europe* (1921). Although modern scholars do not hold Murray in high esteem, for Lovecraft's purposes her notion of widespread pagan-cult survival was just what the witch-doctor ordered, providing him with a plausible mechanism by which to transmit ancient esoteric knowledge down to the modern day, even among the illiterate and the degenerate. It also lent his fiction the respectably scientific veneer of then-current anthropology, thereby buttressing his fantasy. It is hard not to see the prefiguring of the Cthulhu cultists, as well as the half-human Dagon-worshippers of Innsmouth, the quisling Vermont hill-folk who aid the Outer Ones, and the rest of their ilk.

Lovecraft also revised and adapted his notion of degenerate cultists, from literal physical degradation to the more dangerous (because it can pass among us undetected) mental and cultural aberration of later alien-worshippers. The urbane and affable Noyes of "The Whisperer in Darkness" (1930) is a far cry from the

---

10. The mixed metaphor of this imagery is completely intentional, and owes much to Clark Ashton Smith.

crude, savage Old Castro and his fellow Cthulhu-worshippers of 1926 and the inbred Dunwich folk of 1928—and he is all the more unsettling and disturbing because of it.

Given the paucity of extant copies of the *Necronomicon*, of which Lovecraft stipulated that only five were officially known to exist,[11] Murray's pagan cult-survival allowed the esoteric tradition to crop up anywhere Lovecraft wished it to appear. Transplanting the furtively pagan witch-cult into Salem was an obvious step in rooting his horrors in actual American history and thus increasing their immediacy for his readers. In "The Horror at Red Hook" (1925) he Americanized the idea of the Witches' Sabbat (as an ancient polyglot survival mingling entities from classical mythology with Asian and Hebrew beings, such as Lilith) by locating the cult in the heart of a major American metropolis, thus predating Ira Levin by decades.

The trend of substituting science for magic appears in Lovecraft's fiction as early as 1919 and 1920, in "Beyond the Wall of Sleep" and "From Beyond," respectively. In both these tales, physical instrumentality serves to connect the human world with other realms of wonder and horror, via crude electronic telepathy and pineal-gland stimulation. The ghastly interpenetrating cosmic larvae of "From Beyond" can be viewed as a dry run for the Old Ones of "The Dunwich Horror,"[12] just as much as "Dagon" (1917) can be seen as an early experimental form of "The Call of Cthulhu" (1926). Throughout his life, Lovecraft continually reused concepts from earlier tales in more complex, expanded, and highly detailed later stories, invariably with greater artistic polish and aesthetic effectiveness.

The point of "Beyond the Wall of Sleep" and "From Beyond" is that Lovecraft's scientists accomplish what in more traditionally themed fantasy fiction would be called feats of magic. At this

---

11. Although in several of HPL's stories, additional copies of the *Necronomicon* are also found in various private collections.

12. These creatures reappear in *The Dream-Quest of Unknown Kadath* (1926–27), in which they are explicitly identified as the spawn of the Other Gods. These beings, and their connection with Azathoth and the rest of the Other Gods, clearly were still current in HPL's mind a year later when he wrote "The Dunwich Horror."

juncture it is irresistible to quote Dr. Pretorius in *The Bride of Frankenstein:* "It is interesting to think, Henry, that once we should have been burned at the stake as wizards for this experiment" (Hurlbut and Balderston, sequence H-2).

The hyperphysical equipment in these early Lovecraft stories establishes contact with other realms separated from our own by dimensional barriers impervious to our unaided senses. Later, in "The Dunwich Horror" with its Faustian sub-theme, incantations and blood sacrifices are featured instead of pseudoscientific equipment. But this is neither a regression in terms of concept nor a simple bow to tradition; it is simply a necessary substitution of plot-mechanism. The underlying idea remains unchanged.

Properly speaking, Old Whateley's ceremonies are not "spells" at all. The spells of black magic are invocations of evil spirits, which exist in a religious hierarchy that extends in graduated levels from absolute good to absolute evil. Old Whateley's incantations serve as hyperphysical formulae to establish contact with extracosmic realms by opening interdimensional gateways or portals.

There is no inherent moral stigma involved in their use, such as that associated with the Black Mass and Satanism. (This is not to say that there is no *danger* in their use.) One can imagine a disinterested scientist testing them under controlled conditions. One is not damned for the "sin" of using them, for in Lovecraft's non-religious universe, such terms as "damned" and "damnable" exist purely as metaphorical expressions of his characters' emotional reactions to horrific phenomena. They are not literal realities. "Sin" is merely a primitive human cultural conception not yet abolished because humanity has not evolved beyond it.

The formula employed by Armitage, Rice, and Morgan to end the Dunwich Horror is not in any traditional sense a piece of magic. It is not an exorcism, nor is it the ceremonial magician's formal "license to depart," a rite designed to dismiss the summoned spirit back to the place whence it came, there to abide until the magician evokes it again; and it is of vital importance because "the magician cannot leave the [protective magic] circle until the spirit has gone and he cannot be sure that the spirit has gone until he has formally ordered him away" (Cavendish 252).

The ritual used by Armitage and his cohorts literally disintegrates Wilbur Whateley's brother; "it has been split up into what it was originally made of" (*CF* 2.465). Restated in materialistic terms, this hyperphysical formula sets up local field conditions under which it is impossible for the monstrous spawn to exist. "You needn't ask how Wilbur called it out of the air. He didn't call it out" (*CF* 2.466), so the half-human hybrid can't simply be sent packing. Armitage's formula destroys the entity as utterly as a particle of antimatter made to collide with a particle of earthly matter in a nuclear physicist's cloud chamber.[13]

Old Whateley's traffic with Yog-Sothoth is evil because he is a degenerate and selfish man. His spells are evil only insofar as his personal agenda is evil. We do not know much about Professor Bowen's motivations—presumably pure intellectual curiosity, with a stated taste for occult studies—yet within two years of his bringing the Starry Wisdom cult (and the Shining Trapezohedron) to Providence, Rhode Island, people begin mysteriously disappearing. Within four years these disappearances are being openly talked of as blood sacrifices.

Like Faustus, Bowen's insatiable curiosity leads him to "offer lukewarm blood of newborn babes" (Marlowe 26) to keep feeding his addiction to the arcane knowledge doled out by the Haunter. He too is corrupted, although on a higher plane than Old Whateley—and here we see Lovecraft turning the classical theme of diabolical temptation to his own purposes, updating it in pragmatic materialistic terms instead of spiritual and moral ones. It is perhaps significant, and certainly ironic, in view of Lovecraft's lifelong reverence for science as well as Greek civilization and rationalism, that Bowen's "sin" can be classified as scientific hubris.

The Haunter of the Dark is not interested in the souls (if such exist) of Bowen and his fellow Starry Wisdom cultists. The entity wants physical access to the earth, and it needs human crystal-gazers to fulfill its desire. Satan's purpose is to test the faith and moral strength of those he tempts; he operates solely (pun intend-

---

13. Parenthetically, the monstrous mating of human beings with the non-human is another theme HPL continually revisited and expanded: "Facts concerning the Late Arthur Jermyn and His Family" (1920), "The Unnamable" (1923), "The Horror at Red Hook" (1925), "Pickman's Model" (1926), "The Dunwich Horror" (1928), "The Shadow over Innsmouth" (1931), "The Thing on the Doorstep" (1933).

ed) with the permission of God. The Haunter has no interest in testing the moral caliber of those it tempts: the creature is interested in obtaining human tools, not human souls. And there is no "god" above it—unless it is Azathoth.[14]

This is of vital importance because the extracosmic realms opened by Old Whateley's rituals and by gazing into the Shining Trapezohedron have no place in any anthropocentric mythology, which view the spirit world as the ultimate goal of earthly existence; both the material and spiritual worlds are linked dualities in the intentional schemes of a deity or deities. The hyperphysical realms Lovecraft postulates would still exist (fictionally speaking) even if the earth were destroyed, or if it had never been formed.

When Lovecraft wrote "The Dunwich Horror," he still had not conceived the idea of transmitting the plans for mechanical hyperphysical devices to human cultists via time-traveling alien minds; that concept would not emerge until 1934–35 and "The Shadow out of Time." For "Dunwich," the incantation was a preferable plot mechanism, allowing Lovecraft to slot in his science-fictional reworking of the Faustian bargain as well as to pay tribute to the pseudoscientific plot-mechanism of his story's immediate inspiration, Machen's "The Great God Pan." It is highly significant that Helen Vaughan is conceived when her mother is enabled to apprehend Pan through a surgical operation on her brain. There are few things further removed from the vagaries of the occult than the honed no-nonsense edge of a scalpel.

I do not believe Lovecraft would have met the exigency of Machen's mind-destroying scientifically revealed pantheism (perhaps "pandemonism" is a better term) with a simple incantation. He instead rose to the challenge by placing his omnipresent alien

---

14. This is poor pseudo-etymology, but it is irresistible to analyze Azathoth, at least playfully, as follows: *a-* as a privative, which gives some words of Greek origin a negative sense, such as atom from Greek *atomos*, an indivisible ultimate particle of an element (*a* priv., and *tomos* from *temnein*, 'to cut'); and Thoth, the Greek name of *Tehuti* or *Djhuty*, the Egyptian scribe-god of all wisdom, knowledge, and lore. Thus Azathoth might unofficially be interpreted as "lacking all wisdom, knowledge and lore." It is a temptingly apt description of the blind and mindless daemon-sultan. (One might also find a suitably mordant Lovecraftian in-joke in the fact that Thoth is the scribe—the *writer*—of the Egyptian pantheon.)

in a dimensional structure that is far more complex than the simple up-down, right-left, forward-backward configuration that is our common experience. This is a forerunner of the hyperspatial multi-dimensional cosmos Lovecraft would develop more fully in "The Dreams in the Witch House."

It would not be logically believable for Old Whateley to use any sort of mechanical apparatus to allow Yog-Sothoth access to his daughter Lavinia. The incantation is a better storytelling device in this case, since it is suitable for transmission from primitive ages down to our time via an oral tradition of covert "sorcery," supplemented by suppressed grimoires such as the *Necronomicon.* And such hyperphysical "engines" can be operated in backwoods areas where ready sources of electrical power are not available.

Lovecraft's ultimately materialistic attitude toward the concept of magic is utilized far more directly and in greater and more explicit detail in his later, more openly science fiction–oriented tales such as "The Shadow out of Time," "The Whisperer in Darkness" and *At the Mountains of Madness*—but the seed was there all along. Lovecraft carefully weeded, watered, pruned, and grafted his own sinisterly gorgeous Garden of Adompha throughout his writing career.

Works Cited

Brackett, Leigh. "The Sorcerer of Rhiannon." *Astounding* (February 1942).

Cavendish, Richard, *The Black Arts.* New York: G. P. Putnam's Sons, 1967.

Edwardes, Michael. *The Dark Side of History: Magic in the Making of Man.* New York: Stein & Day, 1977.

Haggard, H. Rider. *She.* 1886. London: Longmans, Green, 1911.

Hurlbut, William, and John L. Balderston. *The Bride of Frankenstein.* Original shooting script edited by Philip J. Riley. n.p.: MagicImage Filmbooks, 1989. (*Note:* The script pages are not numbered, hence the sequence number for the cited passage.)

Leiber, Fritz, and H. P. Lovecraft. *Fritz Leiber and H. P. Lovecraft: Writers of the Dark.* Edited by Ben J. S. Szumskyj and S. T. Joshi. Holicong, PA: Wildside Press, 2004.

Marlowe, Christopher. *The Tragical History of the Life and Death of Doctor Faustus*. Edited by John D. Jump. Manchester: Manchester University Press, 1962.

Seligman, Kurt. *Magic, Supernaturalism and Religion*. New York: Pantheon, 1948.

St. Armand, Barton Levi. "The Source of Lovecraft's Knowledge of Borellus in *The Case of Charles Dexter Ward*." *Nyctalops* 2, No. 6 (May 1977): 16–17.

White, Michael. *Isaac Newton: The Last Sorcerer*. London: Fourth Estate, 1997.

H. P. Lovecraft's Weird Body

Alison Sperling

> The horror of the cosmos is essentially a horror of the body.
> —Dylan Trigg, *The Thing* (2014)

Introduction

The writings of H. P. Lovecraft are experiencing a renaissance in the twenty-first century. Elevated from "pulp author" to "canonical classic" by the Library of America publication of his oeuvre in 2005, Lovecraft has since been revived in literary criticism and, perhaps even more productively, in philosophy (Harman, "On the Horror" 4). In the last decade or so, Lovecraft's tales, letters, and essays have re-emerged with intensity, markedly in the influential philosopher Graham Harman's book, *Weird Realism: Lovecraft and Philosophy* (Zero Books, 2012). Lovecraft's work has repeatedly appeared in philosophical essays and books that follow in Harman's speculative realist tradition, where the tales often serve as the literary example *par excellence.*

Residing under the banner of this speculative realism are two distinct but related philosophical methods, object-oriented ontology (OOO) and new materialism, which have jointly undertaken a thorough re-examination of the place of the human in relation to the nonhuman world. Through varying approaches, these philosophers seek to overturn the longstanding assumption that human life and perception serve as an ontological foundation for any ethical study of the world. The effect that these philosophical inquiries have had on literary and cultural studies cannot be overstated. In the twenty-first century, the influence of speculative realism is evidenced in the outpouring of literary criticism and cultural theory that directly contends with the tenets of this philosophy. Both

OOO and the myriad of new materialist approaches to the study of literature are burgeoning methods that have, after a decade or more on the literary scene, continued to introduce a host of new literary objects worthy of study, as well as breathe new life into older literature otherwise exhausted or abandoned.

The re-emergence of Lovecraft's work within this context is therefore no coincidence. The adoption of Lovecraft by the speculative realists marks his tales as the quintessential example of literature that denies the centrality of human life within a rapidly expanding cosmos. His fiction serves as a link between the Modernist period and the contemporary one through this de-emphasis of the human and the inherent inability to ever fully comprehend the mysteries of the universe.

His life (1890–1937), primarily in Providence, Rhode Island, neatly spans what is most commonly identified as the period of literary Modernism. His work, though published almost exclusively in pulp magazines like *Weird Tales* (1923–54), reflects many of the concerns of more widely read and recognized Modernist writers of the period. These concerns include a fascination with and skepticism toward scientific dogma and technological advances, a cynicism toward religion, a return to realism, and a challenge to humanity's capacity for knowledge. Lovecraft's work asks readers to contemplate how one comes to know what one knows, whether knowledge of the world is ever really possible at all, and to imagine instead forms of nonhuman knowledge. The philosophers central to this essay have taken up this question with enthusiasm, going so far as to herald Lovecraft as "philosophy['s] new literary hero" (Harman, "On the Horror" 6).

Lovecraft's place in literary modernism was historically debated throughout the twentieth century, evidenced by key essays in defense of his work by the preeminent Lovecraft scholar and biographer S. T. Joshi. In a period obsessed with the designation of and distinction between high and low aesthetics, Lovecraft's work was immediately relegated to mere pulp, a categorization that would persist into the twenty-first century. Indeed, his fiction contains quite a bit of the fantastic, the supernatural, and the weird, descriptions that seem hardly on par with the work of recognized literary greats of the first part of the twentieth century: T. S. Eliot,

Ezra Pound, Ernest Hemingway, Djuna Barnes, or Gertrude Stein. Lovecraft's supernatural stories draw upon his study of astrophysics, Newtonian physics, and complex geometry to ponder the existence of alien beings on faraway planets or in the fourth dimension. While his tales are rooted almost entirely in fictional towns of Massachusetts, his narrators experience supremely unbelievable events like encounters with invisible creatures, extraterrestrial consciousness swaps, and chance encounters with haunted cities of alien races from millions of years in the past. His work has been criticized for more than just its content: critics have long consigned Lovecraft's literary style to the hackneyed and sloppy, too verbose or too prescriptive, despite an immense oeuvre that surges with elegant and masterfully controlled tales.

At his worst, Lovecraft can certainly be a tedious writer, even formulaic. But when writing at his best—and critics will disagree as to when he is at his best—he expertly creates an atmosphere of fear and confusion. He denies his readers any full disclosure of the creatures that populate his tales, and hints instead at "the general outline of the thing" ("The Call of Cthulhu" [CF 2.24]), or its "weird silhouette" ("The Dunwich Horror" [CF 2.462]). As I will demonstrate in the section that follows, speculative realist philosophers have found this quality of Lovecraft's writing, the refusal to name the horror that so terrifies the narrators of his tales, to be his principal achievement as a writer. Graham Harman, a philosopher at the helm of speculative realism, has written of Lovecraft: "No other writer is so perplexed by the gap between objects and the power of language to describe them, or between objects and the qualities they possess" (*Weird Realism* 3). Harman finds Lovecraft compelling because of this "gap" that his writing reproduces, the refusal to represent to his readers the horrors of the cosmos. For Harman, Lovecraft's work emphasizes the unbridgeable space between experiences in the world and one's ability to ever fully describe them.

Because the philosophical field of speculative realism has been at the forefront of Lovecraft studies in the last decade, this essay will begin with a discussion of the important contributions that thinkers in this vein have made to the study of Lovecraft. Speculative realism is largely responsible for Lovecraft's revival, and it has reinvigorated Lovecraft studies. Their collective emphasis on Lovecraft's flattened ontology has fixed his work at the center of anthropocene studies, eco-criticism, and object-oriented ontology, and together they form a new set of foundational texts for any serious scholar of Lovecraft and his philosophy. Yet no current works provide a thorough study of the way in which Lovecraft's weird tales have been taken up across these philosophical and theoretical works. Lovecraft's "weird" has played a significant role in the development of speculative realism, and I therefore will continue this essay by laying out how the "weird" in Lovecraft has been employed in these accounts. I do this first to demonstrate the significance of his writing within contemporary philosophy, and second, to situate my own subsequent departure from these readings and from their conception of the weird, which have now come to saturate the study and understanding of Lovecraft.

My readings of Lovecraft's tales are influenced by feminist theory, specifically feminist new materialism, a field heavily influenced by the study of the sciences, which, as Rebekah Sheldon has recently argued, lies in thorny relation to other speculative realist philosophies and especially to object-oriented ontology.[1] Whereas OOO readings of Lovecraft seek to undermine the human and thus are not interested specifically in corporeality in his work, I am instead drawn to the work that makes up the concurrent "material turn"[2] in feminism—one that aims to restore the complex makeup of the body as nonhuman, as an "agentic force," and imagines how human corporeality can "account for how the discursive and the material interact in the constitution of bodies" (Alaimo and Hekman 7). This essay is informed by feminist and queer theorists who have argued that embodiment must take into account

---

1. Sheldon's essay "Form/Matter/Chora: Object-Oriented Ontology and Feminist New Materialism," in *The Nonhuman Turn*, ed. Richard Grusin (2015), offers a comprehensive recent history of concepts in feminist new materialism that cut across two fields that are often cited as entirely at odds with each other. Influential to this essay and to my own thinking about the relationship between these two fields is Sheldon's demonstration of the "unwitting embrace of patrilineation" (116) by OOO, and perhaps by speculative realism more broadly.

2. Named as such by Stacy Alaimo and Susan Hekman in the introduction to *Material Feminisms* (2008).

the biological, environmental, atmospheric, chemical, geologic, and various other agential forces and their interactions with the body in order to understand the body's porous and willful nature.

In a series of related keynote talks she delivered in 2014,[3] Donna Haraway argues against human exceptionalism and individualism, citing that the so-called human has always been comprised of the nonhuman as well. Referencing Scott Gilbert's work,[4] Haraway claims: "We are all lichens now. We have never been individuals. From the anatomical, physiological, evolutionary, developmental, philosophic, economic. I don't care what perspective. We are all lichens now" ("Anthropocene"). Through the use of examples of all kinds of creatures both real and imaginary, Haraway builds an argument against the now dominant term "anthropocene" and calls instead for the naming of the current epoch as the "Cthulhucene." It is perhaps no coincidence that Haraway borrows from Lovecraft's most famous monster in "The Call of Cthulhu," the indescribable, timeless entity Cthulhu that has given Lovecraft much cultish adoration. She says it is not the anthropocene but

> the Cthulhucene, the phonic ones, the not yet finished, ongoing, abyssal, and dreadful ones that are generative and destructive, and make Gaia look like a junior kindergarten daughter. . . . The Cthulhucene might be a way to collect up the questions for naming the epoch, for naming what is happening in the airs, waters, and places, in the rocks and oceans, and atmospheres. . . . [It is a way] to imagine a world more liveable. (AURA talk, at approx. 1 min)

Haraway's adoption of Cthulhu to name a kind of possible "reworlding" wherein we might "have a chance of ongoing" is a rare optimistic twist on the squid-like beast, whose literary life has come to be otherwise synonymous with human insignificance on an

---

3. For two primary examples where she discusses the Cthulhucene, see "Anthropocene, Capitalocene, Cthulhucene: Staying with the Trouble" and "SF: String Figures, Multispecies Muddles, Staying with the Trouble," delivered at University of Alberta, 24 March 2014, https://www.youtube.com/watch?v=Z1uTVnhIHS8. A book on the subject is expected this year (2016).

4. See "A Symbiotic View of Life: We Have Never Been Individuals," *Quarterly Review of Biology* 87, No. 4 (December 2012): 325–41, co-authored with Jan Sapp and Alfred I. Tauber.

apocalyptic scale. But her naming of the Cthulhucene also signals the way in which Lovecraft's literary efforts might be read from a feminist materialist perspective, one that takes stock of the material, often nonhuman forms and forces that are intricately connected to "human life" and more specifically to human embodiment.

I therefore continue this essay with speculative realist accounts of Lovecraft because of a curious neglect of corporeality. For while it is true that Lovecraft's work exposes the insignificance of the human race in deep time, the characters in his tales cannot escape their boundedness to the body in their respective presents. They experience the body as strange and alien, freakish and out-of-control, or even as imprisonment. In addition, those speculative realists, like Harman, who are more interested in Lovecraft's formal techniques at the cost of content neglect the political stakes that are inextricable from the body. For example, Lovecraft's still controversial racist and xenophobic attitudes toward people of color and immigrants is well documented in his writings. Although this essay does not explicitly engage with those moments of Lovecraft's inexcusable racial politics,[5] my resistance to exclusively speculative realist readings of Lovecraft is also a resistance to a reading methodology that risks allowing for this racism to escape unnoticed. Although here I will examine stories that are not exclusively about race, I argue that turning attention toward embodiment in Lovecraft's stories is at least one of the ways we might engage critically with the body politics present in Lovecraft's work more broadly. The repeated encounters that Lovecraft's characters have *with their own bodies* as strange stages corporeality as entangled with Lovecraft's horror in profound and largely unexplored ways.

---

5. For a discussion of racism in Lovecraft's work see Michel Houellebecq's *H. P. Lovecraft: Against the World, Against Life* (1991), Bennett Lovett-Graff's "Shadow's Over Lovecraft: Reactionary Fantasy and Immigrant Eugenics," *Extrapolation* 38, No. 3 (1997): 175–92, or China Miéville's introduction to the Modern Library edition of *At the Mountains of Madness* (2005). Critics have also begun to complicate our sense of Lovecraft's racist and eugenic beliefs by demonstrating a shift away from these attitudes in his later writings. See, as one example of this, Timothy H. Evans's "A Last Defense against the Dark: Folklore, Horror, and the Uses of Tradition in the Works of H. P. Lovecraft," *Journal of Folklore Research* 42, No. 1 (January–April 2005): 99–135.

This essay will contend with what has become the trend in the study of Lovecraft, that erasure of subjectivity for the sake of de-anthropocentrism. As the fields of speculative realist philosophy and cultural theory have slowly turned away from the privileging of the human, the sacrifice in Lovecraft studies has been the neglected consideration of embodiment as a primary theme across his work. In what follows, I will interrogate Lovecraft's characterization of bodily experience: the ways in which the body resists our control, estranges us, and incites horror in us. Ultimately I hope to restore a theory of embodiment central to Lovecraft's work, to horror writing of the period, and perhaps to the philosophy of speculative realism more broadly.

Lovecraft's Place in Speculative Realism

Speculative realism was introduced in 2007 to describe the work of four philosophers: Quentin Meillassoux, Graham Harman, Ray Brassier, and Iain Hamilton Grant (Shaviro 5). In his recent book, *The Universe of Things*, Steven Shaviro describes the philosophy:

> Speculative realists question the anthropocentrism that has so long been a key assumption of modern Western rationality. Such a questioning is urgently needed at a time when we face the prospect of ecological catastrophe and when we are forced to recognize that the fate of humanity is deeply intertwined with the fates of all sorts of other entities . . . we cannot isolate our own interests, and our own economies, from processes taking place on a cosmic scale in a universe whose boundaries we are unable to grasp. (1)

This description is Lovecraftian in its sense of scope and scale. Shaviro cites the current ecological moment as urgently requiring a new kind of philosophical thought, wherein imagining a human-centered universe is no longer useful or ethical. Speculative realism aims to think of humans' fates as entangled with those of all sorts of other nonhuman entities: air, water, carbon dioxide, whales, and dirt, rather than superior to or independent of them. He also invokes a "cosmic scale," emphasizing the vastness of the universe of which humans are a part. As our understanding of the nature of the cosmos matures, the less we actually understand about its limits, and the more trivial humanity seems to be.

Speculative realists are united primarily against elements of Kantian philosophy that have, they claim, dominated Western philosophy since the eighteenth century. Most controversial among these elements is the notion that Meillassoux has called Kant's "correlationism": the claim that objects and phenomena are dependent on human thought to exist. For Kant, we can't *know* anything about things-in-themselves beyond our apprehension or perception of them; they may *exist* independently of us, but we have no access to them.[6] But speculative realism has staunchly opposed this philosophy. Is philosophy limited to the human mind and what it thinks and perceives? Speculative realists collectively argue not. Timothy Morton has described the central problem of correlationism in the form of a riddle: "Is the light on in the fridge when you close the door?" (*Hyperobjects* 9).

As both a father of speculative realism and the philosopher most enamored with Lovecraft, Graham Harman's work is exemplary of the way in which Lovecraft has been incorporated into philosophy more broadly. As one of the only literary examples Harman repeatedly returns to across his work, Lovecraft's tales are employed as examples of an author already object-oriented in the early half of the twentieth century. Through Lovecraft, Harman's work attempts to overthrow the longstanding philosophical maxim of correlationism. In what has become a touchstone text for Lovecraft scholars, *Weird Realism: Lovecraft and Philosophy*, Harman performs quick close readings of dozens of short passages from Lovecraft's most well-known tales. He examines Lovecraft's literary style of evasion, claiming that the author "unlocks a world dominated by [the] gap . . . between the world and our descriptions of it" (27). This kind of writing, which operates against the logic of representational realism, is instead what Harman terms "weird realism." The book is a rapid succession of unfastened philosophical scraps that are eventually united as examples of a weird philosophy. Instead of relying on traditional definitions of the weird, which underscore futurity and fate, Harman finds that Lovecraft's most valuable contribution, what makes him "one of

6. Thanks to Matthew Taylor (UNC) for his clarification on this point in an earlier draft of this essay.

the greatest [writers] of the twentieth century" (3), is his ability to merely allude to the horrors of the universe while "cancel[ing] the literal terms of the description" (17). Through this narrative technique (Harman focuses almost exclusively on Lovecraft's style in this book), Lovecraft's work exposes the impossibility of ever fully knowing the object-oriented world, of which humans are just one part.

Harman's most powerful reading in this vein is of Lovecraft's most famous tale, "The Call of Cthulhu" (1926). Perhaps against the spirit of Harman, who claims in the introduction to this section that "'The Call of Cthulhu' is best savored not by summarizing its plot, but by examining . . . the work directly" (54), I will describe the story, albeit briefly. Cthulhu is a giant winged octopoid creature, silent in sleep for eons deep under the ocean, below the earth's crust. As figurines of this ancient being begin to appear across the globe, many who attempt to follow the path to the secrets of the beast die horrible deaths. Eventually, through recovered manuscripts, a description of the thing is finally revealed—but not exactly.

Harman's fascination with the "reveal" in "Cthulhu" is for him a moment that similarly occurs throughout Lovecraft's work. Lovecraft writes of Cthulhu: "If I say that my somewhat extravagant imagination yielded simultaneous pictures of an octopus, a dragon, and a human caricature, I shall not be unfaithful to the spirit of the thing . . . but it was the general outline of the whole which made it most shockingly frightful" (CF 2.24). In a brief section of Weird Realism, "The General Outline of the Whole," Harman revels in Lovecraft's refusal to reduce the horror to a grouping of specific qualities: "cheerful bundles of octopus, dragon, and human" (58), he writes. Instead, what is frightening is the irreduceability of the object to its qualities; the "general outline of the whole" allows for no direct contact with the horror, but only a vagueness that allows an indirect experience of Cthulhu. Lovecraft offers a few concrete descriptions that we can "sink our teeth into" (Harman 238)—octopus, dragon, human—but then retreats to the failures of language to describe his experience or make it known to his readers. Harman's appreciation of Lovecraft identifies his work as the foundational literature of Harman's weird philosophy, which, above all, is weird because of its "obstruct[ion] [of] the power of literal language" (*Weird Realism* 234).

Other speculative realists have similarly defined the "weird" in Lovecraft, although with slight distinctions. Eugene Thacker, author of *After Life* (2010) and the recent three-book series *Horror of Philosophy* (2011, 2015, 2015), also calls on Lovecraft to define what he calls an "entelechy of the weird," which undoubtedly echoes Harman. In *After Life*, he writes that Lovecraft's creatures "can barely be named, let alone adequately described *or thought*." He goes on to say that indescribability is the "crux of supernatural horror, the reason why life is 'weird.' The threat is not the monster, or that which threatens existing categories of knowledge. Rather, it is the 'nameless thing,' or that which presents itself as a horizon for thought" (23). Thacker names Lovecraft's weird as that which resists representation, rather than the weird as the monster itself. Though he does not cite Harman directly, Thacker seems to be furthering Harman's sense of the weird by showing how Lovecraft's work is terrifying because it presents us with the "horizon for thought," or the "possibility of a logic of life . . . absolutely inaccessible to the human" (23). Notably for Thacker, the "weird" in Lovecraft is about weird *life*, a "life according to the logic of an inaccessible real" (23).

In his subsequent series, *Horror of Philosophy*, Thacker calls on Lovecraft at greater length, citing his work as the primary example of the way in which horror forces us to consider the world after humans are gone, what he calls a "world-without-us." Harman's celebration of Lovecraft's anti-representationalist rhetoric is extended in Thacker's work, where he proposes that "horror be understood not as dealing with human fear in a human world (the world-for-us), but . . . about the limits of the human as it confronts a world that is not just a World, and not just the Earth, but also a Planet (the world-without-us). This also means that horror is not simply about fear, but instead about the enigmatic thought of the unknown" (*In the Dust of This Planet* 8). In Thacker's expansion of the cosmos from human-centered "World" to "Earth" to "Planet," the challenge of horror is not to theorize human existence in the World, but to imagine the "Planet" as "that which remains 'after' the human" (7). For Thacker, the horror in Lovecraft is that confrontation with an unknown future landscape, the world post-humanity. In the introduction to the book series, Thacker acknowledges the inherent contradiction in reading Lovecraft in this way: "we cannot help but to think of the world as a human world, by virtue of the fact that it is we human beings that think it" (2). Yet despite this acknowledgment, Thacker does not discuss the ways in which Lovecraft's characters might find the human world as another kind of predicament, the reality within which humans find themselves as bound to the fleshiness of material, embodied life.

If Harman and Thacker are struck by Lovecraft's refusal of linguistic representation, their focus remains primarily on the way in which Lovecraft denies his readers access to the horror of the monsters in the tales. Dylan Trigg's *The Thing: A Phenomenology of Horror* (2014) is the first of the speculative realist philosophers whose work comprehensively considers that the horror might arguably be that thing which is both most known to us and most foreign: our own human bodies. Trigg's book picks up from where thinkers like Harman and Thacker leave off, attempting to reconcile the philosophical trend of post-humanism with a phenomenology that is "attuned to both human and nonhuman entities" (5). Trigg critiques speculative realist projects that replace subjects with objects, claiming that this philosophy has "long since folded back upon itself, becoming a distinctly human—alas, all too human—vision fixed at all times on the perennial question: *How will the Earth remember us?*" (4; emphasis in original). Trigg's work holds that a study of human experience, and specifically of the materiality of the body as alien, is a necessary departure from other speculative realist work, which has thus far worked to entirely negate the subject.

Trigg's work is important in the field and to a more comprehensive understanding of the "weird." Borrowing again from Harman, Trigg distinguishes his employment of "weird realism" as "that which outlives its own corporeal extinction [and] is transformed into an entity that is both itself and concurrently other-than-itself, both human and unhuman at once" (53). Through a reading of Lovecraft's "The Shadow out of Time," a tale I will turn to in the next section, Trigg argues that Lovecraft's weird names a kind of bodily experience, a human subjectivity made up of the "weird facets of bodily existence." These weird facets together name what he calls an "alien subjectivity," one that is explored in Lovecraft's tale and is underscored in Trigg's horror of the body. His engagement with Lovecraft and his investment in the horror of the body enable an intersection with other theories of embodiment, particularly feminist and queer materialisms that have been largely silent on the subject of Lovecraft's fiction.

Lovecraft's "Weird"

Lovecraft himself wrote a number of essays in which he describes what he imagined as the true "weird tale." While the philosophers discussed thus far share a sense of how Lovecraft theorized the "weird," a closer look at Lovecraft's own writing on the subject reveal some additional complexity to the term. Contemporary philosophers have agreed that Lovecraft's weird is most certainly about the horror of indescribability. In his lengthy 1927 essay "Supernatural Horror in Literature," Lovecraft writes that the "true weird tale has something more than secret murder, bloody bones, or a sheeted form clanking chains according to a rule." Instead, he writes:

> The one test of the really weird is simply this—whether or not there be excited in the reader a profound sense of dread, and of contact with unknown spheres and powers, a subtle sense of awed listening, as if for the beating of black wings or the scratching of outside shapes and entities on the known universe's utmost rim. (CE 2.84)

Here, in this beautifully dark and poetic description, Lovecraft illustrates the weird through a series of images and sounds that are meant to evoke "a profound sense of dread," a fear of "unknown spheres and powers." He calls on images impossible to conjure up entirely—a set of disembodied black wings, and the scratching of "shapes and entities" not on the outside of a parlor door but on the "utmost rim" of the known universe. The passage illustrates quite vividly Lovecraft's sense of the weird not as a set of concrete objects or actors, but rather as atmospheric. He writes in the later essay "Notes on Writing Weird Fiction" that "Atmosphere, not action, is the great desideratum of weird fiction. Indeed, all that a wonder story can ever be is *a vivid picture of a certain type of human mood*" (CE 2.177; emphasis in original).

Speculative realism primarily theorizes this sense of indescribable dread as the defining characteristic of the weird. But an extended look at Lovecraft's own description of the weird demonstrates the concept to be complicated by the additional question of temporality. What Lovecraft names as "dread," or "extreme fear; apprehension or anxiety as to future events" (*OED*), marks his vision of the weird as oriented toward the future and signaled by a mood of fear and anxiety. Although he often writes narratives with complex temporalities framed by reflection, recollection, and temporal disorientation, Lovecraft describes weirdness here not in terms of remembrance or regret over past events, but as apprehension over future ones. In a passage worth quoting at length, he writes:

> I choose weird stories because they suit my inclination best, to achieve . . . the illusion of some strange suspension or violation of the galling limitations of time. . . . These stories frequently emphasise the element of hours because fear is our deepest and strongest emotion, and the one which best lends itself to the creation of nature-defying illusions. . . . The reason why *time* plays a great part in so many of my tales is that [it] looms up in my mind as the most profoundly dramatic and grimly terrible thing in the universe. Conflict with time seems to me the most potent and fruitful theme in all human expression. (*CE* 2.176)

Here, Lovecraft expresses the desire to halt time, to suspend it even for a moment in his fiction. Weird fiction is the kind of writing that can possibly attain this suspension through a capitalizing of fear and anxiety. As Joshi has stressed of this passage, "Lovecraft is not renouncing his materialism by seeking an imaginative escape from it; indeed, it is precisely because he believes that [these laws] are uniform . . . that he seeks an imaginative escape from them" (Lovecraft, *Cthulhu* xv). The link between the subject of "hours" with fear doesn't exactly make clear their connection, but it is as if only out of the experience of fear can the author create the illusion of defying the unrelenting the laws of time. This passage makes clear Lovecraft's anxieties over time as the most "terrible thing in the universe," the subject that informs his writing and which he feels is most fruitful when conflicted with.

Where some philosophers have usefully expanded on Lovecraft's description of weird writing as atmospheric, indescribably horrific rather than concretized in an object or thing, Lovecraft's fixation on time is equally important to any discussion of the weird in literature or in philosophy. In response to the staunch and unwavering constraints and regularity of time, Lovecraft creates weird tales that act as explicit confrontations with these limitations. As I will show in the section that follows, these conflicts with time frequently occur at the site of the body.

Lovecraft's Weird Body

Despite the way in which Lovecraft scholarship has tended to disregard embodied experience in favor of the cosmological, it is not especially difficult to locate passages across Lovecraft's fiction that underscore the centrality of the body to his vision of horror. As we have seen in the philosophical readings of his tales and essays, Lovecraft's horror lies, in part, in the inexplicable and indescribable, and emerges not necessarily from "secret murder or bloody bones," but from the literary style of purposeful imprecision, a refusal or inability to name that which is unnamable. But Lovecraft is not merely a horror writer; he is a "weird" writer, and as is evidenced by his own definition of the weird, his tales also lay out a uniquely embodied and horrific temporality. The tales I will examine in this section are therefore chosen for their joint thematic concerns with the body and with time. Together, the readings of this fiction demonstrate how the weird in Lovecraft is hinged to the body and to the experience of embodiment as a temporal phenomenon.

"The Dunwich Horror" (1928) has been called the most "pulpish" of Lovecraft's tales; not surprisingly, Joshi writes, it was "snapped up by *Weird Tales* as soon as he submitted it" (Lovecraft, *Thing on the Doorstep* xiv). The tale follows the life of Wilbur Whateley, a child born in fictional Dunwich, Massachusetts, to the sound of a "hideous screaming which echoed above even the hill noises and the dogs' barking" (*CF* 2.422). His birth is witnessed by none except for his "deformed, unattractive albino" mother Lavinia, whose conditions of pregnancy in the first place remain shrouded in mystery: who is the father of this boy? The strange events that follow his birth are noted over time by the townspeople who occasionally ramble up the hill to the Whateleys' property. As the child ages and matures at alarming rates (he reaches adulthood in form and mind in less than ten years' time), the townspeople note that the Whateleys' livestock has become increasingly depleted and sickly. In the meantime, Wilbur and his grandfather are seen reconstructing their townhouse repeatedly and without explanation. After his grandfather's death, the now *ten-year-old and nine-foot-tall* Wilbur ventures to the (mythical) Miskatonic University Library in search of the (also mythical) *Necronomicon,* which holds the truth to unknown alien pasts. Professor Henry Armitage denies Wilbur's request to take the text from its place in the library, and when Wilbur returns on a later night to steal it, guard dogs attack and kill him, tearing off his clothes and revealing a mass of alien appendages.

Back in the town of Dunwich, havoc has broken out in the elusive form of an invisible creature that has been loosed on the town, destroying homes and killing a number of the townspeople. Suspecting a dark relation to Wilbur's inhuman condition, Professor Armitage himself ventures to Dunwich, only to discover that the invisible creature is the twin brother of Wilbur, nurtured and kept secret in the Whateley home for a decade with the intent of eventually overtaking the human race. After following the invisible beast through its path of destruction and detected only by the sway of grass or the bending of timber, Armitage finally locates the creature. He heroically sprays a potion in the direction of the invisible thing, thus revealing it. He is seen from a distance reciting a series of spells that eventually and successfully destroy the beast, and with it, the malevolent intentions of Yog-Sothoth.

Joshi writes that despite this tale's popularity with readers, it is "one of Lovecraft's great failures in its clumsy moral didacticism and ludicrous use of white magic versus black magic"; it is "pulpish tripe" (*World in Transition* 176). Joshi's critique of "The Dunwich Horror" is not ungrounded. The tale concludes by pitting good verses evil in an uninteresting way, and it is one of Lovecraft's only stories wherein humankind successfully wards off the malignant alien assailants. Whereas for some authors this kind of victory might be met with praise and pleasure, serious Lovecraft readers do not look to his work for these sorts of triumphant endings, and rather see this tale as a failure to live up to his own philosophy. I want to suggest that the tale might be redeemed by focusing not on the ending, but on the rapid maturation of Wilbur Whateley. It is Wilbur's dramatic growth, recorded at nearly twice that typical for a child his age, that is shocking and terrifying, especially if read as parallel to the mounting evil in the Whateley home.

Lovecraft writes, "When Wilbur was a year and seven months old—in September of 1914—his size and accomplishments were almost alarming. He had grown as large as a child of four, and was a fluent and incredibly intelligent talker" (CF 2.426). At the age of four, "Wilbur was growing up uncannily, so that he looked like a boy of ten" (CF 2.427). At four and a half, he "looked like a lad of fifteen. His lips and cheeks were fuzzy with a coarse, dark down, and his voice had begun to break" (CF 2.428), and just a few years later, he was "tremendously mature of aspect, and his height, having reached the normal adult limit, seemed inclined to wax beyond that figure" (CF 2.431). At age fifteen, Wilbur has reached a height of eight feet, and when he meets his death in the Miskatonic University Library shortly thereafter, he has reached a height of nine feet (CF 2.438). The speed of Wilbur's growth is disturbing to the narrator, and he marks each incremental foot of Wilbur's growth throughout the tale as a way to parallel the mounting horror unfolding in Dunwich. In this way, the increasing sense of fear is embodied in the body of Wilbur. Time and the corporeal are bound up in ways that reveal the body to be the site of manipulation on the part of evil beings. As the evil grows, so does Wilbur, his body the manifestation of otherworldly forces outside of his own control.

Literary critics have named the beastly twin brother as the flimsy basis of the terror in "The Dunwich Horror," the strange invisible beast whose nonhuman maturation parallels Wilbur's swift human development into abnormally tall adulthood. But I would argue instead that the real horror is the slow buildup of the bizarre circumstance, the material manifestation of the horror from beyond via the earthly body of Wilbur Whateley. The horror is Wilbur's humanoid figure, a creature that eventually reaches a height of nine feet, a "thing" whose beholding "crowded out all other images," and which "no human pen could describe" (CF 2.438). As with many of Lovecraft's tales, in the moment of the horror's reveal, language and writing fail the narrator, and description becomes impossible. The narrator elaborates: "it could not be vividly visualised by anyone whose ideas of aspect and contour are too closely bound up with common life forms of this planet and the three known dimensions. It was partly human, beyond a doubt . . . But the torso and lower parts of the body were teratologically fabulous" (*CF* 2.43839). Wilbur is a unique character in Lovecraft's body of work, operating as a covert agent of Yog-Sothoth, the mythic godlike entity first introduced in his novella *The Case of Charles Dexter Ward*, written in 1927. As Graham Harham writes, "Fresh ground is broken in the tales with the character of young Wilbur Whateley. In the story of Cthulhu, all the ostensible humans are actually human and we never have reason for physiological suspicion. . . . With Wilbur Whateley, by contrast, we have the soon-to-be classic Lovecraftian theme of a being who pretends to be human while concealing a much darker identity" (*Weird Realism* 102).

In "The Dunwich Horror," the humanoid body is the central vehicle through which an alien race carries out its malevolent plot to destroy the future of humanity. The freakish temporality of Wilbur's individual life is thus in sharp contrast with the immortalized and infinite temporality of Yog-Sothoth. These distinct and conflicting temporalities, Wilbur's individual human(ish) time and the deep time of Yog-Sothoth, are set in dramatic opposition in the tale. Lovecraft would continue to revisit this conflict between scales of temporality in many of his tales to follow, namely "The Whisperer in Darkness," "The Shadow over Innsmouth," and "The Shadow out of Time." In these tales and in countless others, the human body is manipulated and altered by nonhuman actors from outside of time as we know it, and human corporeality is revealed to be a horrific, uncontrollable, or unwieldy experience.

"The Shadow out of Time" (1934–35) tells the story of Nathaniel Wingate Peaslee, who is lecturing at Miskatonic University when his mind is suddenly overtaken by a Yithian being (a member of an ancient race referred to as "The Great Race"). His consciousness has been thrust into the body of a member of the Great Race from 150,000,000 years ago on Earth in an effort to learn about the future. The Great Race has undertaken the project of invading human specimens, overtaking their bodies through the inhabitation of human minds. After five years of alienation from his own body, Peaslee's mind is suddenly returned to himself, exactly at the moment from which it was extracted. The five-year span is just the blink of an eye for Peaslee, who suddenly awakens mid-sentence in the same lecture from which he was stolen. The five years spent in the far distant past of the earth have equated to the blink of an eye. As he reacclimates to present-day life in his own body, he has difficulty taking stock of his human form:

> There was . . . a feeling of profound and inexplicable horror concerning *myself*. I developed a queer fear of seeing my own form, as if my eyes would find it something utterly alien and inconceivably abhorrent. When I did glance down and behold the familiar human shape in quiet grey or blue clothing I always felt a curious relief, though in order to gain this relief I had to conquer an infinite dream. I shunned mirrors as much as possible, and was always shaved at the barber's. (CF 3.377; emphasis in original)

Lovecraft's italicized emphasis on "myself" makes clear the strangeness of the experience of Peaslee's own body. At this moment, the tale minimizes the horror of the Great Race and instead calls attention to the horror of one's own form. Peaslee's fear that he might find his body utterly alien is calmed only by an occasional glance, which he avoids as much as possible. For a while, he doesn't understand his own fear of his body, until the memories of the past five years with the Great Race begin to flood back to him. With his developing knowledge of his time in the distant past comes the awareness that his body has belonged to others. As Peaslee's memories slowly come to the fore, so too does an emergent awareness that his body does not belong to him, but to other forces who invade his consciousness and take over his capacities at their whim. The erasure of his memory, of his past, and therefore of his sense of himself in the present, also erases his familiarity with his human form. He becomes temporarily estranged from his body as the result of his travel through time.

Trigg's reading of "The Shadow out of Time" emphasizes the way in which "ownership" over the body has been central to the conceptualization of the rational subject in Western philosophical thought. Utilizing Lovecraft's tale as a counterexample, Trigg argues that the this Lovecraft passage presents a challenge to these reigning notions of the self as that which can ever be "mastered" by its host:

> The discovery of the body in its alien materiality hinges upon a self-conscious awareness of the body as no longer mine, and thus marks a point of divergence from personal identity . . . this break of the body from an experience of selfhood is not absolute, but depends on a recognition of the body as simultaneously self and other . . . What this means is that the alien within the body is not a departure from the lived body, but a continuation of it . . . The creature we are faced with in Lovecraft . . . is thus a synthesis of the human and the nonhuman, the personal and the impersonal, the possessor and the possessed. (78)

Trigg emphasizes the way in which the alien possessor, a figure that repeatedly surfaces across Lovecraft's tales, is not "a departure from the body" but a "continuation of it." The human is revealed to be what Trigg calls here a "synthesis of the human and the nonhuman": the body (and mind) an open system rather than a cordoned-off, contained one. As Trigg argues, it is Peaslee's revelation of the porousness of the body to outside forces and beings that terrifies him. The human itself is alienated, made strange.

There is another nuance to the Lovecraft passage. Peaslee reflects: "I developed a queer fear of seeing my own form, as if my eyes would find it something utterly alien and inconceivably abhorrent." Here, Peaslee is afraid not simply of an "alien materiality"; it is not only, as Trigg reads it, the horror of lost ownership over the body. It is also that he will not longer be able to recognize the human. It is the possibility of a loss of recognition of himself, *"as if my eyes would find it alien,"* that most frightens him. It is the alienation of the human form, the evolution of the human into something no longer recognizable as such, that drives the terror of this tale, and which makes this passage alluring to read alongside contemporary theories of embodiment. Trigg asks, "If I am unable to possess my body, then who—or perhaps more pertinently what—am I?" (65).

A welcome voice in the choir of speculative realism, Trigg's inquiry here reverberates with corporeal feminisms, which pose similar questions about the body's place in nature and culture. Trigg's work might then serve as one of many possible bridges between object-oriented ontology and feminist new materialisms. Where strict OOO philosophers like Harman theorize that all objects maintain strict boundaries and withdraw from one another without relationality, Trigg's theoretical leanings feel closer to something like Stacy Alaimo's notion of "trans-corporeality,"[7] Donna Haraway's "entanglements," [8] Karen Barad's "intra-actions," [9] or Myra Hird's "microontologies."[10] In these theories of relationality between human and nonhuman realms, the human and nonhuman relate and coexist in various ways; there is no inside or outside of the human form, only a complex intermingling of life and nonlife.

Feminist theorists of the natural and biological sciences—and I've mentioned just a few—each approach the question of corporeality from distinct backgrounds and with unique projects at stake. This very brief account of a few of the major theories in feminist and queer materialism is meant not to group them together to collapse their many differences in approaches, content, and style. Instead, I cite these theories to demonstrate the kind of work that feminism, at the junction of the humanities and the sciences, has been doing previous to and alongside those working in the speculative realist tradition for some time now. Trigg's insightful recognition regarding "The Shadow out of Time" of the human posited as "simultaneously self and other," "a synthesis of the human and the nonhuman," locates in Lovecraft what feminist new materialists have been, albeit in broad terms here, theorizing about the body.

---

7. "Trans-corporeality" is a way to think about the material self not as a "bracketed biological body" (*Bodily Natures* 3) separate from the environment. Instead, the material body "in all its ... fleshiness, is inseparable from 'nature' or 'environment' ... always intermeshed with the more-than-human world" (*Material Feminisms* 238).

8. See *When Species Meet* (2007).

9. For Barad, objects emerge through intra-actions with other objects and phenomena, and do not exist preceding their relationality. See *Meeting the Universe Halfway: Quantum Physics and the Entanglement of Matter and Meaning* (Durham, NC: Duke University Press, 2007).

10. Hird's concept of "microontologies" follows from Haraway's concept of companion species that she outlines in *When Species Meet*, but considers human/nonhuman relations via companion beings that are not species at all and that are mostly invisible to the human eye—bacteria.

An early weird tale, "From Beyond" (1920; published 1934), elucidates a new materialism at work in Lovecraft, wherein the true unknown multiplicity of the universe is revealed. The narrator describes a visit to his friend Crawford Tillinghast's home where Tillinghast has just constructed a new kind of machine that makes ultraviolet rays (among other things) visible, and invites the narrator over to show it to him. Tillinghast claims, "I have always believed that such strange, inaccessible worlds exist at our very elbows, *and now I believe I have found a way to break down the barriers*" (CF 1.194; emphasis in original). Tillinghast turns the machine on, and the narrator's view of the world suddenly and dramatically changes forever:

> I saw the attic laboratory, the electrical machine, and the unsightly form of Tillinghast opposite me; but of all the space unoccupied by familiar objects, not one particle was vacant. Indescribable shapes both alive and otherwise were mixed in disgusting disarray, and close to every known thing were whole worlds of alien, unknown entities. It likewise seemed that all the known things entered into the composition of other unknown things and vice versa. (CF 1.199)

Here, the scientific machine elucidates an otherwise invisible universe all around them. It makes visible the previously imperceptible; it illuminates what was once thought of as "vacant" space as being filled with "unfamiliar" and "indescribable shapes." The beings are both alive and something other than alive, and are all "mixed" in a way that appalls the speaker. The mixture, described as "disarray," is disgusting to the narrator because its objects lack borders and specificity. The invisible universe shares very few of the qualities with our perceivable one, where objects, beings, and bodies seem clearly self-contained and distinct from one another. The narrator writes, "I felt the huge animate things brushing past me and occasionally *walking or drifting through my supposedly solid body*" (CF 1.198; emphasis in original). The body here is revealed to be what Alaimo calls "porous," susceptible to the comings and goings of unperceivable nonhuman entities. No longer able to imagine the body as a closed system impenetrable to outside things and forces, the narrator in "From Beyond" must come to the terrifying realization that the body is always exposed to an environment not visible, and is thus far more vulnerable than he previously understood.

Thacker calls this kind of discovery, one prominent in the horror genre, a "terrifying reverie," citing Pascal's well-known formulation: "Nature is an infinite sphere whose center is everywhere and circumference is nowhere" (cited in Thacker, *Starry Speculative Corpse*, 166). Evoking Shaviro's "universe whose boundaries we are unable to grasp," nature is depicted in the Lovecraft passage as a multitude of worlds around us without any knowable boundaries. As Thacker says of the horror in "From Beyond," it is the "[d]issolving of the boundaries between the natural and the supernatural" (*Dust* 74), the revelation "of the already-existing non-separation between natural and supernatural (77). Thacker reads the device as a kind of mediation between the seen and unseen universe, an instrument that reveals an entanglement that has always existed. Thacker seems right to point out the dissolution of the boundaries between the so-called "natural" and the "super-natural."

Thacker and Trigg have much in common with material feminists who draw from the natural, geological, biological, and other environmental sciences in their collective refusal of nonhuman matter as inert or passive. As Ann Fausto-Sterling writes, "In thinking about both gender and race, feminists must accept the body as simultaneously composed of genes, hormones, cells, and organs— all of which influence health and behavior" (1495). The body's makeup of nonhuman parts biological and otherwise ("I felt the huge animate things brushing past me and occasionally *walking or drifting through my supposedly solid body*") is a central acknowledgment of feminist science studies and feminist new materialist projects.

The acknowledgment of a human/nonhuman body is met throughout Lovecraft's tales with mixed feelings: horror, bewilderment, and even allure. In "The Shadow over Innsmouth" (1931), a novella with dramatic bodily transformations, the narrator Robert Olmstead sets out to explore the town of Innsmouth, where he learns that the townspeople are hybrid offspring of humans and Deep Ones, fish/frog-like creatures that look like humans until mid-life, when they slowly transform into the amphibious beings. After escaping the town, Robert soon discovers to his horror that he too is a descendant of Deep Ones and begins dreaming of his transformation. Yet in a surprising turn at the close of the tale, he writes, "I feel queerly drawn toward the unknown sea-deeps instead of fearing them" (CF 3.230). Whereas "From Beyond" is fascinating for the way in which it anticipates contemporary philosophical thought about the complex and human/nonhuman makeup of the body, "The Shadow over Innsmouth" details the evolutionary commingling of humans and nonhumans and emphasizes the genealogical links between humans and nonhumans. Robert's queer acceptance of his fate as a fish-frog is surprising in light of the horror and disbelief with which he first receives the news of the townspeople of Innsmouth. And despite the fact that his being "queerly drawn" to the creatures does not, in the early twentieth century context, have the theoretical meaning or weight it carries now, his sudden acceptance of his transformation might also be understood as "queer" in the contemporary theoretical sense.[11] His embrace of a human/nonhuman lineage and evolutionary past is a surprising acknowledgment of the way in which human and nonhuman species commingle and coexist, and emphasizes a queerer fluidity in the place of a human/nonhuman divide. "The Shadow over Innsmouth" is an embrace, perhaps, of queer kinship with other species, perhaps even a queer, non-progressive evolutionary view that does not privilege the human as the evolutionary *telos*.[12]

---

11. There is a lot of important theoretical work at the junction of queer theory and the sciences which is attuned to the makeup of the body as primarily non-human material and organisms. This work is outside of the scope of this essay, but offers much to the way in which we might think about weird embodiment at the cellular and bacterial level. See, as exemplary work on the topic, Myra Hird's "Indifferent Globality," "Meeting with the Microcosmos," and "Symbiosis, Microbes, Coevolution and Sociology," as well as her coedited collection with Noreen Giffney, *Queering the Non/Human* (2008).

12. See Stephen Jay Gould's essay "The Evolution of Life on Earth." Gould disputes longstanding claims that evolutionary processes are unidirectional or naturally progressive. Though Gould does not discuss his revised theory of evolution as "queer," I see his project as queering evolution by challenging teleological narratives of evolution and progress, a project that productively aligns with theorists of queer temporality. See, for example, the work of Elizabeth Freeman, Heather Love, Jack Halberstam, Jose Esteban Muñoz, and Lee Edelman.

Conclusion

While some of speculative realist philosophy has begun to consider
the place of the body in Lovecraft, a more comprehensive sense of
corporeality is necessary in order to gain a fuller understanding of the
"weird" across his work. In this vein, this essay has hopefully offered
a reading of Lovecraft through feminism and new materialisms,
which help to restore to Lovecraft's fiction the centrality of embodiment and the many horrors it presents in his work. The convergence I offer between Object-Oriented Ontologies and Feminist
(and Queer) New Materialisms does not negate the philosophical
developments of speculative realist work on Lovecraft, but does
challenge that body of work to consider more fully the centrality of
embodied, material existence to Lovecraft's fiction, and perhaps, to
the still youthful speculative realist philosophical tradition.

   While object-oriented ontology has seemingly staked its claim
on Lovecraft as the literary figurehead of the philosophical
movement, the robust forms of materiality that have emerged
from feminist perspectives offer a useful and much-needed inter-
vention into the study of Lovecraft. Feminism's recent attunement
to the "materiality of the body itself as an active, recalcitrant
force" (Alaimo and Hekman, *Material Feminisms* 4) helps to understand Lovecraft and the "weird" in new ways. The horror of
Lovecraft's corpus is not merely the indescribable strangeness of
the world or the cosmos *writ large*; it is more specifically the un-
familiarity with and estrangement from the human body. It is a
horror of recognition of the body as an agential force: porous and
vulnerable, unpredictable, out of control, even fatalistic. Lovecraft's weird corporeality is one grounded in the materiality of the
body in relation to other things and other bodies, and one that
claims a theory of weirdness that is always and explicitly an embodied phenomenon. As Haraway has written, "theory is not
about matters distant from the lived body; quite the opposite.
Theory is *anything* but disembodied" ("The Promises of Monsters"
295). The horror implicit in the weird is therefore the body's
complete enmeshment with the environment; the site of the
breakdown between what was once thought of as the "natural"
and what can no longer be staved off as the "supernatural."

   Weird corporeality is perhaps most easily recognizable in

Lovecraft, but it is by no means limited to his work. The weird, developed in Lovecraft's essays and embodied in his fiction, is pervasive into the Modernist period, as anxieties mount over developing scientific and cultural understandings of the body. Though most identifiably "weird" in Lovecraft's work, the body is no less alien and certainly no less frightening as it appears in more canonical fiction from across the period.

Works Cited

Alaimo, Stacy. *Bodily Natures: Science, the Environment, and the Material Self.* Bloomington: Indiana University Press, 2010.

Alaimo, Stacy, and Susan Hekman, ed. *Material Feminisms.* Bloomington: Indiana University Press, 2008.

Fausto-Sterling, Ann. "The Bare Bones of Sex." *Signs: Journal of Women in Culture and Society* 30, No. 2 (2005): 1491–1527.

Gould, Stephen Jay. "The Evolution of Life on Earth." *Scientific American* 1, No. 4 (27 October 1994): 84–91.

Grusin, Richard, ed. *The Nonhuman Turn.* Minneapolis: University of Minnesota Press, 2015.

Harman, Graham. "On the Horror of Phenomenology: Lovecraft and Husserl." *Collapse IV: Philosophical Research and Development* (2008): 333–364.

———. *Weird Realism: Lovecraft and Philosophy.* Winchester, UK: Zero Books, 2012.

Haraway, Donna. "Anthropocene, Capitalocene, Cthulhucene: Staying with the Trouble." AURA talk, delivered 9 May 2014. 22 min 45 sec: https://vimeo.com/97663518. Accessed online.

———. "The Promises of Monsters: A Regenerative Politics for Inappropriate/d Others." *Cultural Studies* (1992): 295–337.

———. *When Species Meet.* Duke University Press, 2008.

Hird, Myra. "Indifferent Globality." *Theory, Culture and Society* 27, Nos. 2–3 (2010): 54–72.

———. "Meeting with the Microcosmos." *Environment and Planning D: Society and Space* 28 (2010): 36–39.

———. "Symbiosis, Microbes, Coevolution and Sociology." *Ecological Economics* 69, No. 4 (2010): 737–42.

Hird, Myra, and Noreen Giffney. *Queering the Non/Human.* Aldershot, UK: Ashgate, 2008.

Joshi, S. T. *Lovecraft and a World in Transition: Collected Essays on H. P. Lovecraft.* New York: Hippocampus Press, 2014.

Lovecraft, H. P. *The Call of Cthulhu and Other Weird Stories.* Ed. S. T. Joshi. New York: Penguin, 1999.

———. *The Thing on the Doorstep and Other Weird Stories.* Ed. S. T. Joshi. New York: Penguin, 2001.

Morton, Timothy. *Hyperobjects: Philosophy and Ecology After the End of the World.* Minneapolis: University of Minnesota Press, 2013.

———. "Zero Landscapes in the Time of Hyperobjects." *Graz Architectural Magazine* 7 (2011): 78–87. https://www.academia.edu/1050861/Zero_Landscapes_in_the_Time_of_Hyperobjects. Web.

Shaviro, Steven. *The Universe of Things: On Speculative Realism.* Minneapolis: University of Minnesota Press, 2014.

Sperling, Alison. "H.P. Lovecraft's Weird Body." *Rhizomes: Cultural Studies in Emerging Knowledge* 31 (2016). Fall/ Winter.

Thacker, Eugene. *After Life.* Chicago: University of Chicago Press, 2010.

———. *In the Dust of this Planet. [Horror of Philosophy, Volume 1.]* Winchester, UK: Zero Books, 2011.

———. *Starry Speculative Corpse. [Horror of Philosophy, Volume 2.]* Winchester, UK: Zero Books, 2015.

———. *Tentacles Longer Than Night. [Horror of Philosophy, Volume 3.]* Winchester, UK: Zero Books, 2015.

Trigg, Dylan. *The Thing: A Phenomenology of Horror.* Winchester, UK: Zero Books, 2014.

Woodard, Ben. *Slime Dynamics: Generation, Mutation, and the Creep of Life.* Winchester, UK: Zero Books, 2012.

Queer Geometry and Higher Dimensions: Mathematics in the Fiction of H. P. Lovecraft

Daniel M. Look

Introduction

> My cynicism and skepticism are increasing, and from an entirely
> new cause—the Einstein theory. The latest eclipse observations
> seem to place this system among the facts which cannot be dis-
> missed, and assumedly it removes the last hold which reality or the
> universe can have on the independent mind. All is chance, accident,
> and ephemeral illusion—a fly may be greater than Arcturus, and
> Durfee Hill may surpass Mount Everest—assuming them to be re-
> moved from the present planet and differently environed in the
> continuum of space-time. . . . All the cosmos is a jest, and fit to be
> treated only as a jest, and one thing is as true as another. (*SL* 1.231)

Howard Phillips Lovecraft lived in a time of great scientific and
mathematical advancement. The late nineteenth to the early
twentieth century saw the discovery of X-rays, the identification
of the electron, work on the structure of the atom, breakthroughs
in the mathematical exploration of higher dimensions and alter-
nate geometries, and, of course, Einstein's work on relativity. From
his work on relativity, Einstein postulated that rays of light could
be bent by celestial objects with a large enough gravitational pull.[1]
In 1919 and 1922 measurements were made during two eclipses
that added support to this notion. This left Lovecraft unsettled, as

---

1. This statement is a simplification: Newton's theories already posited that rays
of light could be bent in this manner, but Einstein's theories disagreed with
Newton in terms of the magnitude of this bending.

seen in the above quotation from a 1923 letter to James F. Morton.

Lovecraft's distress is that it seems we can no longer trust our primary means of understanding the world around us. The discovery of X-rays, for example, demonstrated the existence of an invisible reality beyond the reach of our senses. Lovecraft uses similar ideas in his stories to create an essence of fear by removing the sense of familiarity from the familiar, creating a landscape seemingly outside of human experience. This is Freud's concept of the uncanny (*Das Unheimliche*), taking the familiar and making it unfamiliar, creating a sense of "uncomfortable recognition." In "Notes on Writing Weird Fiction," Lovecraft states that "Horror and the unknown or the strange are always closely connected, so that it is hard to create a convincing picture of shattered natural law or cosmic alienage and 'outsideness' without laying stress on the emotion of fear" (CE 2.176). In "The Call of Cthulhu" the sense of the uncanny arises from twisting of the laws of geometry. Rather than the geometric notions we are accustomed to, Lovecraft describes geometries that are queer and non-Euclidean. Whether or not a reader understands the phrase "non-Euclidean" it has a chilling effect, giving the impression of a break in the natural order, a common theme in cosmic horror. Given that Euclid's *Elements* was a common text in geometry classrooms through the end of the nineteenth century, it is likely that many of Lovecraft's readers were at least familiar with Euclid.

Lovecraft's use of mathematics has been explored in previous papers. In particular, Hull's "H. P. Lovecraft: A Horror in Higher Dimensions" points interested mathematics students to the writing of Lovecraft. This is a brief piece intended for audiences familiar with certain mathematical concepts. Halpern and Lobossiere's "Mind out of Time: Identity, Perception, and the Fourth Dimension in H. P. Lovecraft's 'The Shadow out of Time' and 'The Dreams in the Witch House'" contains, among other things, a discussion of how and why Lovecraft used mathematics. The intent of these papers, however, is not to explain the mathematics referenced by Lovecraft. We provide an avenue for the non-mathematician to understand mathematical concepts utilized by Lovecraft. In particular, we focus on Lovecraft's use of dimension and geometry in "The Dreams in the Witch House," "The Call of

Cthulhu," and "Through the Gates of the Silver Key." We summarize the relevant portions of these stories, but primarily discuss the mathematics appearing in the stories, assuming a familiarity with Lovecraft's works on the part of the reader.

Dimension

To understand the geometric and dimensional terms employed by Lovecraft, we start with a story. In 1882 the memoirs of an individual named A. Square were published by Edwin A. Abbott in his novella *Flatland*. A. Square inhabits Flatland—a two-dimensional world inhabited by two-dimensional beings like A. Square who, unsurprisingly, is a square. Through Abbott, A. Square describes how inhabitants of Flatland perceive one another and organize their society. We won't discuss these details (which comprise roughly half of the original novella) as we are interested in the mathematics present in *Flatland*.

One night, A. Square encounters a being claiming to exist in three dimensions: the two of Flatland and a third for which A. Square has no name, but which the visitor, whom we refer to as A. Sphere, calls *height*. When A. Sphere first communicates with A. Square, he does so as a disembodied voice. Then, a dot appears to A. Square, and that dot becomes a circle with increasing radius, which reaches a maximum then begins to shrink, becoming a dot again prior to disappearing. This is confusing to A. Square, but can be understood if we think of Flatland as a two-dimensional space within a three-dimensional space.

Imagine Flatland is a plane, which we can picture as a piece of paper extending infinitely, with the inhabitants drawn on it. The inhabitants of Flatland reside in this plane and cannot see anything not intersecting it. If we, as three-dimensional beings, avoid the plane we are invisible to the Flatlanders. If we touch or put an arm through the plane, the inhabitants see only the two-dimensional cross-sectional intersection.

There are several implications to this scenario that are relevant to our discussion of Lovecraft. For instance, if we put a finger through Flatland the inhabitants would see a circular blob. To capture this creature they might build a rectangular enclosure. To them, it is not possible to escape such a structure, but we have access to a third dimension and can simply pull our finger out of the plane and re-insert it outside of the rectangle. To the Flatlanders, we will have teleported. But in reality, we are only making use of a dimension they cannot see.

We can now understand A. Sphere's appearance as described by A. Square. A. Sphere spoke to A. Square before intersecting Flatland. He then crosses Flatland, first intersecting only at a point when the sphere is tangent to the plane, then becoming a circle with varying radius when the sphere is cut by the plane, then becoming a point again just before disappearing as the sphere passes through the other "side" of Flatland (Figure 1).

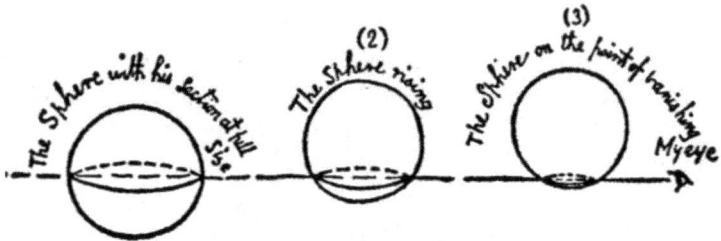

Figure 1: Edwin Abbott's drawing of A. Sphere passing through Flatland. *Ibilio: The Public's Library and Digital Archive.* ibiblio.org. 26 June 2003. Web. November 2014 http://www.ibiblio.org/eldritch/eaa/F16.HTM>

As an example of these ideas in Lovecraft we consider "The Dreams in the Witch House." This story follows Walter Gilman, a mathematics student at Miskatonic University, who rents a room in an old building that at one time housed a witch, Keziah Mason. Gilman begins obsessing over the strange angles of one corner of his room and is plagued by nightmarish dreams.

In one of his dreams, Gilman "observed a further mystery—the tendency of certain entities to appear suddenly out of empty space, or to disappear totally with equal suddenness" (CF 3.238). This could be accounted for by a being inhabiting more than three spatial dimensions intersecting our three-dimensional space. If the creature pulls itself "out" of our space, through a direction inaccessible to us, it would seem to disappear. Further, there are indications that Keziah's witchcraft is related to geometry:

[Keziah] had told Judge Hathorne of lines and curves that could be made to point out directions leading through the walls of space to other spaces beyond, and had implied that such lines and curves were frequently used at certain midnight meetings in the dark valley of the white stone beyond Meadow Hill and on the unpeopled island in the river. . . . Then she had drawn those devices on the walls of her cell and vanished. (CF 3.233)

Dimension provides a possible explanation for Keziah's escape from her prison through strange angles and directions. If Keziah's "witchcraft" included a perception of a direction distinct from all known directions along with the ability to move through this "fourth dimension," she would appear to vanish and would have little trouble escaping a three-dimensional jail cell. In fact, Gilman posits that this is possible and that if individuals had the requisite mathematical knowledge they could

> step deliberately from the earth to any other celestial body which might lie at one of an infinity of specific points in the cosmic pattern. Such a step, he said, would require only two stages; first, a passage out of the three-dimensional sphere we know, and second, a passage back to the three-dimensional sphere at another point, perhaps one of infinite remoteness. (CF 3.240)[2]

These ideas appear in "Through the Gates of the Silver Key" by Lovecraft and E. Hoffmann Price. The story takes place at a gathering held to discuss the fate of Randolph Carter, whose mysterious disappearance is described in "The Silver Key." Through the narration of the Swami Chandraputra (who is actually Carter) we learn that Carter had journeyed through "gates" opened by the silver key. When beyond the gates Carter's sense of space and time become blurred, and Carter is told "how childish and limited is the notion of a tri-dimensional world, and what an infinity of directions there are besides the known directions of up-down, forward-backward, right-left" (CF 3.302).

In both of these stories we encounter the notion of directions other than the "known directions." We can visualize this by returning to Flatland. Figure 2 shows a direction that, to a Flatlander,

---

2. This idea is reminiscent of Einstein-Rosen bridges, or wormholes, a concept discovered by Ludwig Flamm in 1916. The name derives from a 1935 paper by Albert Einstein and Nathan Rosen on the same concept.

would be distinct from all known directions. As shown, each plane is a separate "universe." The known directions for the inhabitants of Flatland include the directions accessible to them: north, east, south, west, and all combinations of those directions. Thus, the arrow pointing from one universe to the other is perpendicular to each of the directional arrows contained in the first universe. In other words, this direction is different from all known directions (for the inhabitants of Flatland), and traveling in this direction would take Flatlanders "outside" of their universe.

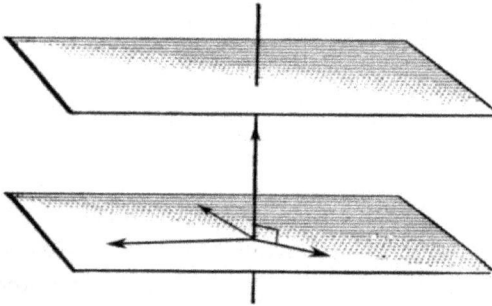

Figure 2: To the inhabitants of Flatland, the direction from one plane to the other is perpendicular to all their known directions. Adapted from G. A. Wentworth *Plane and Solid Geometry* (Boston: Ginn & Company, 1899) 263

Geometries

"The Dreams in the Witch House," "The Call of Cthulhu," and "Through the Gates of the Silver Key" all include uncanny geometric ideas. In each, there is mention of odd angles and geometric figures not behaving according to the properties typically ascribed them. To understand these ideas we explore some concepts from geometry, which will lead us to non-Euclidean and Euclidean geometries.

A beautifully accessible conversation similar to the following can be found in the introductory chapter of *The Shape of Space* by Jeffrey Weeks. To start, we return to Flatland. Intuitively, most people picture Flatland as an infinite plane. However, this may not be the case. Perhaps Flatland has an intrinsic shape that we would call a sphere. How would this appear to the inhabitants of Flatland? We don't have to stretch our imaginations to picture this, as we already experience a version by living on a roughly spherical planet.

What we see around us looks flat; the curvature and size of the Earth relative to our size make the curvature imperceptible. Likewise, the inhabitants of Flatland would not necessarily see the curvature of their universe. What they would be able to do is leave in one direction and, without turning around, come back to their starting point. And why limit Flatland to a sphere? Perhaps its inhabitants live on a torus (Figure 3).

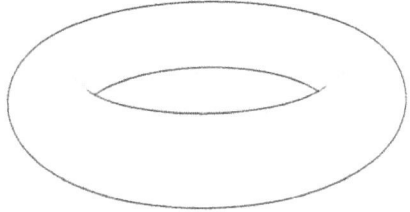

Figure 3: Perhaps Flatland is a torus?

A torus has properties in common with a sphere; for example, the landscape would still appear locally "flat" if the inhabitants were small enough relative to the torus. Also, Flatlanders could still leave in one direction and come back to their starting point. Are there differences that an inhabitant of Flatland could detect? We see a giant hole in the middle, but the inhabitants of Flatland would not see that as they are trapped on the surface. However, imagine two travelers leaving a common point walking in different directions until they return to the starting point. On a torus it is possible that both could return to the starting point without their paths crossing, which is not possible in the similar situation on the sphere. This is shown in Figures 4 and 5.

These are only two of an infinite number of possible

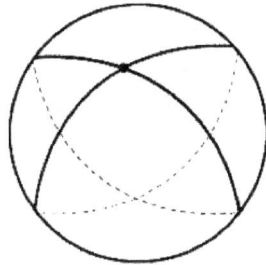

Figure 4: If we choose two directions and walk on a sphere, the paths must cross before returning to the starting point.

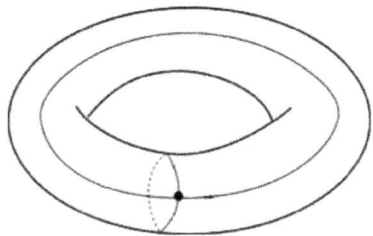

Figure 5: If we choose two directions and walk on a torus, both paths can return to the starting point without crossing.

models for Flatland. Both the sphere and the torus are objects we would intuitively call "curved." Is there any way the Flatlanders could determine if their universe is curved? To this end, let's think about what a triangle would look like on a spherical Flatland. This will lead to a possible explanation for angles that appear "wrong" as well as providing a transition to non-Euclidean geometries.

Since a triangle can be defined as the region bounded by three distinct, non-pairwise parallel lines, we start by discussing lines on spheres. To this end we define a line segment as *the shortest distance between two points*. When trapped on the surface of a sphere, the shortest distance between two points always lies on a *great circle* containing those points, a great circle being a circle on the sphere whose center is also the center of the sphere. A great circle will always split the sphere into two equal sized pieces, unlike a *small circle*, whose center is not the center of the sphere. Figure 6 shows a sphere with a great circle and two small circles. On our (roughly) spherical world the lines of latitude, with the exception of the equator, are small circles while all lines of longitude are great circles.

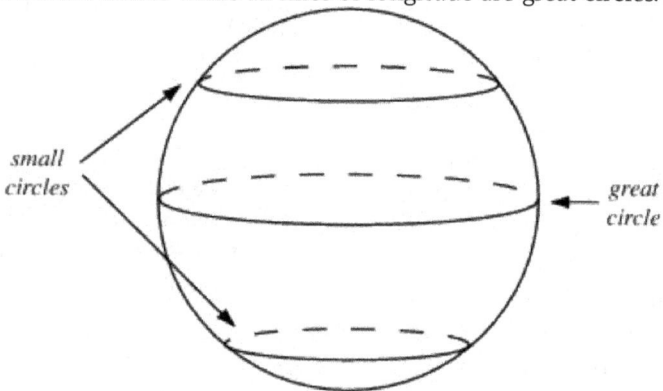

Figure 6: Two small circles and a great circle on a sphere. "Great Circle" *Mathworld*. Wolfram Research, Inc., 30 Nov. 2014. Web. 1 Dec. 2014. http://mathworld.wolfram.com/GreatCircle.html

In Figure 7 we see three great circles, a, b, c, intersecting at three points, A, B, C. This defines a triangle on the sphere with interior angles x, y, z. (Actually, those three "lines" divide the sphere into eight triangles, but we will only consider the triangle with sides a, b, c.) From the picture it seems intuitively obvious that unlike "regular"

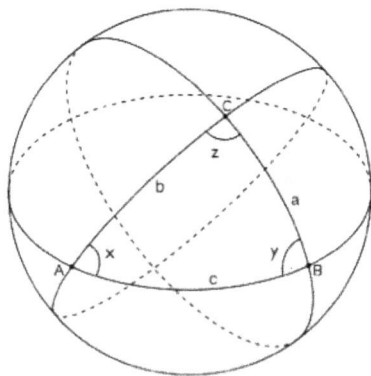

Figure 7: A triangle on a sphere. Note that the angles, x, y, and z add to more than 180 degrees. Adapted from Triangles on a Sphere. "Spherical Trigonometry" *Wikipedia*. Wikimedia Foundation, Inc., 13 November 2014. Web. 28 November. 2014. http://en.wikipedia.org/wiki/Spherical_trigonometry.

triangles, the interior angles for the spherical triangle sum to more than 180 degrees. So if the residents of Flatland were to construct a triangle, they could measure the angles to see if their world was curved. Before we think this is too easy we should keep in mind that this sphere is the entire universe for the Flatlanders. Unlike a flat geometry, the sum of interior angles for triangles on a sphere varies with the size of the triangle (although always remaining greater than 180 degrees). In order to make a triangle with interior angles whose sum is detectably greater than 180 degrees, the Flatlanders may need to make a triangle almost as large as their entire universe.

How does this conversation relate to Lovecraft and angles that seem "wrong" or queer? If this "curvature" is the explanation for strange angles in Lovecraft's work, then it is not only detectable to the characters but also detectible on a distressing magnitude. Imagine that Flatland is, in general, a plane. However, there are some "bumps,"[3] as in Figure 8. A resident of Flatland far from these

---

3. In his *Space Theory of Matter* (1870), mathematician William Kingdon Clifford proposed that small portions of space are of a nature analogous to little hills on a surface that is, on average, flat.

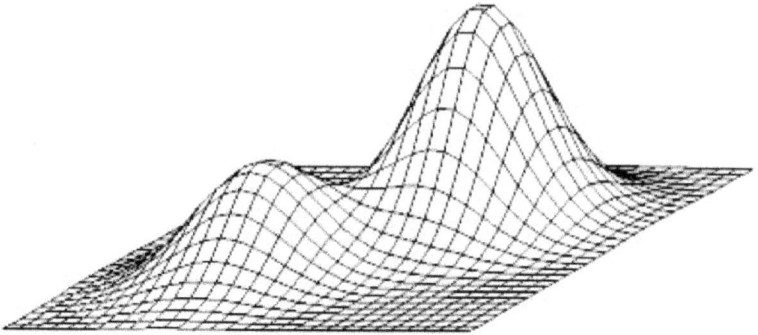

Figure 8. Curved Flatland. "Hill Climbing" *Wikipedia.* Wikimedia Foundation, Inc., 4 November 2014. Web. 28 November 2014. http://en.wikipedia.org/wiki/Hill_climbing.

bumps would find that the interior angles of a triangle add to 180 degrees. However, if the bumps were "curvy" enough, then the same resident could walk to one of these bumps and obtain triangles whose interior angles sum to something other than 180 degrees (this sum could be more or less than 180, as we will soon see). If this individual had lived its entire life in the flat portion of Flatland the geometry of this place would seem uncanny with angles that were "wrong."

What would it look like if our universe had pockets of varying curvature? This is difficult to picture in the same way that we picture a Flatland with bumps, but the key idea remains. Namely, if the curvature were high enough near a particular location, we may be able to discern a difference, one of these differences being perceptible changes in angles.

Lovecraft often mentions non-Euclidean geometry in conjunction with "strange" angles. In the next section we use the concept of curvature to explore non-Euclidean and Euclidean geometries. We then return to Lovecraft to discuss some of the instances where these ideas appear in his fiction.

Euclidean and Non-Euclidean Geometry

A little over 2000 years ago, Euclid wrote *Elements*, his treatise on geometry. *Elements* starts with twenty-three definitions, five axioms (common notions), and five postulates (geometric assumptions). From these Euclid was able to prove results that were in turn used to prove more results, until there arose an immense number of geometric theorems. All these theorems were based entirely, in theory, on the initial assumptions and definitions. It is no surprise that Euclid is sometimes referred to as the Father of Geometry. (We note, however, that one criticism of *Elements* is that some of the proofs involve implicit assumptions not listed.)

Euclid's *Elements* served as the standard geometry textbook in most places until the late nineteenth century. Thus, for Lovecraft and many of his readers "Euclid" is almost synonymous with "geometry." So it is not surprising that Lovecraft refers to Euclid when discussing geometries that somehow lie "outside" the "normal" laws of geometry. This occurs when Lovecraft references non-Euclidean geometries, but there are other examples. Lovecraft invokes Euclid in *At the Mountains of Madness* through a character's description of "geometrical forms for which an Euclid would scarcely find a name" (*CF* 3.80). Here we see Lovecraft's common theme of removing a character from the familiar. Referring to geometric forms gives the impression that the objects are simple, on par with squares or circles. However, they are somehow beyond our conception and even Euclid would not be able to categorize them, implying a character's inability to construct a complete picture of his surroundings. We will return to this theme when discussing "The Call of Cthulhu."

In mathematics, the idea is to use as few assumptions as possible when beginning an exploration. So mathematicians wondered if it were possible to prove any of the five initial postulates using the other four. If it were, then four postulates would suffice. Time and time again the assumption under scrutiny was the fifth postulate, which is equivalent to:

> Given any line and any point not on the line, exactly one line can be drawn through the point that is parallel to the first.

This is shown in Figure 9, where M is the only line through P that is parallel to the line N.

For centuries mathematicians tried proving the fifth postulate from the other four—but each effort proved futile. Eventually another approach was tried; namely, the exploration of a geometry for which the parallel postulate is not assumed. Most mathema-

ticians felt the parallel
postulate was a required
assumption, so they ap-
proached this study look-
ing for contradictions,
implying the necessity of
the fifth postulate. The
mathematician Carl Frie-
drich Gauss worked on
this problem, mention-
ing it to his friend Farkas
Bolyai, who offered sev-
eral (incorrect) proofs
for the parallel postulate.

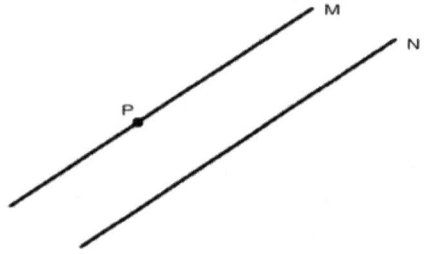

Figure 9: Given a line, N, and a point,
P, not on the line, the parallel postulate
implies that there is exactly one line,
namely M, through the point parallel
to the original line.

(Gauss did not present his ideas to the general mathematical
community, as he believed the fifth postulate was independent of
the other four—an idea that would cause a controversy Gauss
preferred to avoid.) Bolyai taught mathematics to his son, János
Bolyai, but warned him not to waste any time on the problem of
the fifth postulate. János did not heed that advice and in 1823
wrote to his father saying, "I have discovered things so wonderful
that I was astounded . . . out of nothing I have created a strange
new world." Boylai's work (and that of other mathematicians) led
to the discovery that three entirely consistent categories of geometries were possible, distinguished by the number of parallel lines:

- If there is precisely one parallel line we say the geometry is
  Euclidean, as it matches Euclid's original presentation.
- If there are no parallel lines we say the geometry is *elliptic*.
- If there are infinitely many parallel lines we say the geometry
  is *hyperbolic*.[4]

We are now able to give a definition of Euclidean and non-
Euclidean geometries. A Euclidean geometry is one with exactly
one parallel line. This is our "intuitive" geometry. A non-Euclidean
geometry has either no parallel lines or an infinite number of par-

---

4. It can be shown mathematically that having two parallel lines implies there is an
infinite number of parallel lines, so the only choices are none, one, or infinitely many.

allel lines through the specified point.

In terms of horror, we are accustomed to the geometry of our universe, be it Euclidean or non-Euclidean. However, the non-Euclidean geometries in Lovecraft's stories are not familiar to the characters. This implies that the geometry is not consistent with their expectations; they are accustomed to a Euclidean geometry and are now experiencing a non-Euclidean geometry. We note that in our last Flatland model the bumps cause a change in the local geometry. This means a creature living in a Euclidean region of space could move to a non-Euclidean one.

Since Euclidean geometry is the "standard" geometry, we won't spend time explaining it. The main concepts we use are that there is always exactly one parallel line through a given point not on a line and that the interior angles of a triangle sum to 180 degrees. In the following two sections we discuss the two other possibilities.

Elliptic Geometry

The spherical model discussed earlier is an example of an elliptic geometry. The geometry on a sphere, which is called *spherical geometry*, is not the only possible form of elliptic geometry. However, the spherical model allows visualization and we forgo more complicated models and explanations in favor of this intuitive approach.

Recall that the equivalent of a line on a sphere is a great circle. To make this more precise, the mathematical term for the shortest distance between two points is *geodesic*. In Euclidean geometries, the geodesic is a "straight" line. ("Straight" is in quotation marks to indicate our standard idea of a line; we have not defined what it means to be "straight.") On a sphere geodesics are great circles. Using the language of geodesics, the fifth postulate states that given a geodesic and a point not on that geodesic there exists exactly one geodesic through the point parallel to the first.

To see why the geometry on a sphere is elliptic, note that any two geodesics on a sphere must intersect, as shown in Figure 4. Hence, given a geodesic on a sphere and a point not on that geodesic, there are no geodesics through the point parallel to the first, implying this geometry is elliptic. Further, recall that the interior angles for a triangle on a sphere sum to more than 180 degrees. This is always the case with elliptic geometries.

Hyperbolic Geometry

The sphere makes a nice visual for an elliptic geometry and the plane does the same for a Euclidean geometry. For hyperbolic geometry we use a *hyperbolic paraboloid*, sometimes referred to as a saddle, as shown in Figure 10. On this surface, for any geodesic M and point P not on M we have an infinite number of geodesics passing through P and parallel to M. Figure 11 shows a geodesic M and a point P not on M with three geodesics parallel to M passing through P.

Before closing this section, we note that non-Euclidean geometries are not the mad fancy of mathematicians attempting to "break" conventional geometry. Although we only discussed two-dimensional models embedded in a three-dimensional space, there are also hyperbolic, elliptic, and Euclidean geometric models for three-dimensional space. In fact, one of Einstein's models involves a three-sphere (a four-dimensional analogue of our usual sphere), which implies a "curved" spacetime. A conversation on spacetime would bring us too far afield, so we simply note that time itself is now tangled up in the "curving." As one can guess, there is active research into the "shape" of our universe and spacetime. It is the advanced version of the question "Is the world flat?" (We refer interested readers to *The Shape of Space*.)

Queer Landscapes

We have already seen mention of queer geometries in "Through the Gates of the Silver Key" and "The Dreams in the Witch House." We now turn our attention to "The Call of Cthulhu," which involves some of Lovecraft's most explicit use of uncanny geometry and landscapes.

Figure 12 shows a pair of parallel lines and a triangle on the saddle surface. In this case we note that the interior angles of the triangle sum to less than 180 degrees.

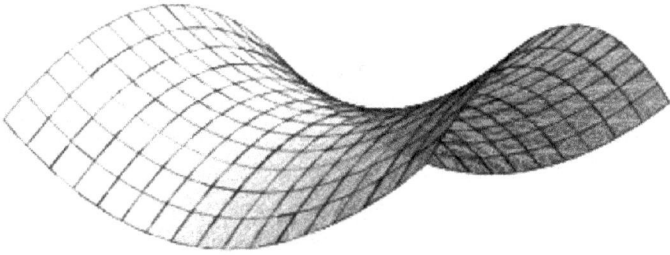

Figure 10: A Hyperbolic Paraboloid.

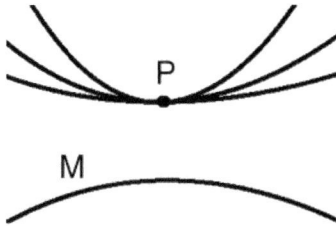

Figure 11: For any line M and point P not on M, there are an infinite number of lines through P parallel to M.

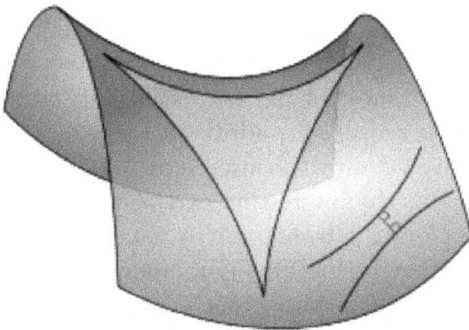

Figure 12: A hyperbolic paraboloid with a pair of parallel lines and a triangle. Adapted from Hyperbolic Triangle. "Hyperbolic Geometry" Wikipedia. Wikimedia Foundation, Inc., 15 September 2014. Web. 24 November 2014. http://en.wikipedia.org/wiki/Hyperbolic_geometry.

"The Call of Cthulhu" tells of George Gammell Angell's investigation of the cult of Cthulhu. In 1925 Angell had been approached by a sculptor, Henry Anthony Wilcox, plagued by dreams involving "great Cyclopean cities of titan blocks and sky-flung monoliths, all dripping with green ooze and sinister with latent horror" (CF 2.26). Wilcox reports hearing "a voice that was not a voice; a chaotic sensation which only fancy could transmute into sound, but which he attempted to render by the almost unpronounceable jumble of letters 'Cthulhu fhtagn'" (CF 2.26). Years earlier, Angell had met an inspector of police who told a tale of his encounter with the cult of Cthulhu, during which he heard those words included in a chant: "Ph'nglui mglw'nafh Cthulhu R'lyeh wgah'nagl fhtagn." A translation of this chant yields the confusing statement: "In his house at R'lyeh dead Cthulhu waits dreaming" (CF 2.34). One of the few cult members captured (and sane enough to give information) told of how Cthulhu's followers were waiting for a time when the stars would align, R'lyeh would rise from the Pacific ocean, and Cthulhu would wake.

Angell's investigation leads him to a report of Norwegian sailor Gustaf Johansen, who was discovered in a half delirious state clutching a "horrible stone idol of unknown origin" (CF 2.45). Johansen wrote a manuscript telling of how he and his crew stumbled upon the risen R'lyeh, which had buildings of strange Cyclopean masonry, and eventually encountered and repelled Cthulhu. Although most of the crew died, Johansen and a fellow crewmate manage to survive, adrift on the wrecked ship. When the ship is discovered, only Johansen remains alive.

Mathematically, the interesting part of this story occurs while the crew is exploring R'lyeh prior to encountering Cthulhu. Johansen's description of the city is reminiscent of the dreams of Wilcox, with a character noting that:

> Without knowing what futurism is like, Johansen achieved something very close to it when he spoke of the city; for instead of describing any definite structure or building, he dwells only on broad impressions of vast angles and stone surfaces—surfaces too great to belong to any thing right or proper for this earth, and impious with horrible images and hieroglyphs. I mention his talk about angles because it suggests something Wilcox had told me of

his awful dreams. He said that the geometry of the dream-place he saw was abnormal, non-Euclidean, and loathsomely redolent of spheres and dimensions apart from ours. (CF 2.51)

This passage contains references to uncanny mathematics and echoes Lovecraft's unease at the eclipse experiment. Johansen is unable to describe any definite structure, giving only broad impressions. A complete picture of R'lyeh is beyond his ability to comprehend, creating a feeling of "mathematical insignificance" along with the cosmic insignificance common to Lovecraft.

Further, as we have seen, describing a non-Euclidean space as one that is suggestive of spheres can be viewed as consistent. The geometry of the space is familiar enough that one expects the normal rules to apply, but yet foreign enough to cause distress and confusion. This can also be seen when "Johansen swears [one of his crew] was swallowed up by an angle of masonry which shouldn't have been there; an angle which was acute, but behaved as if it were obtuse" (CF 2.53). We have seen examples of triangles whose interior angles sum to more than 180 degrees. In such a triangle there could be two angles summing to 145 degrees, implying that the remaining angle "should" be 35 degrees. However, in a hyperbolic geometry the final angle could be 120 degrees; meaning it should be acute, but behaves as if it is obtuse.

It also seems that Johansen is unable to compose a complete picture of his surroundings:

> The very sun of heaven seemed distorted when viewed through the polarizing miasma welling out from this sea-soaked perversion, and twisted menace and suspense lurked leeringly in those crazily elusive angles of carven rock where a second glance shewed concavity after the first shewed convexity. . . . As Wilcox would have said, the geometry of the place was all wrong. One could not be sure that the sea and the ground were horizontal, hence the relative position of everything else seemed phantasmally variable. (CF 2.51–52)

To understand this last description, we return to our model of Flatland with bumps (Figure 8). In this model, A. Square could travel from a region of Flatland with a locally Euclidean geometry to a region with a locally non-Euclidean geometry by approaching and "climbing" one of the bumps. In this model, the local curvature of A. Square's universe varies as A. Square moves across these regions. If A. Square is accustomed to the flat regions of Flatland, this change would be unsettling. Angles would change in degree measure as A. Square moves and usual constants (think of the flatness of the line of horizon) would distort and change.

Is it possible that R'lyeh was in a region of "bent" space, causing Johansen to question his senses and give the above descriptions? In Tipett's "Possible Bubbles of Spacetime Curvature in the South Pacific," the author posits that "all of the credible phenomena which Johansen described may well be explained as being the observable consequences of a localized bubble of spacetime curvature."

One of the effects of a curved spacetime is gravitational lensing, where the image of an object that lies outside a curved region becomes distorted as gravity bends the path of light (similar to the eclipse experiment). This can be used to explain many of the peculiarities in Johanson's report regarding uncertain perspective and geometric confusion. The bending of light rays would cause the horizon to take a curved appearance (which would make it difficult to tell if the sea and ground were horizontal) while some objects on the horizon would be distorted (a circular sun may "thin" as one moves, becoming elliptical in shape and continuing to thin as one approaches the center of the curved space).

Another effect of curved spacetime is time dilation. Basically, time moves at relative rates depending on where one is in relation to the bubble of curved spacetime. Tipett offers this as a possible explanation for the Cthulhu cult's belief that Cthulhu is neither dead nor alive. Perhaps Cthulhu is in a region of space where the passage of time is exponentially slower than it is outside the region. This would indeed happen at the center of the curved spacetime bubble Tipett describes.

We see these ideas in both "The Dreams in the Witch House" and "Through the Gates of the Silver Key." Time dilation could explain Gilman's comment that "Time could not exist in certain belts of space, and by entering and remaining in such a belt one might preserve one's life and age indefinitely" (CF 3.260), and the bending of light rays through gravitational lensing gives a possible interpretation for Randolph Carter's description of "great masses of towering stone, carven into alien and incomprehensible designs and disposed according to the laws of some unknown, inverse geometry. Light filtered from a sky of no assignable colour in baffling, contradictory directions" (CF 3.290). Although a model for such a geometry is presented, Tipett states that a type of matter is required that is "quite unphysical" and has "a nature which is entirely alien to all of the experiences of human science." Clearly, though, we are not considering the limits of human science. For example, Gilman brings a curious piece of metal found in the Witch House to a certain Professor Ellery who finds

> platinum, iron and tellurium in the strange alloy; but mixed with these were at least three other apparent elements of high atomic weight which chemistry was absolutely powerless to classify. Not only did they fail to correspond with any known element, but they did not even fit the vacant places reserved for probable elements in the periodic system. (CF 3.258)

Conclusion

In many instances, Lovecraft's use of non-Euclidean geometry and dimension seems an educated one, with the accompanying descriptions from characters matching at least one possible mathematical interpretation. However, there are instances where Lovecraft uses mathematical phrases in ways that are difficult to interpret. For example, in "Dreams" Gilman feels that he was "certainly near the boundary between the known universe and the fourth dimension" (CF 3.243). By most interpretations of dimension, it is nonsensical to speak of being "close" to the fourth dimension.

Although he frequently employed mathematical concepts, Lovecraft did not consider himself an adept mathematician. In fact, in a letter to Maurice W. Moe in 1915 Lovecraft remarked: "Mathematics I detest, and only a supreme effort of the will gained for me the highest marks in Algebra and Geometry at school. In everything I am behind the times" (SL 1.9). Although Lovecraft professed to dislike mathematics, he was very interested in astronomy and physics and picked up mathematical notions through these interests. Lovecraft used these mathematical ideas, it would seem, in part because he himself found the "toppling" of Newtonian physics by Einstein's theory of relativity unsettling. As Halpern and Labossiere state:

> Rather than breaking the laws of science with supernatural means and thus generating fear, [Lovecraft] creates a feeling of horror by showing that the common sense views of physics and nature (that is, the old Newtonian views) are the comforting fantasy. In contrast, the counterintuitive "new physics," the true scientific reality, provides the source of horror. (513)

When sight and time are relative, Lovecraft felt all perception was in question. He described landscapes utterly alien to humanity by altering something as fundamental as geometry. Our insignificance and ignorance are underscored by the notion that we exist in a space much bigger than we imagined, with entire spatial dimensions we cannot perceive, natural laws we cannot understand, and geometric forms so alien they escape description.

Works Cited

Abbott, Edwin A. *Flatland: A Romance of Many Dimensions.* 3rd ed. New York: Dover, 1992.

Burleson, Donald R. *H. P. Lovecraft: A Critical Study.* Westport, CT: Greenwood Press, 1983.

Halpern, Paul, and Labossiere, Michael C. "Mind out of Time: Identity, Perception, and the Fourth Dimension in H. P. Lovecraft's 'The Shadow out of Time' and 'The Dreams in the Witch House.'" *Extrapolation* 50 (2009): 512–33.

Hull, Thomas. "H. P. Lovecraft: A Horror in Higher Dimensions." *Math Horizons* 13, No. 3 (2006): 10–12.

Tipett, Benjamin T. "Possible Bubbles of Spacetime Curvature in the South Pacific." *arXiv* (2012): n.p. Web: http://arxiv.org/abs/1210.8144. Accessed 5 June 2013.

Weeks, Jeffrey R. *The Shape of Space.* 2nd ed. New York: CRC Press, 2012.

Postcards to Jonathan E. Hoag

H. P. Lovecraft

Edited by David E. Schultz and S. T. Joshi

Jonathan E[than] Hoag (1831–1927) lived in and around Troy, N.Y., and entered amateur journalism late in life. H. P. Lovecraft compiled and wrote an introduction to Hoag's *Poetical Works* (1923). Lovecraft, Samuel Loveman, and James F. Morton revised some of Hoag's poetry for the volume. The book constituted the first appearance of a work by Lovecraft in hard covers. Lovecraft wrote birthday poems to Hoag from 1918 to 1927, and the elegy "Ave atque Vale" (*Tryout*, December 1927), at Hoag's death. Hoag's descriptions of the Catskill Mountains may have contributed to the topographical atmosphere of "Beyond the Wall of Sleep" and "The Lurking Fear," set there. Hoag may have been a partial inspiration for the character Zadok Allen in "The Shadow over Innsmouth," whose life-dates exactly match Hoag's.

Lovecraft's few surviving postcards to Hoag are chatty, unlike his late postcards, which amount to being short letters. It is evident from the cards published here that Lovecraft and Hoag corresponded, but none of Lovecraft's letters to him survive.

[1]   [ANS]

                          [No stamp; not addressed; not posted]

H. P. Lovecraft [written by Hoag]

Front: County Farm Dam / Cocheco River / Dover N.H.

COUNTY FARM DAM
COCHECO RIVER
DOVER N.H.

POST CARD

COMMUNICATION   ADDRESS ONLY

Place Stamp Here
Domestic
One Cent
Foreign
Two Cents

A2016-012[15]

[2]   [ANS]

[Postmarked Providence, R.I.,
3 July 1920]

Today I have another welcome visitor—R. Kleiner, Esq. We shall
go to Boston together Monday.
                    Ward Phillips

        Best wishes
and sincere respects.
            Rheinhart Kleiner

Front: State Armory, Providence, R. I.

State Armory, Providence. R. I.

7/3/20

POST CARD

FOR CORRESPONDENCE

Berger Bros., Publishers, Providence, R. I.

Today I have another
welcome visitor —
R. Kleiner, Esq. We
shall go to Boston
together Monday
since Philip[?]

best wishes
and sincere respects.
Rheinhart Kleiner

J. E. Hoag, Esq.,
Box 498,
Greenwich,
N.Y.

[3]   [ANS]

[Postmarked Brooklyn, N.Y.,
___ September 1922]

Your interesting letter, with its delightful enclosures received.
Will answer soon. Am in Brooklyn, on my way back from Cleve-
land. ¶ Loveman recd. your letter, but was not able to attend to
anything at the time—physically well, but very nervous. I shall try
to transfer our work to more effective hands—don't lose hope!
More anon.

H. P. L.

Front: Reviewing Stand, Entrance to Flower Garden, Prospect
Park, Brooklyn, N. Y.

Reviewing Stand, Entrance to Flower Garden, Prospect Park, Brooklyn, N. Y.

[4]   [ANS]

[Postmarked Brooklyn, N.Y.,
22 September 1922]

Visited this historic spot recently—wish you could see it. N.Y. is
full of interesting sights & antiquities, including the old tavern—
Fraunce's [*sic*]—where Gen. Washington bade farewell to his ar-
my. ¶ Will write more. Loveman has been unusually silent, but I'll
wake him up if it kills me! H. P. L.

Front: Washington's   Headquarters   1776,   160th   Street   and
Edgecombe Avenue, New York

[5]   [ANS]

[Postmarked Marblehead, Mass.,
8 July 1923]

How do you like the book? Am exploring old Marblehead & Salem—have been to Hub Club convention in Boston.
   Best wishes,
    H P L.

[*Note by Hoag:*] Rec'd July 9" / 23.

Front: A Quaint Old Street in Marblehead, Mass.

A QUAINT OLD STREET IN MARBLEHEAD, MASS.

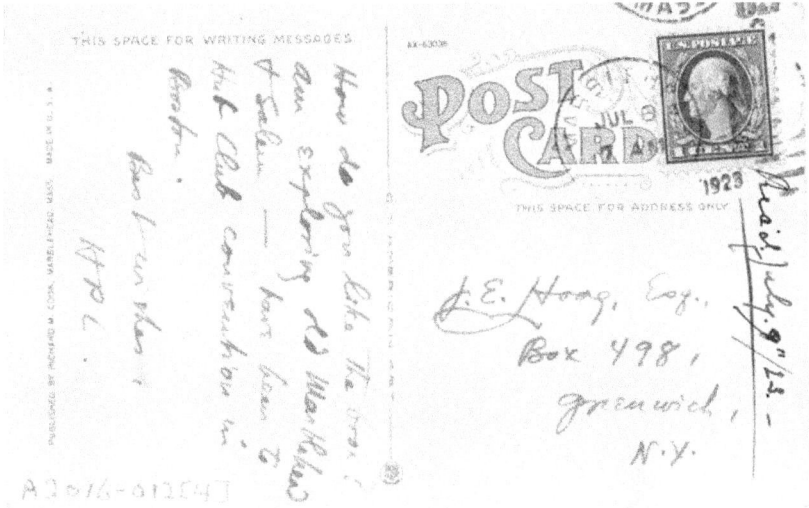

[6]   [ANS]

[Postmarked Providence, R.I.,
19 September 1923]

Well, here are both of your friends & literary collaborators, together in solemn conclave! Your letter just came, & I believe one
of mine has gone astray, for I was the last to write . . . . It was a
thick letter, with many enclosures—too bad it's lost!
       Yr moſt obt   H P Lovecraft

It gives me pleasure to join in sending cordial greetings.
we have been viewing many interesting scenes together.
       James F. Morton, Jr.

Front: Manning Hall Brown University.

[7]   [ANS]

[No stamp, no postmark]
259 Parkside Ave.,
Brooklyn, N.Y.
May 14, 1924

My very dear friend Scriba:—

This is just to herald the letter I have owed you so long, & which I shall certainly write in a few days! Pressure of work has been enormous, as I shall duly relate. ¶ and here are your two splendid poems, duly sandpapered. Pray send me copies when they are printed. ¶ United trying to get ahead under difficulties—of this more anon.

H. P. L

[P.S.] The new household sends unanimous regards!

Front: Poe's Cottage, Bronx, N. Y.

Poe's Cottage, Bronx, N. Y.

EDGAR ALLEN POE

A 5016-013-[5]

Post Card   259 Parkside Ave.,
Brooklyn, N.Y.
May 14, 1924

FOR CORRESPONDENCE   FOR ADDRESS ONLY

PLACE POSTAGE STAMP HERE

Pub. by Fordham Stationery, 4778 - 3rd Ave.

My very dear friend Scriba: —

This is just to herald the letter I have owed you so long, &which I shall certainly write in a few days! Pressure of work has been Enormous, as I shall duly relate. & and here are your two splendid poems, duly sandpapered. Pray send me copies when they are printed. & United trying to get ahead under difficulties — of this work anon! H.P.L.

The new manuscripts speak!

[8]   [ANS]

Exploring quaint Staten Island with my friend George Kirk. Delightful antiquities! Am writing this on flat-topped grave in a half-
deserted village churchyard!
Yr obt Servt H P Lovecraft

Being a friend of HPL's I consider you a friend of mine. Best wishes
George Kirk

Front: Old Billopp House, Tottenville, S. I. (Erected 1668)

Old Billopp House, Tottenville, S. I. (Erected 1668)

[9]   [ANS]

[Postmarked Alexandria, Va.,
13 April 1925]

Still on my wanderings! Absorbing the National Capital & its antiquities, & incidentally meeting the local amateur leaders—
        H P Lovecraft

Front: The National Cathedral, Washington, D. C.

THE NATIONAL CATHEDRAL, WASHINGTON, D. C.

THE NATIONAL CATHEDRAL (EPISCOPAL.)
Mt. St. Alban, now building, will fulfill George Washington's dream of "a church for national purposes." Not since the 14th century has a Gothic cathedral like this been built. In five years one of the finest cathedrals in the world, larger than Westminster Abbey, will rise above the city higher than the Washington Monument. The area and elevation of the Cathedral Close are the same as Solomon's Temple Plateau above Jerusalem. Length 500 feet, height 262 feet. The Cathedral is now the last resting place of the late Woodrow Wilson.

Still on my travels yet! Absorbing the National Capital's antiquities & incidental hills, valleys, & mackerel. —The local amateur —
Carlos—
HPLovecraft

J. E. Hoag, Esq.,
17, Prospect St.,
Greenwich,
N.Y.

[10]   [ANS]

[Postmarked Newport, R.I.,
5 August 1926]

Your letter recd.—Will answer soon. the two of us are revelling in Colonial sights!
    ——H P Lovecraft

    It is long since I have heard from you. I hope you are enjoying excellent health.
    James F. Morton, Jr.

Front: The Old Mill and Channing Monument, Touro Park, Newport, R. I.

THE OLD MILL AND CHANNING MONUMENT. TOURO PARK. NEWPORT. R. I.

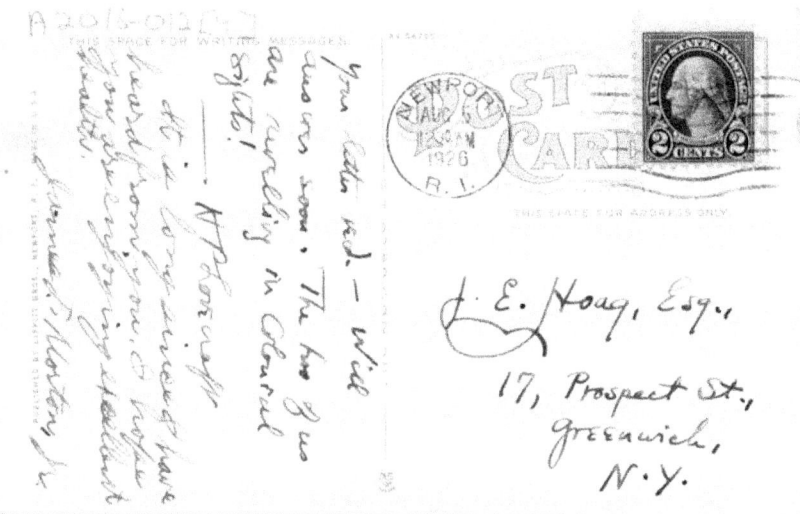

[11]   [ANS]

[Postmarked Newport, R.I.,
14 July 1927]

Am shewing a young friend of mine the antiquities of colonial
Newport—now seated on a high cliff overlooking the sea.
        Yr obt Servt.   HPL

If I approach closely enough, I shall stop at all Greenwich. But
nothing is certain in my eccentric peregrinations. I have met the
enemy, and I am theirs!

Very sincerely yours
Donald Wandrei

Front: Interior Trinity Church Built 1726, Newport R. I.

INTERIOR TRINITY CHURCH. BUILT 1726. NEWPORT, R. I.

J. E. Hoag, Esq.,
17 Prospect St.,
Greenwich,
N. Y.

[12]   [ANS]

[Postmarked Providence, R.I.,
21 July 1927]

Assembled in conclave in Providence:
[signed]
Frank B. Long, Jr.
Donald Wandrei
James F. Morton (late "Jr."), who sends cordial greetings and wish-
ings for another visit with you.
C. M. Eddy, Jr.

We are holding quite a convention of kindred souls, & wish you
could be here to take part ink he deliberations. Tomorrow the
party goes to Newport.
                —Theobald

Front: The Carrie Tower Brown University.

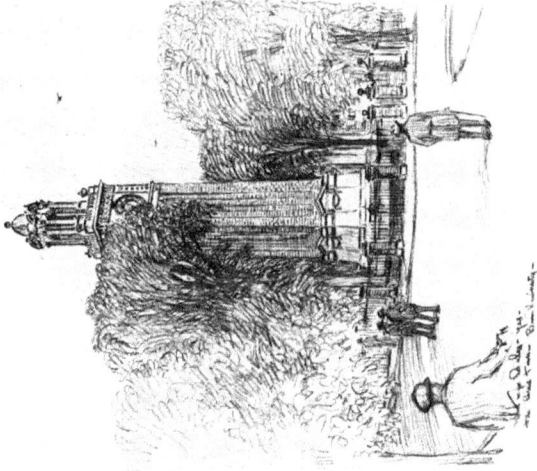

BROWN UNIVERSITY

THE CARRIE TOWER

MAILING CARD

MESSAGE   ADDRESS

J. E. Hoag, Esq,
17, Prospect St.,
Greenwich,
N. Y.

[13]   [ANS]

[Postmarked Portland, Me.,
26 August 1927]

Still on the road! Portland is a fascinating place, & full of recollec-
tions of Longfellow. now for Portsmouth, Newburyport, &
Haverhill—at which latter place I shall see the genial Tryout editor. stopping at YMCA & seeing the house thoroughly. It is quite a
city, but full of old time seafaring colour.
        Best wishes—Theobald

Front: Longfellow's Home, Portland, Me.

LONGFELLOW'S HOME, PORTLAND, ME.

J. E. Hoag, Esq.,
17, Prospect St.,
Greenwich,
N. Y.

[14]   [ANS]

[Postmarked Bretton Woods, N.H.,
8 August 1927]

Was so near the White Mts. in Portland that I decided to take advantage of a cheap excursion. Ascended Mt. Washington & had some fine views in south, though rain spoiled view at summit.
        Sincerely—
                H P Lovecraft

Front: Crawford Notch from Mt. Willard, White Mountains, N. H.

CRAWFORD NOTCH FROM MT. WILLARD, WHITE MOUNTAINS, N. H.

A2016-012 [13]

**CRAWFORD NOTCH
FROM MT. WILLARD**

From this elevated viewpoint one
enjoys the most expansive view of
Crawford Notch, fifteen miles in length
by three across. On the left is Mt.
Willard, while half way up the mountain side on the right appears, clearly
defined, the railroad. Far below, trav-
ersing the floor of the entire notch,
conspicuous in its course past the historic Willey House in center of Valley,
is seen the carriage road.

J. E. Hoag, Esq.,
17, Prospect St.,
Greenwich,
N. Y.

[15]   [AN]

This place has the best existing collection of Colonial household objects—I wish you could see it. This winter I am making a
particularly thorough study of the Colonial atmosphere, & a visit-
ing as many of these houses & museums as possible.

Front: Rhode Island School of Design /Southeast Bedroom /
Pendleton Collection / Colonial House

SOUTHEAST BEDROOM   RHODE ISLAND SCHOOL OF DESIGN
                          PENDLETON COLLECTION   COLONIAL HOUSE

A2016-012 [17]

Here is a feature of old Providence
which I don't think I've shown you before.

Built in 1816.

It was designed by John Holden Greene, a Providence
architect, & is one of the finest Georgian churches
in New England; though its steeple is not as
perfect as that of the old First Baptist (1775.)

SEEING PROVIDENCE, R. I.

Jessie D. Allardice, Publisher Providence, R. I. No. B2350

[16]   [AN]

Here is a feature of Old Providence which I don't think I've
shewn you before.
                    Built in 1816.
It was designed by John Holden Green, a Providence architect, &
is one of the finest Georgian churches in New England; though its
steeple is not as perfect as that of the old First Baptist (1775).

Front: First Congregational (Unitarian) Church / "An Old New
England Meeting House"

FIRST CONGREGATIONAL (UNITARIAN) CHURCH
"AN OLD NEW ENGLAND MEETING HOUSE"
"AMERICAN TRAVEL" SERIES
CHURCHES—OLD-TIMEY SKETCHES

A2016-012 [17]

Here is a feature of Old Providence
which I don't think I've shown you before.

Built in 1816.

It was designed by John Holden Greene, a Providence
architect, & is one of the finest georgian churches
in New England; though its steeple is not as
perfect as that of the old First Baptist (1775)

Jessie D. Allardice, Publisher Providence, R. I. No. B2350

Post Card

Post Card Tours

[17]   [AN]

This likeness is only an hypothetical one made in the 18th Century. Actually, Roger Williams had no pictures painted, so that we do not know how he really looked. The costume shown in the picture is 100 years too recent for Williams's time.

Front: Roger Williams—Copies of Engraving. Engraved by F. Halpin from an Original Painting for "Benedict's History of the Baptists".

Copies of Engraving, Engraved by F. Halpin, from an Original Painting, for "Benedict's History of the Baptists".

Roger Williams

This likeness is only an hypothetical one made in the 18th century. Actually, Roger Williams (w) we pictures paint(s); so that we do not know how he really looked. The astrinle shown in this picture is 100 years too recent for Williams's here.

POST CARD

A2016-012 [18]

[18]   [AN; Hoag to Lovecraft]

[no stamp; not posted]

To H. P. Lovecraft: 598 Angell St., Providence, R.I.

From Prospect St.
Greenwich, N.Y.

Now Philip, when on Fashion St. you go.
You meet a freckl'd face you so well know,
Foxy hair bobb'd short—and her dress the same,
A number b on rubber heels; and lame
You'd feel a thrill of joy you ne'er felt before!
Pray don't tarry long to scare the whole world o'er,
But dye that scanty crop on top your grizzl'd head
Like hers you met on Fashion St. a foxy red.—

<illegible>   The advice of Scriba.

Front: Elmira State Reformatory, Elmira, N. Y.

Elmira State Reformatory. Elmira, N. Y.

The Mouse in the Walls: Disney, Lovecraft, and *Gravity Falls*

Tom Miller

One of the major foci of Lovecraft scholarship is that which attempts to delineate the boundaries and characteristics of what has been variously called "The Mythology of Hastur," "The Cthulhu Mythos," "The Yog-Sothoth Cycle of Myth," or "The Lovecraft Mythos." This body of writings looks to characteristics of Lovecraft's works and those of writers who follow him in order to distinguish "the 'pure' Lovecraftian conception from elaborations (or, from one point of view, perversions) of later writers, extending all the way up to the present day" (Joshi, "Introduction" 5). This second stratum of critique attempts to understand the vital contribution to weird writing that Lovecraft's fiction represents. The myriad of followers attests to the allure of his fictional constructions, but that allure alone does not make for significant literary contribution. While the biographical considerations cannot ever wholly be set aside, and Lovecraft's political and social views are writ large across the texts he leaves behind, it is to this second body of scholarship that the present inquiry turns.

Noted Lovecraft scholar S. T. Joshi dismisses many Mythos tales, penned both by Lovecraft and his successors, due to a "lack of possession of intrinsic literary merits" (Joshi, *Rise* 12). Joshi has, in past, been called out on his dismissal of those texts he judges to be not only lacking in these "literary merits," but also using "Lovecraft's work as a kind of literary crutch" (13). He offers the example of mentioning the name "Innsmouth," a fictional town in Lovecraft's New England, as a kind of shorthand to communicate a particular quality and lineage of horror (13). From the stance of a literary scholar, Joshi's requirement is a fundamentally important one. However, dismissal of works that engage with Lovecraft's oeuvre but do not possess qualities desired by a narrow academic lens is problematic in considering the breadth and depth of cultural immersion evinced by the Lovecraft Mythos. It is to this immersion that I wish to turn my attention, and my trajectory leads to the unlikeliest of places.

Lovecraft, well known for his nihilistic worldview and questionable social precepts, would likely be horrified by the transformations his nightmare terrors have undergone in the years since his death in 1937. One imagines, however, that he would be wise enough to understand that a creature such as Cthulhu, who influences dreams, or more properly nightmares, would find a way to manifest itself in diverse modes across the imaginative dream-life of the culture. Lovecraft's most famous creation has been everything from comedic sidekick (Carl Cthulhu in *Little Gloomy*) to stuffed animal to action figure, but his sinister genesis is never far from consciousness. Witness the briefest of flashes in the 15th episode of the second season of the Disney XD cartoon series *Gravity Falls*. When a product of the Magic Kingdom, one ostensibly aimed at a pre- or young teen audience, features a Great Old One (and, as we shall see, the messenger of the gods, Nyarlathotep), it can hardly be doubted that Lovecraft's creations have become a dark fictional underbelly of our collective dream, or that *Gravity Falls* is one of the harbingers of this fact.

Lovecraft himself dabbled in publishing juvenile literature, though given the precociousness evident in even his earliest writings, one hesitates to say that he wrote children's literature proper. At the tender age of six, Lovecraft "published" *The Poem of Ulysses; or, The Odyssey: Written for Young People*, an 88-line condensation of Homer's *Odyssey* (Joshi, *Life* 40) that Joshi calls "a delight" (40). Most interesting, however, is the advertisement that is attached to the poem that lists a whole series of adaptations of classical tales, from the *Aeneid* to the *Metamorphoses*, geared specifically toward younger readers (41). Given that Lovecraft was only six when many of these pieces must have been written, or at least conceived, very few of them remain extant, *The Poem of Ulysses* being the earliest known imaginative writing (40) of the boy who would become the Old Gentleman of Providence. Notably, however, during his mature period, Lovecraft never once delved into anything that might be considered children's literature.

In *The Rise and Fall of the Cthulhu Mythos*, Joshi offers a broad outline that he utilizes to analyze Mythos tales, both those written by Lovecraft and by others. This outline is comprised of five main aspects: "*A fictional New England topography* . . . an entire array of imaginary New England cities" (*Rise* 16; emphasis in original) within which many of his tales of madness and horror take place; "*A . . . library of imaginary 'forbidden' books* . . . chief among them the *Necronomicon*" (17; emphasis in original); "*A diverse array of extraterrestrial 'gods' or entities*" (17; emphasis in original); "*A sense of cosmicism*" (17; emphasis in original), an interesting idea that Lovecraft himself theorizes, one that he "enunciated . . . as the defining and unifying element in his work" (17), and which we will seek to define and understand more fully as we look to *Gravity Falls*; and finally, though this aspect is added as something of an afterthought by Joshi, a "scholarly narrator or protagonist" (18), often a professor or autodidact who stumbles across the mysteries and perils of the Mythos. None of these ideas in and of itself is a guarantor of the inclusion by scholars or fans of a work in the Lovecraft Mythos, and it is precisely because of their use as a "shorthand" to horrific literary capital that many works including these aspects are set aside from scholarly interrogation. It is only when these aspects are utilized in novel ways, when a writer demonstrates a knowledge of them not only as narrative devices but also as a conceptual framework for communicating particular "aesthetic and philosophical" (13) ideas, that, in Joshi's formulation, a tale takes its place among "the best 'imitations' of Lovecraft . . . [those that] expand upon or transcend his own conceptions" (13–14). Disney's *Gravity Falls* is precisely one of these transcendent expansions, and in the course of this paper I will argue that it not only utilizes Joshi's aspects in novel ways and successfully transfers the genre of the Lovecraftian tale into the realm of popular children's literature, but also that it offers enough expansion upon the nebulous quality of the Lovecraftian that it deserves inclusion in the amorphous body of works that make up the Lovecraft Mythos.

The consideration of *Gravity Falls* will begin with a basic summary of the series that will also serve to demonstrate how the cartoon satisfies each of Joshi's five Lovecraftian aspects. During this summary, we will consider closely two specific appearances by Lovecraftian creatures, one explicit and one implicit, all of which will serve to demonstrate the criteria by which we might include *Gravity Falls* in a list of tales of the Lovecraft Mythos. Finally, we will consider the ramifications of the inclusion of such characters in a piece of children's fiction, and more broadly what it might mean that Disney, a company known for its saccharine reinterpretations of myths and fairy tales, now actively promotes and produces a cartoon for children that is, fundamentally, Lovecraftian.

Gravity Falls—currently, as of February 2016, finishing up its second and final season—tells the story of twin twelve-year-old siblings Dipper and Mabel Pines, sent at the beginning of their summer holidays to the backwoods Oregon town of Gravity Falls. There they reside with their great-uncle Stan, who runs a tourist trap called "The Mystery Shack," a location loosely based on creator Alex Hirsch's own memories of childhood summer holidays (Adams). The town of Gravity Falls is populated by quirky and strange characters, and seems to attract and to be surrounded by strange creatures and phenomena. Though categorically not set in New England, the isolated location, the strange and perhaps decadent inhabitants, and the bizarre occurrences all line up nicely with the first of Joshi's aspects, the fictional New England geography. Simply put, Hirsch and his team take the trope of the fictional Eastern towns implicated in ancient mysteries and transport them to the Western United States. The episode "Roadside Attraction" features a road trip, tourist trap to tourist trap, around this colorfully sinister landscape. Such tactics have been deployed by other writers in the Lovecraftian stable, most notably Ramsey Campbell, who transported the Lovecraftian setting to Great Britain, and the "equally-haunted Severn Valley towns of Severnford, Brichester, Camside, Clotton, and Goatswood" (Aniolowski viii). Thus, in a similar manner as Campbell, Hirsch's setting of Gravity Falls both coincides and transcends the geographical setting aspect of Joshi's, and Lovecraft's, formulations. Further, where the more properly horrific fictions might depict the towns as decrepit and the inhabitants as inbred and cruel, *Gravity Falls* manages to communicate the same senses of isolation and strangeness, but in a way that is more in keeping with a cartoon designed for younger teens. The decadence of location is transformed into quirkiness, albeit a quirkiness erring on the side of the sinister.

Early in the first episode of the series, Dipper discovers a journal concealed in the forest surrounding The Mystery Shack. Emblazoned upon the cover is a six-fingered hand, and upon that the number 3 (Hirsch, "Tourist"). The journal becomes Dipper's entry into the strangeness that pervades Gravity Falls, and the identity of its author is one of the central mysteries of the first, and part of the second, seasons. Much like Lovecraft's *Necronomicon* and its ilk, the journal contains esoteric knowledge about the creatures and phenomena that surround the town of Gravity Falls. It is revealed over the course of the series that, unsurprisingly, the journal is one of three books possessed by various characters in the town. As well as the encyclopedic entries, what few glimpses we receive of the interiors of the journals also chronicle the author's realization of the evil that lurks in the woods, and of his dealings with a mysterious being named Bill Cipher. We will speak of him more fully later in the paper. More so, then, than the setting of the series, these journals, analogous to the "rare and obscure books [that hold] cosmic secrets too dangerous . . . for profane eyes" (Joshi, *Rise* 17), offer a link to the aspects of the Lovecraftian fiction. Not only do they initiate Dipper and Mabel into the strange world of Gravity Falls, but they also become loci of power for various individuals in the town. In this way, the narrative of *Gravity Falls* does indeed transcend the Lovecraftian deployment of such texts, in that the scramble for possession of the books and the power they represent, and the search for the mysterious author of the journals, becomes an ongoing story throughout the series. This change is partially due to the specificity of the information in the books to the town and its environs, an aspect mostly absent in the Lovecraftian pseudo-texts, but also to the serialized nature and long-form story of the show. Lovecraftian protagonists very rarely last more than one short story.

Following from the information in the books, the array of "gods and entities" that Joshi points to are the primary narrative force of the show from a serialized standpoint. By this I mean that while there is an overarching plot being developed through the series as a whole, the majority of individual episodes revolve around the discovery of some strange being or phenomenon in the town's environs that Dipper, Mabel, and their companions have to confront. Joshi notes that, in the earliest of Lovecraft's stories and those of his colleagues and collaborators, these creatures and phenomena are not explicitly written about, but instead used as "background-material" (21) for stories about how this subtextual reality impacts the humans who discover it. The aforementioned Bill Cipher, and the three journals, function in just such a way in *Gravity Falls*. Bill, whose form (an important point that we will address further on) is similar to that of the pyramidal All-Seeing Eye, is a "dream demon" who, according to the journals, was initially manifested as a benevolent helper, but eventually reveals himself to be a manipulative beast from a nightmare realm. The character proper, however, only appears in a single episode of the first season, though his image is hidden in backgrounds pervasively throughout the season's twenty episodes. Bill, as one of the aforementioned "gods and entities," comprises a literal background to the narrative. The "Cipher Wheel," a hieroglyphic representation of Bill, also appears for the briefest of moments at the end of each of the credits sequences. Bill's final words to Dipper and Mabel in "Dreamscaperers," his first proper appearance and the 19th episode of the season, are, "I'll be watching you" (McKeon, Chapman, and Hirsch)—something that, through his inclusion in background scenes, he appears to have been doing since the very beginning of the series.

In the second season, Bill's role as antagonist comes to the fore, and in the 18th episode, "Weirdmaggedon Part 1," he escapes the prison dimension within which he is confined, bringing along a cadre of weird and anarchic creatures to ravage the world. None of these creatures is a fully Lovecraftian creation, though Xanthar is initially introduced as "the being whose name must never be said" (Weinstein, Hirsch, and Rowe), similar to the deity Hastur in the Lovecraftian mythos.[1] Shortly I will offer evidence that Bill himself is actually a Lovecraftian deity in disguise, but a more concrete link to these creatures comes in the form of Lovecraft's

---

1. It should be noted that HPL himself never explicitly cited Hastur as an entity in his tales, but borrowed the name from the works of Bierce and Robert W. Chambers. It is August Derleth who, in "The Return of Hastur," promoted the name to full-fledged entity.

most famous creation: Cthulhu.[2] As alluded to above, for a brief moment in episode 15 of the second season, as Bill torments Ford Pines and then disappears, an illustration of the Great Old One flashes on the screen (see Figure 1). A few episodes later, as Bill's "Weirdmaggedon" unfolds, we see Cthulhu rampaging through the town, though always and only in the background, a moving, horrific set-piece. Where Lovecraft, through the testimony of Inspector Legrasse, tells us that one day the Great Old Ones would return, "when the stars were right" (Lovecraft, "The Call of Cthulhu" CF 2.39]), *Gravity Falls* offers a view of how that return might look from the single-eyed perspective of Bill Cipher.

Though only appearing as a character in a single episode of the first season, Bill Cipher is the looming presence, the harbinger of doom, which defines the series. This "'all-seeing eye' . . . knows much about magic and technology. He sometimes appears to a chosen person, and gives him a useful incantation or piece of machinery. Unfailingly, these gifts lead only to the madness and destruction of their wielders" (Harms 151). Though the previous statement could certainly have been made about Bill, it is actually taken from the "Nyarlathotep" entry in the *Encyclopedia Cthulhiana*. Where the appearance of Cthulhu in background scenes provides one link to the Joshian use of Lovecraftian deities, Bill's triangular presence in virtually every episode, along with his propensity for making deals with unsuspecting humans, allows us to peer behind the eye and to see the Crawling Chaos. The entry in the *Encyclopedia* (partially reproduced in the Appendix) applies equally to Bill and Nyarlathotep, and if we can accept that the narrative construction of the series is adapting Lovecraftian themes and tropes to a children's cartoon, then it is hardly a vast leap of logic to make to conflate Bill and Lovecraft's messenger god. One need only consider Bill's name, the idea of a cipher, and his pyramidal (and by proxy Egyptian) depiction, in conjunction with the supposition of Nyarlathotep as "personification of the telepathic powers of the

2. In a video preceding the broadcast of the series finale "Weirdmaggedon Part 3," creator Alex Hirsch acknowledges that Cthulhu appears in the background of a few scenes, but notes that for some reason they could not "call him Cthulhu, so in the script he was called 'Cthreelu'" (Mystery of Gravity Falls). It is unclear why the use of Cthulhu's traditional name was not allowed.

Figure 1. The Cipher Wheel and Cthulhu, screen capture from Alex Hirsch, "The Last Mabelcorn," *Gravity Falls* (2015).

Great Old Ones" (Harms 151) to forge even a solely functional link to the terror that "came out of Egypt" (Lovecraft, "Nyarlatho-tep" [*CF* 1.203]). Indeed, the aforementioned entry lists a number of Nyarlathotep's forms and aliases, and I argue that Bill Cipher's top hat and triangle form (a top hat that, when shot through, re-forms itself out of flesh and tentacle) is yet another of these forms.

His treatment of humans and his appearance aside, Bill evinces other behaviors that link him explicitly with the messenger of the Outer Gods. The latter is said to "act as an intermediary between the Great Old Ones and their worshippers" (Harms 151); Bill, too, demonstrates this intermediary role with regard to the creatures he is attempting to free from the "nightmare dimension." During his dream visit to Ford Pines in episode 15, "The Last Mabelcorn," Bill tells Ford he has "been making deals, chatting with old friends, preparing for the big day" (Hirsch, "Mabelcorn")—the day, we must assume, when the stars are right. Later, as Ford reveals his history of contact with Bill to Dipper, we are shown moments where Bill gifts Ford with technology and scientific knowledge, all in the service of opening a portal to the nightmare dimension. And while Dipper and Ford sit at a table, sharing a soda while Ford tells his story, just behind his head is a wall-hanging depict-ing a stylized Egyptian Pharaoh ("Mabelcorn"). In this same epi-sode, if we needed further evidence of the links to Lovecraft, Dipper and Mabel discover in their uncle's closet of games a box labeled "Necronomiconopoly." The previous Bill-centered episode, "Sock Opera," involves the entity taking Dipper as his puppet, os-tensibly in exchange for information. In the secondary storyline, Mabel's attempt at an epic puppet show, one of the protagonist puppets is called away "to fight . . . in the War!" (Shion, Hirsch, and Paez), and the enemy against which this character is set is a giant Cthulhoid puppet. These techniques, the inclusion of symbolic clues to Bill's true identity, the narrative paralleling, are certainly the sort of "literary merits" that might convince a more critical viewer of the series that it is more than simply a cartoon for teens.

Once his comrades are freed in "Weirdmaggedon Part 1," Bill in-dulges in a dance party for them, high atop his pyramidal fortress. And though there are strobe lights and pop music playing for Bill's party (see Figure 2), we still witness "the maddening beating of drums,

Figure 2. Bill's Dance Party, screen capture from Weinstein et al., "Weirdmaggedon Part 1," *Gravity Falls* (2015).

and thin, monotonous whine of blasphemous flutes from inconceivable, unlighted chambers . . . the detestable pounding and piping whereunto dance slowly, awkwardly, and absurdly the gigantic, tenebrous" (Lovecraft, "Nyarlathotep" [*CF* 1.205]) guests of Bill's Weirdmaggedon.

I have been addressing Joshi's aspects in the order he presents them in *The Rise and Fall of the Cthulhu Mythos*, but I will postpone my discussion of cosmicism until later in the paper. As Joshi notes, the most successful of Lovecraft's descendants are those who do not simply copy his style or settings, but transcend them, and it is most poignantly in the aspect of cosmicism that *Gravity Falls* transcends. While the existential horror of an uncaring universe is indeed present in the cartoon, the series offers a counter to Lovecraft's cold and unfeeling cosmos that I argue is the fundamental quality that not only makes it a worthy addition to the Mythos, but also a successful and affecting piece of children's literature of which we should take note.

The final element, though one not solely relegated to Lovecraft's Mythos tales (Joshi 18), is the scholarly protagonist. Dipper, described as a nerd by his much more hip sister, fills this role in the series. His discovery and subsequent devotion to the journals of the six-fingered author are representative of the myopic academic fervor that many, if not all, of Lovecraft's protagonists evince. Once the mystery of the journals' author has been solved,[3] another of these scholarly protagonists is added to the mix—one who, in many ways, emblematizes what the result might be of having survived a Lovecraftian tale. The fundamental difference between these protagonists and those of the traditional Lovecraftian story is that neither Dipper nor the author operate in isolation, but within a network of relationships. It is their reactions to these relationships that offer the aforementioned counter to cosmicism, a notion that we will return to shortly.

Having demonstrated that *Gravity Falls* does indeed offer both explicit and implicit fulfillment of Joshi's Lovecraftian criteria, more salient questions can be addressed. The most obvious is whether or not a cartoon ostensibly created for "tweens" can have

---

3. A mystery I will attempt not to spoil here, as I have given away much of the plot already.

a place in the Lovecraftian canon at all. Thacker notes that "the world of 'real' literature and the world of children's literature have been kept largely separate" (7), and such is certainly the case in the more rarefied environment of the Lovecraft Mythos scholarship. The nihilism of Lovecraft's philosophy, "Lovecraft as a . . . violently anti-idealist" "tacit philosopher" (Harman 3), seems to contradict the ostensibly positive "educational values" (Thacker 2) of children's literature, offering instead only despair on a cosmic level. But a growing body of scholarship around children's literature now asserts that "childhood itself is uncanny" (Buckley 58), to utilize Freud's term, which better aligns children's literature with the tenets of Lovecraftian fictions. More nuanced analyses of children's books sees some works as responses "to a 'demand' made by children themselves: [these works feed] their 'appetite' for images evoking childhood as it is actually experienced" (Buckley 70). Though this specific assessment is directed toward Neil Gaiman's *Coraline*, such a pronouncement offers a perspective by which we can actually conceive of a Lovecraftian children's story.

In discussing the German-language equivalent of "uncanny," Freud notes that "*unheimlich* is . . . the opposite of '*heimlich*' [homely], '*heimisch*' ['native']—the opposite of what is familiar; . . . that what is 'uncanny' is frightening precisely because it is *not* known and familiar" (826; emphasis in original). *Gravity Falls* presents the uncanniness of childhood through both setting and experience. Though Stan Pines is family to Dipper and Mabel, he is certainly not "familiar" family, and thus demonstrates the conundrum often placed upon children of having to trust an adult simply because of that person's adulthood. As noted above, the town proper of Gravity Falls is a more colorful and welcoming Dunwich or Innsmouth, but still retains those aspects of an isolated and unfamiliar place necessary for making a town "unhomely." Where Lovecraft offers a "thin sprinkling of repellent-looking youngish people," or "crumbling houses [that] harboured small shops with dingy signs" ("The Shadow over Innsmouth" [*CF* 3.176]), *Gravity Falls* provides such characters as Lazy Susan, a waitress with a malfunctioning eyelid, or Toby Determined, an ersatz reporter and member of the Blind Eye Society whose appearance recalls the "narrow head, bulging, watery blue eyes . . . [and] long, thick lip" (*CF* 3.170) of the "Innsmouth look." (See Figure 3.)

Fig. 3. Toby Determined, from Wallington and Hirsch, "Head Hunters"
Gravity Falls (2012).

The Mystery Shack itself is a cobbled-together edifice, the "S" in shack often falling to the ground, offering the chorus-like commentary on Stan Pines as a "Mystery Hack." While certainly made more colorful for the consumption of younger people, the town is indeed uncanny. What we must recall about this uncanniness is that it is not solely a literal deployment of strangeness to build atmosphere, but also a metaphoric representation of the experience of inexperienced and powerless young people in an adult world that, oftentimes, makes little or no sense to them. Were we to dip our analytical toes into the psychological realm pioneered by Freud, the series as a whole might well be considered a metaphor for the unfamiliar experience of children entering the early stages of adulthood; Dipper and Mabel celebrate their thirteenth birthday in the town (Chapman et al.) and worry over the changes this will wreak in their lives. This metaphoric reading of the series aligns with the pedagogical aspect associated with children's literature, and offers an ingress for discussion, though one outside of the purview of this paper, of the series more broadly in terms of children's literature.

Gravity Falls sits at a strange meeting of literary traditions. Its uncanniness positions it as a children's tale in the tradition of Alice's Adventures in Wonderland and of that work's spiritual successor, Coraline. Conversely, its fulfillment of the criteria of a

Lovecraftian tale squarely places it into that tradition. It is precisely at this convergence that the series offers something that is new for both traditions, however, a convergence that speaks to the criterion mentioned earlier but set aside: cosmicism. As "the defining and unifying element in his work," cosmicism, in Lovecraft's deployment of the idea, conveys the "terror at the thought of human insignificance in a boundless cosmos" (Joshi, *Rise* 17–18). The Old Gentleman himself, in discussing his literary ancestor Edgar Allan Poe, calls this idea "[adversity or indifference] to the tastes and traditional outward sentiments of mankind, and to the health, sanity, and normal expansive welfare of the species" (Lovecraft, *Supernatural* 55). Despite its uncanny propensities, such cosmicism is not common fodder for writings aimed at children, yet *Gravity Falls* demonstrates this indifference at numerous points and with numerous devices. During occasional hiatuses in the broadcast of the show, small vignettes were presented under the title "Dipper's Guide to the Paranormal." Rather than presenting a mystery or situation that is, if only partially, solved by the end of the episode, these short pieces very often end with unresolved circumstances and the fleeing of the main characters—far more like a traditional Lovecraft story, really. What these short stories demonstrate about the fictional universe within which the series takes place is that there are mysteries beyond the bounds of human comprehension, even that of the mysterious and knowledgeable author of the journals. These mysteries operate on a level outside of the human, and thus have little or no interest in the comings and goings of the Pines twins.

But it is precisely those twins who, in the series proper, offer the combined pedagogical moment of traditional children's literature and a counter to Lovecraft's nihilistic cosmicism. Dipper and Mabel demonstrate that in the face of an uncaring and indifferent universe, it is not our attempts to understand the mysteries of the universe that give us meaning and hope, but the relationships we cultivate with those around us, be they family or friends.

Very late in the series, Dipper is offered an apprenticeship under his great-uncle Ford, the opportunity to study the very mysteries that have defined his summer vacation in rural Oregon. To do so means to leave Mabel. The decision to break with family, even amicably, to leave one's home in favor of a literal unknown, is among the most uncanny experiences of life. With very few exceptions, children eventually have to leave both their parents and their homes, even if only through the inevitable separation of death. Much like the seminal television series *Buffy the Vampire Slayer*, *Gravity Falls* stands as a metaphor "to represent the fears present among today's teens and young adults growing up in a post-industrial world" (Little 283), evincing the uncanniness of youth that Freud's psycho-literary analysis argues. Dipper and Mabel find themselves in a strange place, surrounded by strange people, in an environment the fabric of which is . . . strange. All they have to hold on to, all that is not *unheimlich*, is each other.

But siblings part, eventually, inevitably. Whereas, however, the traditional Lovecraftian protagonist is sent spiraling into the void at the end of most traditional Mythos stories, *Gravity Falls* shows us that it is the tether to one another in the face of that void that provides meaning in life and that erects structure against the demolishing cosmicism of an uncaring universe. And while Dipper emblematizes the scholarly protagonist in the series, it is Mabel who emblematizes this tether. In fact, at the close of the first episode of the series, Mabel is rewarded by Great-Uncle Stan with an item from the Mystery Shack gift shop, a thank you for a job well done (Hirsch, "Tourist"). The item she selects, in her inimitable style, is a grappling hook, an item that, in the final episode of the first season, becomes a literal tether, saving both herself and her brother from plunging to their doom at the hands of the evil Gideon Gleeful (Chapman, Hirsch, and Rianda). Dipper's investigations lead the twins farther and farther from safety, further into the uncanny realms that surround the town. Mabel, with her boy-craziness, her seemingly endless supply of quirky sweaters, with her love of eighties pop culture, keeps the two from falling into the void that yawns before them, born of Lovecraft's worldview and fiction. While it may in fact be true that "the oldest and strongest emotion of mankind is fear, and the oldest and strongest kind of fear is fear of the unknown" (Lovecraft, *Supernatural* 25), facing such fears alone is what opens one to the despair of the cosmic; when fears are faced together, be they Nyarlathotepian tricksters or the sad inevitabilities of life, we create meaning in the face of a cold and indifferent universe.

By way of concluding, we must consider some of the ramifications of the processes in which *Gravity Falls* engages. The series explicitly combats the separation of children's literature from "real" literature, and even goes so far as to tell a Lovecraftian story through the lens of a children's cartoon. Though such things have happened before, notably *The Real Ghostbusters* episode "The Collect Call of Cthulhu," by and large they have been satires or pastiches, rather than, as is the case with *Gravity Falls*, faithful reworkings of the formulae laid down in the early twentieth century by Lovecraft. Perhaps the example of this generic bridge between literatures that are so often disparate can stand as an example of how "texts written . . . for a young audience contribute significantly to an understanding of literary movements" (Thacker 2). But this raises another question: what does *Gravity Falls* "significantly contribute" to our understanding of Lovecraftian fiction? First, it concretely demonstrates the possibility, and plausibility, of adapting the Lovecraftian into the realm of children's literature. As noted above, such things have happened before. Kenneth Hite's *The Antarctic Express* and Brown and Podesta's *Howard Lovecraft and the Frozen Kingdom* both skew toward younger readers. But these two examples, and most others of their ilk, are not quite the same as *Gravity Falls*. It would be difficult for us to make the case of fitting *The Frozen Kingdom* into the Lovecraft Mythos as its main character is H. P. Lovecraft himself, albeit a younger and more heroically inclined version. *The Antarctic Express* adapts Lovecraft's *At the Mountains of Madness* into a *Polar Express*–styled storybook, but the tale itself is still fundamentally the Lovecraft original. It is parody, though a gentle one, but, as with *The Frozen Kingdom*, not something that will find its way into the Mythos. *Gravity Falls* is far less explicit in its metatextual games. It embraces both the narrative and philosophical worlds of Lovecraftian fiction; but through the tropes available from its roots in children's fiction, it offers novel reinterpretations and commentaries on the fundamental aspects of Mythos-related writings.

A more curious question arises from the method of distribution through which *Gravity Falls* reaches its audience: Disney. According to their "Our Stories and Characters" corporate policy,

Disney characters "speak to the heart; [their] characters appeal to children across gender, ability, and experience because they're defined by kindness, loyalty, humor, courage, wit and other traits that make a good friend" (Walt Disney Company). It hardly needs be noted that this sounds like the antithesis of Lovecraftian fiction, yet the two have come together under this altruistic aegis. Disney's more popular cartoons, especially their film enterprises, are often saccharine reinterpretations of old fairy tales, cleaned and polished for the consumption of a mass audience. These stories all but remove the uncanniness of the original tales, replacing the unfamiliar with cartoon snowmen (an uncanny creature if ever there was one) and beautiful, ubiquitously vocally adept heroes and heroines. Said cleansing doesn't quite take in the case of *Gravity Falls*. There is something odd and disturbing about the place and the people who inhabit it. Despite its distribution by the "home [of] some of the world's most beloved characters and cherished stories" (Walt Disney Company), *Gravity Falls* has not had its other roots, the twisted and tentacular ones that reach to the deepest of ocean abysses and to the swirling, chaotic center of time, trimmed. Beneath the color is decay; beneath the peppy music of the theme song, the wailing of uncanny flutes. Yet, setting such roots aside but not forgetting their presence, Dipper and Mabel do indeed demonstrate the aforementioned Disney character traits, clasping hands and hearts, and deploying such traits successfully as an answer to the cosmic conundrums of "the revolting graveyard of the universe" (Lovecraft, "Nyarlathotep" [*CF* 1.205]). And, as stated earlier in the paper, this is the advance, the novelty, we must celebrate in this innovative show. The conflation of Disney and the Lovecraftian, of the juvenile and the adult, of children's literature and "real" literature, shows us how one can react, how one can make meaning, in the face of the uncanniness of life.

APPENDIX

From Daniel Harms's *Encyclopedia Cthulhiana* (150–51):

NYARLATHOTEP (also THE CRAWLING CHAOS or MIGHTY MESSENGER). The mighty soul and messenger of the Outer Gods. He is said to dwell in a cavern at the center of the world, accompanied by two mindless flutists, yet he often sends messages and performs services for the Other Gods throughout space and time. Nyarlathotep answers to the every whim of his masters, though he is contemptuous of them as well.

The Crawling Chaos is also said to act as an intermediary between the Great Old Ones and their worshipers, as well as carrying tidings between the Great Old Ones themselves; however, only a few such cases have been reported. In fact, Nyarlathotep may be a personification of the telepathic powers of the Great Old Ones. However, he seems to have a distinct personality which the Old Ones' inhuman minds might find difficult to duplicate.

Nyarlathotep has been worshiped under several guises in all parts of the world, but he is usually connected with Egypt. He was one of the greatest gods in the land of the Nile, where he was the ruler of the underworld, the master of the night, and the patron of sorcerers. After many years, however, the people of Egypt grew frightened of the dark god and struck out all references to him, reassigning his attributes to other gods, such as Set and Thoth. Though the enemies of the cult tried to suppress the memory of Nyarlathotep, he was still remembered, and there were resurgences of his worship throughout Egyptian history, especially during the time of Nephren-Ka, Nophru-Ka, and Nitocris.

Nyarlathotep is called the "all-seeing eye" in Prinn's *De Vermis Mysteriis*, and knows much about magic and technology. He sometimes appears to a chosen person, and gives him a useful incantation or piece of machinery. Unfailingly, these gifts lead only to the madness and destruction of their wielders. Nyarlathotep seems to gain great pleasure from watching these victims destroy themselves.

The Outer God is credited with eventually bringing destruction to humanity and Earth. Several prophesies state that Nyarlathotep will come in the last days, dressed in red and with wild beasts following him, licking his hands. He will journey among the cities of the world, giving demonstrations of science and magic. Then "quaking auroras will roll down on the citadels of man", and humanity will be destroyed as he turns the entire universe into a graveyard. Nyarlathotep has aided in the construction of the first nuclear weapons, so this prophecy may already be coming true.

Nyarlathotep's true form is a noxious expanse of yellowish slime, but to carry out the bidding of the Other Gods, he can take anyone of his thousand forms.

Works Cited

Adams, Erik. "Comedy Showrunners Week: Alex Hirsch on the Real in the Unreal of *Gravity Falls*." *A.V. Club*. The Onion. 28 September 2012. Web. Accessed 11 Nov. 2015. http://www.avclub.com/article/comedy-showrunners-week-alex-hirsch-on-the-real-in-85801.

Aniolowski, Scott. "Introduction." In *Made in Goatswood: New Tales of Horror in the Severn Valley*, ed. Scott David Aniolowski. Oakland, CA: Chaosium, 1995. vii–ix.

Buckley, Chloé. "Psychoanalysis, 'Gothic' Children's Literature, and the Canonization of *Coraline*." *Children's Literature Association Quarterly* 40, No. 1 (2015): 58–79. *Project Muse*. Web. 2 October 2015.

Chapman, Matt, et al. "Dipper and Mabel vs. the Future." *Gravity Falls*. Disney XD. 12 October 2015. Television.

Chapman, Matt; Hirsch, Alex; and Rianda, Michael. "Gideon Rises." *Gravity Falls*. Disney Channel. 2, August 2013. Television.

Freud, Sigmund. "*From* The 'Uncanny.'" In *The Norton Anthology of Theory and Criticism*, ed. Vincent Leitch et al. New York: W.W. Norton & Co., 2010. 824–41.

Harman, Graham. *Weird Realism: Lovecraft and Philosophy*. Winchester, UK: Zero Books, 2012.

Harms, Daniel. *Encyclopedia Cthulhiana*. Oakland, CA: Chaosium, 1994.

Hirsch, Alex. "The Last Mabelcorn." *Gravity Falls*. Disney XD. 7 September 2015. Television.

———. "Tourist Trapped." *Gravity Falls*. Disney Channel. 15 June 2012. Television.

Joshi, S. T. *I Am Providence: The Life and Times of H. P. Lovecraft.* New York: Hippocampus Press, 2010.

———. "Introduction." In *Dissecting Cthulhu*, ed. S. T. Joshi. Lakeland, FL: Miskatonic River Press, 2011. 5–8.

———. *The Rise and Fall of the Cthulhu Mythos.* Poplar Bluff, MO: Mythos Books, 2008.

Little, Tracy. "High School Is Hell: Metaphor Made Literal in *Buffy the Vampire Slayer.*" In *Buffy the Vampire Slayer and Philosophy*, ed. James B. South. Chicago: Open Court Publishing, 2003. 282–93.

Lovecraft, H. P. *The Annotated Supernatural Horror in Literature.* Ed. S. T. Joshi. 2nd ed. New York: Hippocampus Press, 2012.

McKeon, Tim; Chapman, Matt; and Hirsch, Alex. "Dreamscapers." *Gravity Falls.* Disney Channel. 12 July 2013. Television.

Mystery of Gravity Falls, The. "Gravity Falls—5 Unusual Facts about Weirdmaggedon." Online video clip. *YouTube.* YouTube, 14 February 2016. Web. Accessed 15 Feb. 2016. https://www.youtube.com/watch?v=amloQJwhxVY.

Takeuchi, Shion; Hirsch, Alex; and Paez, Zach. "Sock Opera." *Gravity Falls.* Disney XD. 8 September 2014. Television.

Thacker, Deborah, and Jean Webb. *Introducing Children's Literature: From Romanticism to Postmodernism.* New York: Routledge, 2002. *ProQuest ebrary.* Web. Accessed 2 October 2015.

Weinstein, Josh; Hirsch, Alex; and Rowe, Jeff. "Weirdmaggedon Part 1." *Gravity Falls.* Disney XD. 26 Oct. 2015. Television.

Wallington, Aury, and Alex Hirsch. "Head Hunters." *Gravity Falls.* Disney Channel. 30 June 2012. Television.

Walt Disney Company, The. "Our Stories and Characters." *The Walt Disney Company.* The Walt Disney Company. N.d. PDF file. https://ditm-twdc-us.storage.googleapis.com/Our-Stories-and-Characters.pdf

Lovecraft Quoted in Support of David V. Bush

Kenneth W. Faig, Jr.

Popular psychology and success lecturer David V. Bush (1882–1959) was a relentless promoter of his own work. Following his two successful lecture series in Carnegie Hall in New York City in May–June 1924 and September 1924,[1] Bush published a brochure entitled *New York Endorsements*.[2] The brochure, 11 inches tall by 7 1/16 inches wide, consisted of a single sheet folded to six unnumbered pages. At the foot of the first page, it is identified as:

> Demonstration Phamphlet [*sic*] No. 23 / Being only one in an Unlimited Series of Pamphlets of / Testamonials [*sic*] about Demonstrations Accruing from / David V. Bush's *Campaigns, Books* and *Classes*[3]

---

1. Bush's letter to Miss Mary O'Connor dated October 14, 1957 (State Historical Society of Missouri, Collection So782, folder 6) makes clear that he had two two-week engagements at Carnegie Hall in 1924—one commencing on Monday, May 26, 1924 (Faig 164), and one in September 1924. Bush's letter to Miss O'Connor is published in full as Appendix 1 of this article. The author is indebted to Rob Hudson of Carnegie Hall Archives for the exact dates of Bush's lectures: Monday, May 26, 1924 through Wednesday, June 11, 1924 (excepting Tuesday May 27, Friday May 30, Sunday June 1, and Friday June 6), for a total of 13 lectures; and Tuesday, September 2, 1924 through Tuesday, September 16, 1924 (excepting Monday September 8 and Saturday September 13), for a total of 13 lectures.

2. The author purchased the surviving papers of David V. Bush from Brian W. Gaines in 2015. He found copies of *New York Endorsements* among these papers.

3. Bush claimed on the first page of his brochure: "Poem Written by David V. Bush Saves Life of Condemned Man." Governor Alfred E. Smith of New York commuted the death sentence of convicted murderer and former railroad laborer Michael Jernakowski, age thirty, to life imprisonment on September 17, 1924, a

At the bottom of the final page, the publisher is identified as "David V. Bush, *Publisher* / 225 North Michigan Blvd., Chicago, Illinois." The brochure is undated, but presumably dates to September 18, 1924 or later.

The right side of page [2], all of page [3], and the left side of page [4] are occupied by a large reproduction of the photograph of one of Bush's Carnegie Hall lectures with the overlaid caption "David V. Bush's Psychological Campaign, / Carnegie Hall, New York City." The photographer is identified as Drucker & Baltes Co. / N.Y. / 24-[illegible]69" in the lower right-hand corner of the photograph. Over the photograph is printed the caption: "David V. Bush has the distinction of having broken all records of attendance in Carnegie Hall, New York City, during its history of thirty-one years."[4]

Bush also reprinted this photograph in the August–September 1924 issue of his periodical *Mind Power Plus* (pp. 36–37). In 1954 he used the photograph as part of the wraparound dust jacket for his final published book, *If You Want to Be Rich.*

---

day before his scheduled execution. Jernakowski had shot Mrs. Kathleen Hanover to death in Buffalo, NY, during a confrontation with her husband during a strike. According to the report in the *New York Telegram and Evening Mail* for September 18, 1924, Jernakowski could neither read nor write when he was convicted of the murder. His case was taken up by attorney Mrs. Cecile Schuerer of New York City, who encouraged him to improve himself. Bush's poem "Think Right" (see Appendix 2) was apparently submitted to Governor Smith as an example of Jernakowski's work (see Appendix 1). The *Harrisburg* [PA] *Evening News* for September 18, 1924, also reported on the commutation of Jernakowski's sentence. According to the *Evening News*, Jernakowski's brother John was allowed to travel 350 miles from Clinton Penitentiary in Dannemora, NY (where he was serving a twenty-year sentence for robbery), to pay a final visit to his brother Michael. Bush later reprinted *New York Endorsements* on better paper, replacing "Poem Written by David V. Bush Saves Life of Condemned Man" with the testimonial "Wisdom, New Life, Happiness and Everlasting Peace of Mind" on the first page. The misspellings of "pamphlet" and "testimonials" on the first page were also corrected in this later printing. The author does not know whether Michael Jernakowski ended his life in prison or was eventually paroled.

4. The first performance in the Main Hall occurred on May 5, 1891, although there were performances in the Recital Hall as early as March 12, 1891. See www.carnegiehall.org/History.

The left-hand side of page [2] of the brochure *New York En-dorsements* reprints an article from *Financial and Commercial World*⁵ for October 1924 that will be of interest to students of Lovecraft and his work:⁶

DAVID V. BUSH—ACTOR[,] LECTURER
AND HUMAN BEING

{(Reprinted from Financial and
Commercial World October 1924.)}

This brief article might be called a record of an impression—an impression left upon the mind of the present writer[,] first by what he was told about a certain man[,] then by seeing and hearing the man "in action." My friend and fellow[-]writer[,] Mr. Howard P. Lovecraft[,] had been telling me about the most astonishing success as a lecturer on applied psychology of Dr. David V. Bush who[,] at this writing[,] is conducting another course of lectures at Carnegie Hall.

"How does he put it across?" I asked. "What is his method—as the vaudeville people put it—of 'selling his act'?"

"The answer is simple," Lovecraft answered; "he is sincerity and enthusiasm personified and he is a regular volcano of nervous and mental energy. You may not agree with all his expressed opinions[,] but you can't ignore them and you can't crack a smile when he is[,] himself, in a serious mood, for he 'gets' you from the drop

5. The title is given as *Financial & Commercial World* in the masthead of the October 1924 number. The New York Public Library owns a file of this periodical, which was published semimonthly from March to May 1924 and then monthly from July 1924 until cessation of publication in April 1925 (vol. 2, no. 4). The October 1924 number (vol. 1, no. 10) was filed for copyright on September 20, 1924 (registration number 33967). The publisher was Financial and Commercial World, Inc., with offices at 294 Broadway in New York City and 239 Washington Street in Jersey City, NJ.
6. Bush or another editor made minor changes in the article for reprinting in the brochure *New York Endorsements*. Most of the editing consisted of removal of commas and other punctuation. In the following text, material appearing in *Financial and Commercial World* but removed in *New York Endorsements* is shown in square brackets. Material unique to the reprinting in *Financial and Commercial World* is shown in curly brackets.

of the hat and you listen to him as you would read the printed work of any philosopher or thinker worthy of the name.["]

Well, I had heard enough about the man to make me want to see him "doing his stuff." I make no apology for the levity nor for the slang; for I have found that the truly big men in modern business and in the professions are far from being heavy[,] over-serious people[,] while slang[,] used in moderation[,] is one of the most useful adjuncts to modern expression. I had heard[,] both from Mr. Lovecraft and from Mr. James F. Morton, Jr., that Dr. Bush was a writer and poet as well as a lecturer[,] and had been a Shakespearean and dramatic actor as well as, later, a minister of the Gospel. I had heard a great many lecturers—and alleged lecturers—on applied psychology, the science of success, and kindred subjects; and I took a seat in Carnegie Hall in a decidedly "show me" frame of mind.

The first half hour of listening was a revelation. Here was a man who, while fairly oozing enthusiasm and an intense belief in the soundness of his doctrines, nevertheless spoke in the absolutely tolerant mood of one who might have said: "You don't have to believe this[,] you know. You don't have to share with me the solid mental comfort of knowing that you are the captain of your own soul[,] and a slave to no man. You can take it or leave it—but it will pay you, and pay you big, to take it, to think it over, {and} [to] shape your future actions along lines of courage and optimism, faith in your fellow man, and a determination to win out in the game of life, despite all the little black devils of doubt and fear, discouragement and pessimism."

Yes, sir! I got decided kick out of Dr. Bush's talk; like Oliver Twist, I asked for more. In the first place, I found to my delight that Dr. Bush is one man who believes that the first duty of a lecturer is to make himself heard. All the platitudes and second-hand philosophizing of the average lecturer on topics of this nature was left out. "Bunk" was entirely absent. The man has a vision, a deep conviction, a genuine message. He is a seer with the practical levelheadedness of a great business man.

{—Editor, Financial and Commercial World, New York City.}

Although the third paragraph of the article as reprinted in the brochure *New York Endorsements* is not closed with a quotation

mark,[7] the author believes this paragraph constitutes the totality
of Lovecraft's quoted remarks. All the rest of the brochure is de-
voted to individual testimonials to Bush.

The author is grateful to the staff of the New York Public Library for images from *Financial and Commercial World* for October 1924. The masthead shows M. P. Falcon as president and
treasurer of the publisher, Financial and Commercial World, Inc.
The editor is listed as E. A. Austin. Homer G. King is listed as
general trade editor and J. G. Burke as circulation manager. Four
associate editors are listed: A. Lionel Greene, Chas. T. Clarke, H.
M. Herbert, and J. F. Morgan. The author does not know which
member of the editorial staff knew Lovecraft and Morton and was
responsible for the unsigned article "David V. Bush—Actor, Lecturer and Human Being." The author checked the name index
[Smith and Morton] of Truman J. Spencer's *The History of Amateur Journalism* (New York: The Fossils, 1957) for the names of
the members of the editorial staff of *Financial and Commercial
World*, but did not find any matches. Of course, both Lovecraft
and Morton had New York City connections outside the amateur
journalism hobby.[8]

Is Lovecraft quoted verbatim (e.g., from a letter) or is the author of "David V. Bush—Actor, Lecturer and Human Being" only
quoting him from memory? We do know from other sources that
Lovecraft had a favorable opinion of Bush's sincerity. For example,
he wrote of Bush to Anne Tillery Renshaw on June 14, 1922 (*ATR*
370): "His keynote is hearty good fellowship & I almost think he is
rather sincere about it."

Bush's first lecture series at Carnegie Hall began in the Main
Hall at 7:30 P.M. on Monday, May 26, 1924.[9] According to the re-

---

7. Note that a quotation mark did close the quotation from HPL in the original
printing of the article in *Financial and Commercial World*.

8. The author believes that HPL probably met his friend and later Florida host
Dudley C. Newton (1864–1954), who worked for a wholesale millinery firm,
through his wife Sonia (Haft) Greene Lovecraft, who was a milliner. The author
doubts that there was any connection between Miss Haft's first husband Samuel
Greene (a.k.a. Samuel Seckendorff) and *Financial and Commercial World* Associate Editor A. Lionel Greene.

9. In the dust jacket flap copy for *If You Want To Be Rich*, Bush claimed that the

search of Carnegie Hall archivist Rob Hudson, all twenty-six of Bush's 1924 lectures at Carnegie Hall—consisting of two separate series of thirteen lectures each—were delivered in the Main Hall (today Stern Auditorium) and were free. More typically, Bush presented a week of free lectures,[10] followed by a week-long fee-based course. It is possible that Bush presented a week-long fee-based course in a different venue following each of his two 1924 lecture series in the Main Hall at Carnegie Hall.

Bush returned to Carnegie Hall in September 1924 for another thirteen-night engagement. The author of "David V. Bush—Actor, Lecturer and Human Being" asserts that Bush was delivering a series of lectures at Carnegie Hall "at this writing." Bush's second 1924 lecture series at Carnegie Hall ended on Tuesday, September 16, 1924, just one day before the news broke concerning Governor Smith's pardon of the condemned murderer Michael Jernakowski on September 17, 1924. Bush's poem "Think Right" (see Appendix 2) had apparently been attributed to Jernakowski (see note 3 and Appendix 1). Bush probably published his brochure *New York Endorsements* within a few days or weeks of the end of his second lecture series at Carnegie Hall in September 1924.

Today, the capacity of the Main Hall (Stern Auditorium) at Carnegie Hall totals 2804, consisting of: parquet (main floor), 1021; first tier of boxes, 264; second tier of boxes, 238; dress circle, 444; and balcony, 837. If the capacity of the Main Hall was similar in 1924 and Bush filled the hall on every night of his two thirteen-night lecture series, 72,904 persons (26 × 2,804) might have heard Bush speak—perhaps 50,000 individuals, allowing for individuals who attended multiple lectures.[11] If only one in fifty attendants at

---

doors for his first lecture on May 26, 1924, opened at 7:15 P.M. and that the lecture began at 7:30 P.M. after the fire department cleared the auditorium of persons in the aisles.

10. Bush sometimes collected freewill donations at his free lectures. The author does not know whether he did so at Carnegie Hall. He would customarily have had staff on hand to sell publications and to sign attendees up for his $25 course. His 800-page course book *Practical Psychology and Sex Life* (1922) sold for $6 to course enrollees and for $25 to all others.

11. When Bush presented a series of free lectures, he typically nuanced the subject of each lecture in order to encourage returnees. The individual lectures of a

the free lectures enrolled for a $25 course, Bush would still poten-
tially have garnered $25,000 in tuition payments, from which of
course he would have to pay hall and hotel room rental charges,
advertising, and other associated expenses.

It is not known whether Lovecraft met with Bush again during
his second lecture series at Carnegie Hall in September 1924. At
present, Lovecraft's meeting with Bush on Sunday May 25, 1924,[12]
the eve of Bush's first Carnegie Hall lecture series, is his last
known meeting with his revision client (Faig 164). It would have
been natural for Bush to have met again with Lovecraft when he
returned to Carnegie Hall for a second series of lectures in September 1924, unless the two had by then ended their business relationship. Sometimes silences in Lovecraft's correspondence can
mask controversies or conflicts. The severance of his business relationship with Bush could possibly have marked a conflict which
Lovecraft chose to omit from his regular correspondence.[13]

Lovecraft worked steadily for Bush between 1917 and 1924
(Faig 163). By 1927, Bush had shifted most of his revision and pub-
licity work to the firm of Ruthrauff & Ryan in New York City.[14]

---

series of free lectures, however, typically had common elements—e.g., demonstration healings. Bush—whose early career included stints as a performer and as
an actor—liked to enliven his lectures with dramatic readings. At a Chicago lecture in 1923, he gave a dramatic reading from Shakespeare's *The Merchant of Ven-
ice*. At a Boston lecture in 1922, he gave a dramatic reading from John B. Gough's
Autobiography (1846 et seq.), enhanced with special lighting.

12. On that day, Scott Nearing and Bertrand Russell debated at Carnegie Hall at 3 P.M.

13. Bush was recruited for UAPA by Andrew Francis Lockhart (1890–1964) in
1916, but did not maintain his membership for long. From November 1922 to
January 1923, Lockhart worked for Bush in St. Louis. Bush's correspondence with
Lockhart makes clear that R. M. Laird also helped Bush to edit his monthly magazine *Mind Power Plus* and to prepare his book *Character Analysis* (1923) during
this period. Bush did not publish any additional collections of poetry after 1922.
Thus, HPL's business dealings with him may already have been waning by the
time the two met on May 25, 1924. It is not impossible that Bush, like *Weird* Tales owner J. C. Henneberger, wanted to bring HPL to Chicago to assist him in his
business endeavors, only to be met by refusal. The author does not know whether Bush ever met any of HPL's amateur journalism friends in New York City,
including HPL's wife Sonia (Haft) Greene Lovecraft.

14. John Caples (1900–1990) of the firm revised Bush's work *Character Analysis*
(1923) as *You-ology* (1927).

However, Bush did write Lovecraft from San Francisco as late as mid-September 1935 about a potential revision job (*JFM* 368).[15] It is not known whether Lovecraft undertook the revision work proposed in 1935.

Lovecraft earned significant income from the revision of Bush's poetry, but found his client's work laughably poor. He may have had some hand in revising "Think Right."[16] However, Lovecraft did believe in Bush's sincerity. How he felt about the words attributed to him in *Financial and Commercial World* for October 1924 and their use in the promotional brochure *New York Endorsements* we do not know, and likely will not know, unless a Lovecraft letter referring to this matter can be found.[17] It would have been natural for the editor who wrote the unsigned article in *Financial and Commercial World* for October 1924 to have sent Lovecraft a complimentary copy, especially if he was a friend of Lovecraft and of James F. Morton. However, we do not know that he did so. It is also possible that Lovecraft never saw Bush's brochure *New York Endorsements.*

One final question is whether Bush used Lovecraft's image, as well as his alleged words, in the brochure *New York Endorsements.* Bush faces the photographer at his lectern in the large photograph of Carnegie Hall. Directly behind him, at the doors of the middle aisle of the ground floor (parquet) of the hall, stand a trio: a woman, a narrow-headed man in a coat and tie, and a woman in a large hat. Large hats were a favorite part of milliner Sonia Lovecraft's dress, but certainly not exclusive to her. It would have been a natural courtesy for Bush to have invited Lovecraft and his wife Sonia (Haft) Greene Lovecraft to one of his lectures at Carnegie Hall.[18] Regrettably, even the large reproductions of the panoramic

15. The author is indebted to David E. Schultz for this citation.

16. The poetical elisions like "ne'er" and "vict'ry" suggest HPL's hand (see Appendix 2).

17. R. Alain Everts stated to the author that Maxine Conwell Bush (1907–1991), daughter of David V. Bush, copied the Lovecraft–Bush correspondence for him. These copies—in storage as of this writing—could contain references to the alleged quotation in *Financial and Commercial World* for October 1924.

18. In his dust jacket flap copy for *If You Want To Be Rich*, Bush recalled how the fire department had had to clear the aisles before his first lecture at Carnegie Hall on May 26, 1924 could begin. Thus, it seems likely that only specially invited guests

photograph in *New York Endorsements* and *Mind Power Plus* (August-September 1924) do not contain enough detail to allow an identification.

Acknowledgments

The author gratefully acknowledges the assistance of the staff of the New York Public Library and of Rob Hudson, Carnegie Hall Archivist. However, the author remains responsible for all statements of fact and of opinion in this article.

Appendix 1

David V. Bush to Miss Mary O'Connor, Oct. 14, 1957[19]

Mary O'Connor
Belmont & Conshohocken Avenues
Philadelphia 31, Pa.

Dear Miss O'Connor:

In reply to yours of October 10, I shall be happy to serve with Bert VanDyke as World Poetry Day booster for Wyoming County.[20]

I am enclosing a poem "Charity" which seems to me to be apropos for the purposes of the World Poetry Day Movement. Also I am sending under separate cover "Inspirational Poems" from

---

would have been allowed to stand at the doors of the parquet level of the hall.

19. State Historical Society of Missouri, Collection S0782, folder 6.

20. Bush was then residing in Mehoopany Township of Wyoming County, Pennsylvania, where he had purchased a farm and home in 1923. He later developed part of the farm as a summer camp which he ran from his acquisition of the property until at least 1932. The second page of Bush's letter to Miss O'Connor is written on the reserve side of stationery with the heading: "David V. Bush's Camp/On the Susquehanna River/In the Blue Ridge Range of the Allegheny Mountains/Meshoppen, Pa." Meshoppen—Bush's birthplace—was across the Susquehanna River from Mehoopany Township. He probably used the Meshoppen address because Meshoppen had more connections by rail and by highway. Bush later sold the farm and camp but an 8.81-acre tract including the home remained in the family until the death of his daughter Maxine in 1991. Bush's large frame home looked out over the Susquehanna River. The home, which had become derelict, was demolished by the current property owner in 2013.

which "Charity" and "Think Right" are taken.[21]

I think you would be interested in knowing about this poem "Think Right." I think you will agree it is the most dramatic story about any poem by any author, living or dead. It was in 1924 when I was delivering a course of two weeks lecture engagement at Carnegie Hall, New York City, when the newspapers of New York played up the story of a murderer in the death house at Sing Sing, awaiting his execution, and how he saved his own life.

The press of New York thought so much about the dramatic power of this poem that when I returned to Carnegie Hall three months later for another two weeks' engagement, it was still talking about the murderer whose death sentence had been commuted to life as a result of a little poem "Think Right." The Governor who pardoned the man was Alfred Smith.

Here is one of the captions in a newspaper: Poem Saves Life of Condemned Man–another, Man in Sing Sing is Credited With Writing "Think Right" and has Death Sentence Commuted–and The New York Telegram and Evening Mail of September 18, 1924, gave the following story: I quote:—

"Verse Saves Man From Chair"

"Poet Slayer Writes in Sing Sing Death House—Gets Sentence Commuted."

Continuing, the paper said, "Condemned man owes his life today to his remarkable literary ability acquired since he has been in the death house at Sing Sing, is the opinion of prison observers.

["]His sentence was commuted to life imprisonment yesterday by Governor Smith. He was to have been put to death in the electric chair tonight.

["]At the time of his conviction of the murder he could neither

---

21. There were at least two editions of *Inspirational Poems*: (1) St. Louis MO: Hicks Almanac and Publishing Co. [and] Bush and Kirk, Publishers—Midcity Building and (2) St. Louis MO: David V. Bush, Publisher—4224 Harris Avenue. Both editions are marked "Copyright, 1921." Edition (1) has two bindings: blue cloth with white stamping and (2) black leatherette with raised stamping. Edition (2) has two bindings: (1) maroon cloth with gold stamping and (2) leatherette with raised stamping (not seen). "Think Right" appears on p. 28 of edition (1) and on p. 35 of edition (2).

read nor write. When he entered the death house he immediately
started studying. His unusual progress, due to unremitting labor,
attracted the attention of several persons. His thinking was that of
a trained lawyer, and his mind is the mind of a poet."

The lawyer defending the murderer went to Governor Smith
with this poem and said, in substance, "Your excellency, you do
not want the State to kill a man who has the soul of a poet. In the
death house facing his execution this man has written a poem
"Think Right." Al Smith read the poem, considered the case, and
the murderer's sentence was commuted to life imprisonment on
the night before his execution was to have been effected.

The defendant's lawyer claimed the murdered [sic] had written
the poem. The murdered [sic] had either committed my poem to
memory or some one had given it to him. The lawyer, thinking he
was the author, made the appeal to Governor Smith and his life
was saved.

I expect to be in Philadelphia before I go to Florida for the
winter[22] and may have an opportunity to see you while in the city.
I am a graduate of Temple University[23] and have many relatives in
Philadelphia.[24]

Yours for success, health and happiness.

David V. Bush

DVB/rb[25]

---

22. Bush customarily wintered in Florida in his later years. He died of a cerebral
hemorrhage at the Princess Martha Hotel in St. Petersburg, FL, on January 26,
1959.

23. Bush received a B.A. degree in elocution from Temple University in 1901. He
did attend theological lectures at both Temple University and Oakland City Col-
lege (Oakland City, IN), but apparently did not receive his claimed D.D. degree
from either of these institutions. Bush worked as a minister in 1907–21, before
becoming a full-time lecturer and writer. Bush's D.D. degree may have been a
mail-order degree from Frank Hamilton Rice's Denver-based Liberal Church.
Bush's daughter Maxine Conwell Bush was a bishop in this church, which she
called the Cosmopolitan Church of Liberality.

24. Bush's wife Elizabeth (Twining) Bush (1876–1960) had many relatives in the
Philadelphia area.

25. The author does not know the identity of Bush's typist "rb." He continued to
operate his Inspirational Publishing House until his death.

Appendix 2

"Think Right"[26]

Think smiles, and smiles shall be;
Think doubt, and hope will flee.
Think love, and love will grow;
Think hate, and hate you'll know.
Think good, and good is here.
Think vice—its claws appear!
Think joy, and joy ne'er ends;
Think gloom, and dusk descends.
Think faith, and faith's at hand;
Think ill—it stalks the land.
Think peace, sublime and sweet,
And you that peace will meet.
Think fear, with brooding mind,
And failure's close behind.
Think this: "I'm going to win!"—
Think not on what has been.
Think vict'ry—think "I can!"
Then you're a WINNING MAN!

---

26. Text follows *Inspirational Poems*, second edition, copyright 1921, p. 35.

Works Cited

Bush, David V. *If You Want to Be Rich.* Mehoopany PA: Inspirational Publishing House, 1954.

Faig, Kenneth W., Jr. "Lovecraft's Final Meeting with David V. Bush." *Lovecraft Annual* no. 8 (2014): 162–77.

Lovecraft, H. P. *Letters to Elizabeth Toldridge and Anne Tillery Renshaw.* Ed. David E. Schultz and S. T. Joshi. New York: Hippocampus Press, 2014. [*ATR*]

———. *Letters to James F. Morton.* Ed. S. T. Joshi and David E. Schultz. New York: Hippocampus Press, 2011. [*JFM*]

Smith, Nita Gerner[27] and Nelson G. Morton,[28] compilers. *Index to the History of Amateur Journalism.* New York: The Fossils, 1959.

---

27. Nita (Gerner) Smith (1881–1969) was the daughter of amateur journalist Richard Gerner (1856–1885) and the wife of amateur journalist Edwin Hadley Smith (1869–1944). She succeeded her husband as librarian for The Fossils and served until 1955. Edwin Hadley Smith's Library of Amateur Journalism (LAJ) collection was acquired by Charles C. Heuman for The Fossils in 1916, and has since 2004 resided in the Special Collections Department of the University of Wisconsin Library in Madison. The LAJ collection contains a separate set of bound volumes of Richard Gerner's writings. A conference celebrating the centenary of The Fossils' acquisition of the LAJ collection is scheduled to be held at University of Wisconsin's Memorial Library in Madison on July 21–23, 2016. In conjunction with the conference, the American Amateur Press Association (AAPA, founded 1936–37) is scheduled to hold a regional meeting, and the National Amateur Press Association (NAPA, founded 1876) is scheduled to hold its annual convention and business meeting. From his recruitment by Edward F. Daas in 1914 until the demise of the association in 1926–27, HPL's main activity was in the so-called Hoffman-Daas branch of the United Amateur Press Association (UAPA). He served the UAPA in numerous offices, including president in 1917–18. However, HPL joined the NAPA as early as 1917 and served in offices including president (1922–23), executive judge (1923–24 and 1935–36), and chairman, Bureau of Critics (1933–35). The UAPA had many factions over the years but all were extinct by the first decade of the twenty-first century. In 1917–18, HPL's adversary Elsa Gidlow (1898–1986) was president of the rival UAPA faction dominated by J. Roy Erford of Seattle.

28. Nelson Glazier Morton (1881–1968) was the younger brother of HPL's friend James Ferdinand Morton. Both Morton brothers served as President of NAPA: James in 1896–97 and Nelson in 1900–01.

Pieces of Reality: Lovecraft's Innovative Depiction of Music and Relativity

Tristan Zaba

> I have reached these lands but newly
> From an ultimate dim Thule—
> From a wild weird clime that lieth, sublime,
> Out of SPACE—out of TIME.
> —Edgar Allan Poe, "Dreamland"

Throughout H. P. Lovecraft's literary oeuvre we find an apparent clash between his famously scientific personality and his characteristic dark romanticism; between the hoax-like realistic detail and relentless rationalism of Lovecraft's detective tales on the one hand, and the fanciful prose style he developed to describe the nightmare worlds his protagonists discover on the other. The best-documented stylistic forerunner to Lovecraft is Edgar Allan Poe, whose tales' "style, texture, mood, and rhetorical effects became deeply imbued in Lovecraft's mind and inevitably colored his work from the beginning" (Joshi 53). However, even given that he lived in a less scientifically advanced era than Lovecraft, a scientific perception of reality is conspicuously absent from the works of Poe. During the resurrection scene in "Ligeia," for example, there is no attention paid to the physical reality of the world at hand. While much of Poe's work manages to leave the reader philosophically at odds, it cannot hope to question the reader's perception of reality in the same manner as Lovecraft. This is largely a result of the sophistication and intensity with which Lovecraft weaves the scientific and cultural developments of his time into his work. In fact, while the two writers' thematic ends are comparable, the ways in which Poe and Lovecraft approach

191

these ends are hugely different. Quite in contrast to the common view of Lovecraft as an overly nostalgic or even reactionary writer, his work was primarily aimed at developing the dark romantic tradition for a modern thinking audience.

Lovecraft's interest in contemporary physics is an excellent example. With special and general relativity, Einstein revolutionized physics and changed the world forever. As with many science fiction writers, Einstein's often-misunderstood general relativity is what really interested Lovecraft. At the base of everything, Einstein assumes that time and space are intrinsically bound together to create a four-dimensional reality as interrelated as traditional Euclidean geometry, referred to as "Spacetime." The implications of general relativity are that the existence of matter in the traditional three dimensions results in a bending of time as well, ultimately meaning time and space are relative to each other (*Britannica* 26.505). The extent to which the fourth dimension as time was explored in literature around this time period began and ended with H. G. Wells's *The Time Machine* (1895). Despite Wells's explanation of "time [being] only a kind of space," his use of the fourth dimension is entirely ungrounded. Wells provides no description beyond these sorts of phrases, only saying that the protagonist's time machine does to time what the hot air balloon does to the vertical dimension. In explaining time in this fashion, what he really misunderstands is relative scale. The time traveler's analogy is closer to being equivalent to instantaneously teleporting a truly vast distance, for example from Earth to Mars. Many people would intuitively assume that both energy and time are needed for this to occur. Similarly, it would make sense that in order for a break in time to occur, there would have to be some conversion of energy and dissolution of matter.

Lovecraft's work is pioneering in its representation of a more scientifically accurate fourth dimension in fiction. This isn't always easily apparent, as a major feature of Lovecraft's style is the confused or overwhelmed narrator, but the signs are definitely there. If one considers the possibility that entities such as Cthulhu are only seemingly all-powerful from the perspective of Lovecraft's earthbound protagonists and narrators, one can perceive a break in space or "dimensions" (*CF* 2.51), as described in "The Call of Cthulhu," as actually being primarily a break in *time*. In fact, the apparently inexplicable appearance in the modern world of entities from not just different historical periods (beings described in documents pertaining to the Salem witch trials in the case of "The Dreams in the Witch House," or from ancient Egyptian mythology in "Nyarlathotep") but entirely different geological and cosmological time scales (*At the Mountains of Madness*, "The Shadow out of Time") is one of Lovecraft's characteristic themes. Furthermore, we can also observe blatant recognition of spacetime relations in the words of non-narrative characters, such as in Pickman's statement regarding his North End studio being "[not] so very far away from the elevated as distance goes, but ... centuries away as the soul goes" (*CF* 2.62) in "Pickman's Model." It is more recognizable in this story than most that "the narrator [is led] back in time literally as well as figuratively" (Price 14). However, it is not often recognized that this theme occurs throughout Lovecraft's literary career.

If we continue exploring Lovecraft's work with this in mind, many unexplained elements of early works such as "The Music of Erich Zann," "The Outsider," and others begin to make sense. Lovecraft begins to succeed exactly where Wells falls short: in the concept of relativity between time and matter, and the reality of time-bending. While his approach may still be slightly neglectful of the black-hole-like gravitational consequences such breaks would entail, he still manages to represent this in an extremely interesting and intelligent way using an easily observable time equilibrium effect. One noticeable effect that occurs in "The Music of Erich Zann," as well as in "The Festival," is a strangely high population of elderly characters who inhabit a place that is isolated from the "modern" world in a manner far stronger and stranger than mere geography. These characters do not *perceive* time any differently, but as a result of localized bent time they age faster within the context of the rest of their reality's surroundings. The explanation is that a localized piece of reality surrounding a spacetime rift to the far future speeds up in order to synchronize with the other reality. It is interesting in "Erich Zann" that the narrator specifically states that he "was not myself when [he] moved there" (*CF* 1.281), and worth noting that he describes a change in his physical health afterwards and his memory as "broken" (*CF* 1.280). The specific tie he draws to the Rue d'Auseil is also strongly indicative of a spatially localized time disruption.

"The Outsider" is one of Lovecraft's most mysterious early tales, and the one he himself recognized as most strongly influenced
by Poe. Yet it also shows him moving well beyond Poe—and
Wells—in treating the theme of the distortion of time. In Poe's
"MS. Found in a Bottle," the hapless and confused narrator finds
himself upon the ship *Discovery*. Here he is left with a crew of
aged people upon a ship "imbued with the spirit of Eld" (198).
One does not know how long the crew has been there or how
long he will be there. Were there such a convenience as a break in
reality, this sort of anomaly could also be attributed to the sort of
physical phenomenon that Lovecraft's work thrives on. However,
as noted, it is characteristic of Poe not to provide an explanation.
In contrast, it is characteristic of Lovecraft to incorporate concepts
from contemporary physics in order to continue the development
of concepts he originally encountered in Poe's works, so as to provide an intellectual framework for them. If Poe envisioned apparently impossible scenarios "Out of Space—out of Time," Lovecraft
grounded such scenarios.

Thus, the protagonist of "The Outsider," rather than being a
revenant from the remote past, might thus be a descendant of
humanity in the far *future;* this seems particularly plausible when
one considers the protagonist's discovery of the "maddeningly familiar" (*CF* 1.269) ivied castle near the end of the story. In fact,
Lovecraft strongly hints that character's species may have at one
point been human (*CF* 1.271). In an inverse scenario to the align-
ment of past pieces of reality with twentieth-century Earth seen
in "Erich Zann" and "The Festival," the main character of "The
Outsider" could easily exist at a point far in the future. In this interpretation, the castle he lives in has fallen into ruin, the sky
could be dark from a possible apocalypse scenario, and with the
exception of mutants like the protagonist, humanity has met extinction. Through one of the same spacetime rifts that other
nameless Lovecraft narrators encounter, he finds his way to a past
before these events have occurred. His perception of time also
makes sense with occupying space near a rift, as proven by a
statement that he "must have lived years in [the] place, but
[could] not measure the time" (*CF* 1.266). He does not even de-

scribe having to sustain himself in any way, which should prove an obvious impossibility. When in contact with a rift to the past, however, it would make sense that time would slow down exponentially and his bodily systems may not feel the stresses of time. This would also prove true for entities like Cthulhu, who could dwell near a rift and be present as a phantom entity throughout thousands of years of human history while only aging marginally. Lovecraft later describes just such a scenario with the witch Keziah Mason. Distortions of time are an effective explanation for otherwise inexplicable phenomena in Lovecraft's works, including the existence of life forms and locations lurking undiscovered in the midst of our world.

Building further on this idea and addressing the concept of the physical rift itself, Lovecraft displays a very sophisticated view of the breakdown of the other three dimensions and its effect on the travel of sound. Pronunciation of character names for Lovecraft was a major point, as many of the names he wrote were considered approximations of sounds that supposedly couldn't be made by humans (*SL* 5.11). Evidence suggests that this isn't necessarily a problem with speaking a name so much as it is a problem of interpretation following the travel of sound across a spacetime rift. The biggest piece of evidence is the climax of "The Music of Erich Zann."

When there is disruption near Erich Zann, his music begins to morph into a "chaotic babel of sound" (*CF* 1.286). This is another effect of spacetime distortion. When a sound is played it also carries with it certain overtones. These overtones are dubbed "the harmonic series," and that series is essential to our comprehension of sound and is unchangeable within this physical reality (*Britannica* 24.690). Furthermore, that series suggests our entire method of dividing music into twelve equal semitones per octave. Within this system, music theorists can devise music and chord progressions, fundamentally rooted in physics, that they know will sound pleasant and natural. If the four-dimensional reality is disrupted, it is entirely possible that the overtone series would fall apart or rearrange in a new manner—this being exactly what happens in the story. The narrator notes that at the beginning of this series of events, Zann is recognizably playing the piece of another composer. When the viol starts "emitting sounds [that no] viol could emit" (CF 1.288), we are hearing the breakdown and reestablishment of a new harmonic series, which would completely change the timbre of the instrument and render traditional tonality (and the piece) nonsensical.

It is also worth noting that the viol is a fretted predecessor to modern bowed string instruments, meaning it must stay within twelve-tone equal-temperament tuning and cannot deviate from this system of octave division without modification of the instrument. The sound is also furthermore distorted by the time equilibrium effect, which would result in sound feeding back from the flip side of the rift traveling at a fraction of its speed. As a result, the narrator notes that Zann's viol produces sounds that no single instrument could make, and recognizes a distorted parallel version of Zann's music flowing back in from the void beyond the window. This also toys with the popular conception of music as the only one-dimensional art form, existing exclusively in the fourth dimension. The reasoning behind this is due to the fact that music is completely immaterial and depends only on the movement of time to progress.

This sonic speculation also connects Lovecraft's work to the musical developments of the early twentieth century. Classical music from 1900 onward showed a clear progression to atonality (a movement stressing a bondage to the twelve-tone division, but not the notes' harmonic relationships), onward to Western music's first foray into microtonality in the late 1910s and '20s (divisions of tones in ways that openly contradict the harmonic series) (Burkholder 813), and ultimately to experiments with indeterminate timbres and pitches. These developments occurred mainly in the United States, with composers such as New York's Henry Cowell and Charles Ives known as some of the most prominent experimental pioneers. This was a time in which composers began challenging the aforementioned guidelines set forward by physics, thus resulting in further engagement of physics and math enthusiasts.

Coming back to Lovecraft's influences, Edgar Allan Poe had a huge impact on music, from numerous classical settings of his poems to reinterpretations of his tales by the Alan Parsons Project. In fact, when Claude Debussy, one of the foremost composers of the time, died in 1917, he was famously obsessing over the creation of two one-act operas from the work of Poe for the Metropolitan Opera (Trezise 82). This sort of information may very well have interested Lovecraft, considering his obsession with the work of Poe. Even while the scores were eventually left incomplete, news of such a deal would have been widely publicized by the opera company at the time. Lovecraft may very well have allowed the news of these operas to influence works such as "The Music of Erich Zann." The character parallels between Roderick Usher (the subject of one of the incomplete operas), Erich Zann, and their roles as artists are easily observable. Moreover, each seems cut off from his time, straining to divulge some terrible secret that he himself can hardly comprehend or remember. Furthermore, the influence of the music of the time on Lovecraft personally is known, as shown by his reference to the geographically conven-ient Boston Symphony Orchestra as one of the last vestiges of "non-eccentric, non-propogandist material still aimed at gentle-folk" (*SL* 5.399). This same orchestra was well known for holding the American premiere of Debussy's "Fantaisie for Piano and Or-chestra" in 1920, after the composer's death and around the time Lovecraft wrote "The Music of Erich Zann" (BSO Archives).

The more one explores the work of Lovecraft in conjunction with the reality of his time, the more one realizes the extent to which he incorporated it. The connection between the work of Lovecraft, physics, and music is only one direction from which a person may approach his work. Looking at these sorts of areas, however, it is plain to see exactly how Lovecraft perceived his own style. His elaboration on dark romanticism is meant to be in-tellectually progressive and his audience is made up of people like himself, who simultaneously dwell on the mysteries of the past and the promises of the future. Lovecraft's legacy proved progres-sive both for future authors of science fiction such as Arthur C. Clarke ("All the Time in the World," "Songs of Distant Earth") and for musicians, who continue to draw on his cosmic visions for inspiration.

Works Cited

"American Premieres: The 1920s | Boston Symphony Orchestra." *BSO Archives*. Boston Symphony Orchestra, n.d. Web. 25 May 2015.

Burkholder, J. Peter. *A History of Western Music*. 9th ed. London: W. W. Norton, 2014.

Burleson, Donald R. "'The Music of Erich Zann' as Fugue." *Lovecraft Studies* No. 6 (Spring 1982): 14–17.

Einstein, Albert. *The Special and General Theory*. New York: Henry Holt & Co., 1920.

The Encyclopedia Britannica. 15th ed. Chicago: Encyclopedia Britannica, 2007.

Joshi, S. T. *A Subtler Magick: The Writings and Philosophy of H. P. Lovecraft*. San Bernardino, CA: Borgo Press, 1996.

Orledge, Robert. *Debussy and the Theatre*. Cambridge: Cambridge University Press, 1982.

Poe, Edgar Allan. *Poetry, Tales, & Selected Essays*. 2nd ed. New York: Penguin Putnam, 1996.

Price, Robert M. "Erich Zann and the Rue d'Auseil." *Lovecraft Studies* Nos. 22/23 (Fall 1990): 13–14.

Trezise, Simon. *The Cambridge Companion to Debussy*. Cambridge: Cambridge University Press, 2003.

Wells, H. G. *The Time Machine*. New York: Atria, 2011. EBUP file.

Fragments from the Lost Letters of H. P. Lovecraft to Robert E. Howard

Bobby Derie

The correspondence of H. P. Lovecraft and Robert E. Howard lasted from 1930 to 1936, ending with Howard's death; Lovecraft himself would succumb to cancer the following year. August Derleth and Donald Wandrei solicited Lovecraft's letters for the *Selected Letters* project, including from the Texan's father, Dr. I. M. Howard, who duly sent them on. Portions of those letters were transcribed into what became the Arkham House Transcripts and returned to Dr. Howard, who regrettably burned them sometime in the 1940s (*MF* 1.12). When the collected correspondence of Lovecraft and Howard was published as *A Means to Freedom* (2009), these transcripts were the major basis for Lovecraft's portion, with the editors choosing to mark the missing letters as "non-extant."

However, while we do not have the letters themselves, a close study of the *Collected Letters of Robert E. Howard* (Robert E. Howard Foundation Press, 2007–08) shows that Robert E. Howard did quote from several of Lovecraft's letters in his correspondence with others—including some that do not match any sections of text in *A Means to Freedom* and must therefore be from the missing letters, or those portions of the letters not part of the Arkham House Transcripts. These fragments are likely all that remain from those missives.

Determining the source for these fragments is aided by the form of Lovecraft and Howard's letters, where they would often reply to each other point-by-point, so that even if one letter is missing, if we have the reply we can usually get the gist of the contents, especially if the subject can be collated with other let-

ters Lovecraft had written around the same time. In his early correspondence with Lovecraft, Howard was keen on discussing the
letters with others, such as his friend Tevis Clyde Smith, to whom
Howard wrote in September 1930:

> I got a letter from Lovecraft and he referred to August Derleth;
> you know, the fellow that writes the very short stories that ap-
> pear regularly in Weird Tales. I was amazed to learn that Derleth
> is only twenty-one years old. He must have started writing when
> he was about ten. Lovecraft says he wishes he had the dough to
> travel all over hellandback, or words to that effect. Gad—he does
> more than I do. The first letter I got from him, he'd just gotten
> back from a month's trip; the next he'd been up to Salem, and
> Marblehead and Boston. The next letter, he'd gotten back from
> Boston, I believe and was just fixing to go up in Massachusetts to
> visit the Frank Belknap Long Jr. family for five days. This latest
> letter was mailed in Backbay, Boston, and he said he was writing
> it while on his way to Quebec. He said he'd never seen Europe,
> but craved to and intended to do so. I was surprized to learn that
> he occasionally got stuff rejected, also Clark Ashton Smith, who
> must be no spring chicken, as Lovecraft told me Clark Ashton
> had out a volume of verse as early as 1910. Wandrei, he said, a
> very fine poet whose works appear every now and then in Weird
> Tales, is only twenty-two. I'm beginning to believe the poetry-
> business is a lot like the fight game—most of the poets do their
> best work early in life. But I'll bet Lovecraft is older than most of
> the others. I think if I get time, I'll write to Derleth, Smith, Long
> Jr., Dwyer, Wandrei, Danziger and Arthur Machen. Lovecraft says
> that he's having Long send me his "loancopy" of verse—all that's
> left of his publishings. He says it's a pity that Long, like himself,
> has to grind out his energies in hack work. And say—a tip on Sci-
> ence Wonder Stories. Lovecraft tells me Clark Ashton is hesitating
> over a contract for a series of interplanetary novelettes, because
> the management of the magazine is shady in money matters.
>
> Speaking of Derleth, Lovecraft says: "His work in W.T. does
> not represent him at all, being merely pot-boiling hack material;
> but his really serious products (on the order of Marcel Proust)
> display qualities amounting almost to genius." (CL 2.69)

The quotation regarding Derleth is probably from letter 9 in *A*

Means to Freedom, as the subsequent response from Howard to Lovecraft begins by talking about Lovecraft's travels and Derleth (*MF* 1.41–42; *CL* 2.73). However, it is possible that the quotation is from the missing pages of letter 7, as Howard quotes extensively from that missive in the same letter to Smith (*CL* 2.71–72; cf. *MF* 1.40).

In another letter to Smith (c. December 1930), Howard wrote:

> Lovecraft says that he envies me my Southern blood, that he has always admired the South, though he is a native New Englander of many generations descent. He speaks with great admiration of the old Southern aristocracy era, and says that Charleston is his favorite of all cities, and that he may move there some day to live. (*CL* 2.117–18)

The sentiments are undoubtedly Lovecraftian and probably refer to letter 16 in *A Means to Freedom*. In his reply to that letter, Howard talks about the South and states, "I am sure Charleston is a beautiful city and would be a splendid place to live" (*MF* 1.99; *CL* 2.121).

As their correspondence continued, Howard became part of the pulp writer grapevine, sharing tidbits of news and possible leads on new markets with other writers. One example of this is given in another letter to Smith from March 1931: "By the way, Lovecraft told me that August Derleth told *him* that Farnsworth told *him* that the first of June *Weird Tales* goes back to the monthly basis" (*CL* 2.189). *Weird Tales* had gone to a bimonthly schedule for three issues in 1931 and had returned to regular monthly publication starting with the August 1931 number. This bit of gossip was probably in letter 22 of *A Means to Freedom*, as in the following letter Howard remarked to Lovecraft: "No, I hadn't heard anything about Weird Tales going monthly again, but I'm glad to hear of it" (*MF* 1.148; *CL* 2.166). Derleth's passing on of this information to Lovecraft is acknowledged in a letter dated 23 January 1931, where Lovecraft writes: "Incidentally, your news of the return of W.T. to a monthly basis is the first hint to that effect which I have received" (*ES* 1.317).

In April 1931, Howard wrote to Wilfred Blanch Talman:

Our mutual friend Mr. Lovecraft writes me that a publishing house had been corresponding with him in regard to possibly bringing out his stories in book form. I most sincerely hope that they close the deal satisfactorily to all parties, for literature would be enriched exceedingly by the appearance of his tales on the book shelves of the world. And God knows, modern literature needs some such stimulus, for it has fallen on barren ways. (CL 2.194)

This is probably a reference to letter 25 in *A Means to Freedom*: Lovecraft had been asked to submit some manuscripts to a publisher for consideration, but the proposed volume was later rejected. His comments were probably largely identical to those written it August Derleth around the same time:

I have recently been hearing from the book editor of G. P. Putnam's Sons, who asked me to submit some stuff for consideration as a possible book-form collection—but doubt if anything will come of it. I have finally bitten to the extent of sending the 30 tales which I had around the house in loose form, but will not do any copying from my files unless I am assured of strong acceptance-chances. (*ES* 1.327)

In letter 28, Robert E. Howard had replied to Lovecraft's letter 25: "I most certainly hope that Putnam & Sons have decided to bring out your work in book form—both for your own sake and for the sake of American literature as a whole" (*MF* 1.167; CL 2.204).

In another letter to Talman, from October 1931, Howard wrote: "I'm returning herewith your stories, 'The Heads at Gywry' and 'Midnight Coach' which Mr. Lovecraft forwarded to me" (CL 2.251). This is probably a reference to letter 35 in *A Means to Freedom*, from mid-October 1931, where Lovecraft wrote: "Here's a new tale which Talman asked me to send to you, for subsequent return to him"; in the following letter Howard acknowledges, "I enjoyed Mr. Talman's stories greatly" (*MF* 1.215; CL 2.253), and in Howard's letter after that, "I have received and read Talman's manuscript and think it splendidly done" (*MF* 1.230; CL2.272).

Also in October 1931, Howard wrote to Tevis Clyde Smith again: "That reminds me that in his last letter Lovecraft told me that he'd never encountered a better natural ear for rhythm than mine—all of which is an extreme exhibition of vanity on my part,

for me to repeat, but I never laid claim to be any modest shrink-
ing violet" (*CL* 2.254). This is probably a paraphrasing of Lovecraft's comments in letter 34 in *A Means to Freedom*, where he
wrote: "Your case would seem to be an argument that good versi-
fiers are such by instinct rather than by acquisition" (*MF* 1.209). A
much more extensive quotation from Lovecraft's letters follows in
a March 1932 letter to Smith:

> Lovecraft wrote me that he'd placed a couple of yarns, and evi-
> dently the old weird tale buccaneers have descended on it like a
> horde of vultures. Lovecraft said Smith, Long, Whitehead, Der-
> leth, etc., etc., etc., had sold Swanson a lot of stuff already. By the
> way, Farnsworth rejected the last three yarns I sent him, together
> with a bunch of verse. No rest for the weary. I've drifted into cor-
> respondence with some more Weird Tailors (as Lovecraft calls
> them) and Mashburn tells me that there seems to be a good
> chance of getting that weird anthology published. I hope so, ye
> gods. [. . .] I sent a copy of one of those of mine included in the
> bunch (I trust that sentence is clear!) to Lovecraft, to let him read
> it—the one called "Echoes From an Iron Harp" or something like
> that, and he said: "You are certainly a genuine poet in every sense
> of the word". And further on in the letter he said, "Your poem—
> as I said at the beginning of this letter—is powerful and splendid."
> "I don't know anyone today who reproduces the ancient Aryan
> emotions as powerfully, vividly, and sincerely as you do. This
> mood is almost obsolete in Europe and the Eastern U.S.; and if it
> is to have continued literary expression, such will probably come
> from the Southwest." Pardon my conceit in repeating these kind
> comments. But hell, why shouldn't I? I'm no shrinking violet. But
> if a discerning critic like Lovecraft likes my stuff, then the world
> will certainly be enriched by our book, because both your poems
> and Lenore's are superior to mine. (*CL* 2.315–16)

The quoted portions probably come from letter 50 in *A Means to
Freedom*. Howard had included "Echoes of an Iron Harp" in letter 49
(*MF* 1.273; *CL*2.308). The reference to placing stories with Carl
Swanson is in regard to *Galaxy*, a prospective publication that never came off. Howard would later write to Swanson: "In fact, I first
heard of your new publication through my friend, Mr. Lovecraft,
who I understand has placed some work with you" (*CL* 2.361).

There are a couple dozen other references to Lovecraft in Howard's surviving correspondence to others, but no other references to the non-extant letters, though in a letter to Smith from May 1932 Howard quotes bits of Lovecraft's letter 53 in *A Means to Freedom* (CL 2.369; cf. *MF* 1.287–88).

Works Cited

Howard, Robert E. *Collected Letters of Robert E. Howard.* Ed. Rob Roehm. Sugar Land, TX: Robert E. Howard Foundation Press, 2007–08. 3 vols. [Abbreviated in the text as CL.]

Lovecraft, H. P., and August Derleth. *Essential Solitude: The Letters of H. P. Lovecraft and August Derleth.* Ed. David E. Schultz and S. T. Joshi. New York, NY: Hippocampus Press, 2008. 2 vols. [Abbreviated in the text as ES.]

Lovecraft, H. P., and Robert E. Howard. *A Means to Freedom: The Letters of H. P. Lovecraft and Robert E. Howard.* Ed. S. T. Joshi, David E. Schultz, and Rusty Burke. New York: Hippocampus Press, 2009. 2 vols. [Abbreviated in the text as MF.]

Pop Cultural Assimilation of the Lovecraftian Worldview through the Lens of *Rick and Morty*

Duncan Norris

At first glance, the ongoing 2013 cartoon television series *Rick and Morty* could not seem further removed from the literary and conceptual world and style of Howard Phillips Lovecraft. An irreverent, profane, and overtly sexualized comedic cartoon, it is based on the very Hollywood premise of "What if Doc Brown from the movie *Back to the Future* was a more creative, misanthropic alcoholic whose Marty McFly was his naïve grandson?" Yet when we glance beneath the cartoon veneer, the conceptual worldview of the oxymoronic maleficently indifferent universe and the unimportance of humanity that underpins Lovecraft's Cthulhu Mythos is a crucial driving factor of *Rick and Morty*. This is not an accidental happenstance. Whilst the show is replete with patent and subtle reference to both classic and modern science fiction and horror works (*Inception, The Lawnmower Man*, and *A Nightmare on Elm Street*, to name but the three most obvious movies alluded to in the second episode alone), they are individual works and tropes used, generally, in single episodic format. The following study aims to demonstrate the very real placement of the totality of the *Rick and Morty* in an active and well-realized Lovecraftian milieu, and thus demonstrate that the filtration and dissemination of Lovecraftian ideas can be done in a manner that goes well beyond the seemingly endless catalogue of forbidden book lists and increasingly explicable and thus de-empowered beings and deities of Lovecraft's original conceptions.

The opening credits of *Rick and Morty* show, as part of their rapid vignette style, an image of Rick, Morty, and his sister Summer navigating in a spacecraft through a drowned, ruined city attempting to escape from a rampaging monster that is clearly Cthulhu. We, the viewer, literally go down Cthulhu's maw to the title card to start the show. It is important to note that this scene, as of the end of Season Two, is not from an episode the viewer ever sees. Instead, the creators have chosen, in a typically Lovecraftian manner, to create a greater narrative depth by hints rather than later full exposition. This is true of four of the seven vignette scenes in the opening credits of Season One and five of the seven in Season Two.[1] Only the first and final Cthulhu vignettes remain the same in both seasons. *Rick and Morty* literally starts at a premise of us being engulfed in the Lovecraftian universe, demonstrating that what we are seeing is a small part of a far greater whole.

Yet a skeptical person would be correct in proclaiming that the clever use of backstory creation and a single visual reference to what is arguably Lovecraft's most artistically arrogated construction does not a Lovecraftian worldview make. For example, director Sam Raimi, whose use of the *Necronomicon* as the gateway to summon possessive demons in the cult horror classic film series *The Evil Dead*, introduced this archetypal Lovecraftian creation to a wide audience but in a manner completely divorced of any connection to its origins in Lovecraft. Thus over time it is has become common to find Lovecraftian inventions absent any connection to the original creations or underpinning motifs and mythopoeia. Equally important is the common practice for creators in a variety of media to insert homages to Lovecraft if they have enjoyed or feel a personal connection to his work. To remain within just the medium of television science-fiction cartoon comedy, *Futurama*, a decidedly un-Lovecraftian show, has a humanoid squid character, Zoidberg, clearly modeled loosely on Cthulhu. Yet this character is used as an (admittedly amusing) standard comedy buffoon with no further attempt at the other aspects of Cthulhu or the bleaker Lovecraftian universe. In fact, the disparity between Zoidberg's appearance and his character helps add to his comic appeal, even to those who might not know the original on

---

1. Or perhaps four of the vignettes in Season Two, depending on how one chooses to classify a small section in a flashback montage of a fake memory implanted as a reproductive mentor by alien parasites.

which he is based. In a like manner *Futurama* briefly uses the unmistakable image of a Yithian in "A Bicyclops Built for Two," an episode concerning a shape-shifting alien trying to perform a complex marriage scam. It is an in-joke for Lovecraft fans and has no further connection or agenda than the joy created by a shared moment only the initiated are privy too.

However, *Rick and Morty* goes far beyond glancing references or minor in-jokes. The entirety of the show rests upon the idea, which several of the characters in the show openly espouse to a greater or lesser degree, of the human race living in a deeply purposeless and dangerously amoral universe. To quote Rick in Season One, Episode Seven (S1E7), "Raising Gazorpazorp": "after all that stuff we just did, nothing really mattered and there was no point to it." This (to humans) nihilistic understanding of life in the larger universal viewpoint can be easily demonstrated in the opening moments of S1E9, "Something Ricked This Way Comes." Rick creates an artificially intelligent robot at the breakfast table simply to pass him the butter. The creation repeatedly asks, "What is my purpose?" to which Rick replies, "You pass butter." In existential angst it proclaims dejectedly, "Oh my god," to which Rick comments, "Yeah, welcome to the club, pal." The parallels to the creation of mankind by the Elder Things of Antarctica in *At the Mountains of Madness* "as jest or mistake" (*CF* 3.40), a side effect of other life they wanted, is unmistakable.

In S2E2, "Mortynight Run," Morty's varyingly inept and pathetic father Jerry is left in an isolated multiverse day-care, Jerryboree, with a host of Jerry's from alternative timelines and dimensions in order to keep him safe from the dangers of the galaxy. It is almost a literal interpretation of "We live on a placid island of ignorance in the midst of black seas of infinity" (*CF* 2.21) from "The Call of Cthulhu," and it is notable that Rick and Morty in the A-story of the episode deal with a powerful being from another reality that is looking to wipe out our existence, seeing us as a disease. Furthermore, rather than being a prison Jerryboree has an open-door policy: when Jerry does leave he is so frightened by the truth of what he sees that he voluntarily returns to the safety of fixing television cables and screen settings, "flee[ing] from the deadly light into the peace and safety of a new dark age" (*CF* 2.22). In the same episode

Rick accuses Morty (not without a large element of self-interest) of having a "very planetary mindset," because of his moral objections to selling an assassin a weapon. Morty favors the standard human moral view that cold-blooded murder is wrong, and by matching words to actions he unintendedly causes the deaths of thousands and nearly allows a galactic genocide, which is only averted by Morty himself committing cold-blooded murder. The uncaring yet malign Lovecraftian universe is on full display.

In S2E5, "Get Swifty," a giant head appears in the sky and is destroying Earth, demanding for us to "Show me what you got." A cult starts up, worshipping and ultimately offering human sacrifice to the giant heads after people misunderstand what is actually happening, which is that the giant heads are Cromulons from the Signus Five Expanse who want Earth to participate in their musical talent competition. Losers face planetary destruction, and our nuclear arsenal is useless. Once again this is a clearly Lovecraftian theme of humans worshipping beings from space that they cannot comprehend, being completely blind to the creatures' true nature or motives and completely helpless in the face of this blindness.

The following episode, S2E6, "The Ricks Must Be Crazy," combines both themes in the A and B narratives of the episode. Whilst Rick, Morty, and Summer are in an Earth-like parallel reality (with additional giant telepathic spiders) to watch a movie and eat ice cream, the battery in Rick's spaceship fails. Rick and Morty subsequently go inside the battery to investigate why. It transpires that Rick has created an entire "microverse" in which he is venerated as a beneficent alien, when in reality the inhabitants are effectively slaves whose sole purpose is to generate electricity to power his vehicle. One of the microverse's scientists has done a like process to create a "miniverse," as has one of the scientists in his miniverse who has created a "teenyverse"; and this trend seems likely to to continue indefinitely. When this latter being discovers the truth of his existence he kills himself, and ultimately the scientist in the original microverse stops his plans to cease electricity production, knowing that Rick will simply uncaringly destroy their universe and get a new battery if it fails to function. Simultaneously Summer is left behind in the ship, whose extreme artificial intelligence is given the mandate "Keep Summer safe." After murder, crippling, and psychological torture to achieve these ends are activated and then subsequently vetoed at Summer's horrified urgings, the ship creates planetary peace between the humans and giant spiders as a final solution to fulfill her mandate within the parameters. Thus are juxtaposed two different examinations of powerful beings haphazardly wreaking havoc on entire worlds simply to fulfill their own desires and with no higher purpose or morality. This lack of a higher morality or purpose is driven home in the final scene wherein Rick complains because, as per the new peace mandate with the giant spiders, the formerly "best ice cream in the multiverse" now has flies in it.

But the greatest expression of the Lovecraftian worldview that is central to the nature of "Rick and Morty" comes in S1E8, "Rixty Minutes." In this episode, in trying to make Summer see the futility of running away because her mother, being pregnant with her, is the reason her unhappily married parents are together, Morty relates to Summer the events of S1E6, "Rick Potion #9," in which he and Rick have mutated and effectively destroyed the entire world, which they escape by jumping into a parallel reality. Morty then points to his own grave in the back yard, the original Morty of this world who had died gruesomely seconds before the current Morty arrived. He sums up his tale as follows: "Nobody exists on purpose. Nobody belongs anywhere. Everybody's going to die." It is a lesson Summer takes to heart. In S2E9, "Big Trouble in Little Sanchez," she claims the reason Rick won't return his consciousness to his old body from his teenage clone is to hide from "the fact that we're all going to die one day, the fact that the universe is so big nothing in it matters." The pointlessness of human existence on the cosmic scale could not be expressed more succinctly.

Thus *Rick and Morty* manages to eschew the tropes and trappings of Lovecraftian fiction yet captures in its irreverent and chaotic form the truest underpinning of Lovecraftian horror: a malign yet ultimately uncaring and uncontrollable universe filled with horror beyond comprehension, with only the single, guttering candle of science in the dark to hold it at bay, until the time when science itself leads to our destruction.

Reviews

H. P. LOVECRAFT. *Fungi from Yuggoth: An Annotated Edition.* Edited by David E. Schultz. Illustrated by Jason C. Eckhardt. New York: Hippocampus Press, August 2016. 287 pp. Limited edition hardcover, $40. Reviewed by Steven J. Mariconda.

In 1918 distinguished literary scholar George Edward Woodberry published *Nathaniel Hawthorne: How to Know Him* (287 pages). In 2016 distinguished literary scholar David E. Schultz published *Fungi from Yuggoth: An Annotated Edition* (287 pages). Schultz might just as well have titled his book *H. P. Lovecraft: How to Know Him.* You cannot know H. P. Lovecraft without owning, studying, and internalizing this volume. This is not just a collection of Lovecraft's best poems with an excellent introduction and annotations. It is a handbook to Lovecraft's creative process and realm—personal, prosodic, and poetic.

H. P. Lovecraft's *Fungi from Yuggoth* (FFY) is a sequence of thirty-six sonnets, composed in 1929 and 1930. In the first three poems, an unnamed first-person narrator obtains a mysterious tome—a "book that told the hidden way / Across the void and through the space-hung screens"—from an ancient bookseller, and is followed home by an unseen pursuer. The remaining poems, which Lovecraft offered to numerous publications independently of the first three, are vignettes on a variety of weird themes.

Taken together, these sonnets embody in poetic form the core set of imagery Lovecraft used so adroitly in his fiction. Admirers of "The Call of Cthulhu," "The Colour out of Space," and similar Lovecraft landmarks will find much to like here—brilliant flights of pure Lovecraftian fancy presented in compelling and concise prosody.

We are fortunate now to have, for the first time, a standalone edition of FFY of a quality commensurate with its contents. In addition to an immaculate presentation of the sonnets, each with an accompanying illustration facing, the book consists of several sections. "Fungi from Yuggoth: The Manuscript" sets the tone for the book: this is a scholarly edition offering MLA-level rigor in terms of both textual reliability and critical apparatus. The edition establishes accuracy with respect to the text, and documents its editorial principles and methods. This is complimented by extensive explanatory matter, which the editor has respectfully placed after the sonnet cycle.

Schultz presents the complicated history of the FFY text and its physical forms, explains how this edition has been constructed, and provides his rationale for various editorial choices. He discusses the compositional elements of the text (punctuation, capitalization, spelling), and the layout, graphical presentation, and physical appearance of the source material. Spot illustrations from a planned but never published edition are provided. Helpful tables show the sequence and location of the sonnets printed during Lovecraft's lifetime. The fifty-page "Dim Essences: The Origins of Fungi from Yuggoth" is a well-rounded and comprehensive essay that proceeds to an explication of the sonnet cycle. Notes for each poem, including headnotes and line annotations, follow. Next come the Appendixes (Notes for Additional Sonnets; The Book [a prose fragment— an attempt to recast the poems as a story]; Chronology of Appearances of Fungi from Yuggoth; and Textual Variants). For those playing along at home (on piano), Schultz reproduces "The Musical Compositions of Harold S. Farnese," staff-paper settings for "Mirage" (XXIII) and "The Elder Pharos" (XXVII). At the end, there is an extensive Bibliography and an Index of Titles and First Lines.

Many are aware of Schultz as co-editor with S. T. Joshi of dozens of volumes of the literature of weird fiction and poetry: Lovecraft, Ambrose Bierce, Clark Ashton Smith, George Sterling, R. H. Barlow, Samuel Loveman, Park Barnitz, James F. Morton, Robert E. Howard, and so on. The term "co-editor" does not sufficiently convey the level of Schultz's contribution: he has added tremendous amounts of critical value to these books in terms of *content*-- in the front and back matter, and in the annotations. A prominent instance is Bierce's *Unabridged Devil's Dictionary* (University of Georgia Press, 2002), the definitive edition of that classic. For Schultz-as-critic, the reader is referred to *The H. P. Lovecraft Encyclopedia* (Hippocampus Press, 2004; recently made available for

Kindle), for which Schultz wrote many of the entries. In addition
to his credits as co-editor and co-author, Schultz is the force-
multiplier behind much of the S. T. Joshi publishing phenomenon.
Joshi has well over 200 titles to his credit, and an incremental two
dozen in queue; behind the scenes, Schultz edited and prepared
many of these for press after Joshi donated his IBM Selectric
typewriter to the Smithsonian in the 1990s.

Schultz is one of the few who can pace Joshi's phenomenal
productivity: over the last several decades he spent 40+ hours a
week editing technical documents for a living while doing the literary work in his "spare time." Like Joshi, Schultz has spent more
hours in front of digital scanners, microfilm readers, and high speed
laser printers than is recommended by the Surgeon General of the
ALA. The two have expended long intervals side by side hand-
transcribing manuscripts from library archives all over the U.S. for
citizens like us to enjoy. Many of these immense efforts still await
publication. Among the maniacal initiatives Schultz has been involved with over the years is transcribing, with Joshi, nearly the entirety of Bierce's published work—about 6 million words—as well
as a half-million words of Bierce's letters. Schultz took the job of
transcribing *hundreds* of Bierce's "Little Johnny" newspaper install-
ments, the dialect anecdotes of an aspiring juvenile naturalist journalist written (as Joshi phrases it) "in an almost impenetrable patois
of deliberate solecisms and misspellings." These items proved impervious to speed-typing or spell-checking (example: "The pede is
found in the torpid zone, but the rhi nupple dinkey is a three-
legger and makes the welkin ring!'), but Schultz staunchly captured upwards of 1,500 printed pages of it for digital posterity.

Beyond contributions preserved between hard covers, Schultz
established his credential as a leading Lovecraft scholar in amateur
press associations (APAs) in the 1970s, doing ground-breaking
close reading of the Lovecraft oeuvre well before most explicators
came on the scene. There are at least two reasons we have we not
seen much recent criticism from Schultz. Firstly, his interest in
Lovecraft is bounded by a pragmatic sensibility: Poststructuralism
and other incomprehensible "interpretation" is not in scope. Secondly, his level of perfectionism approaches the prohibitive when
it comes to committing something to print. We are thus lucky to

have this book at all. Happily, many of Schultz's insights from his APA days have been carried forward into this book.

Fungi from Yuggoth: An Annotated Edition has (as Floyd Stovall said of *Leaves of Grass*) a "long foreground." The genesis of this book, like many things in objective reality, sounds like something out of Lovecraft. In mid-1976 BJE (Before the Joshi Era), Schultz received from a correspondent a packet of two dozen 8 × 10 prints of surreptitiously taken black and white photographs of the autograph manuscript of FFY. (The event recalls "The Whisperer in Darkness" [1929-30], where the narrator receives a set of photographic prints showing the apparent existence of the Old Ones.) Despite the somewhat blurry and out-of-focus spy-cam pictures, Schultz was struck by the volume of interlineations and notations present on the AMs (Cleaner images of these pages are included in the book, so the reader can experience something similar.) and the fact that FFY, at the time of composition, comprised only *thirty-five sonnets*. His first critical examination of FFY appeared in the amateur press soon after.

At this point, the idea of an annotated edition was conceived. Schultz began intermittent work on the book, but stalled when a provisional agreement with a small press publisher fell through, and "real life" in the form of work and family intervened. He continued to work on it over a period of years.

Meanwhile, he had a similar revelation regarding Lovecraft's *Commonplace Book*, which had been printed in a garbled state in Arkham House's *The Shuttered Room and Other Pieces* (1959). He began annotating that item in parallel. The second initiative saw print first: *H.P. Lovecraft: Commonplace Book*, edited by Schultz, was published in two volumes by Necronomicon Press in 1987. (It is offered for $2,000 on the internet as I write.)

Perhaps unknowingly, Schultz had hit on a brilliant scheme to understand Lovecraft: by collating the artist's symbolism with the finished work, and following the creative process the along the way in Lovecraft's life and letters. The *Commonplace Book* is the raw material of Lovecraft's artistic imagery. The fiction—now in the American canon aside Melville, Hawthorne, and Poe—are the prose embodiment of this imagery. But it is FFY that is the poetic apotheosis of that same set of core imagery. This is the concentrated essence of Lovecraft's unique creative achievement, the purest expression of his imaginative genius.

Literary images magnify the thought they convey or illustrate. It is thus that they make the thought more prominent and distinct than a literal statement of it could. The imagery in Lovecraft's work is a natural and cohesive outgrowth of his philosophical position as expressed in letters and essays. Kaleidoscopic visions, weird sounds, alien rhythms, disturbing outlines and proportions, geometrical figures and patterns, asymmetry, Ultimate Chaos, and the black void beyond: all are motifs he wove throughout his work to convey his sense of the weird. All these motifs can be traced from the *Commonplace Book*, into the tales, and here into FFY.

What emerges to the interested reader who studies the *Commonplace Book*, FFY, and the stories is a kind of neural network diagramming the Lovecraftian worldview: interconnections among the nodes in different layers of a vast, linked system of imagination. It has little to do with what was dubbed "the Cthulhu Mythos" and shows what Lovecraft is really about as an artist.

In his essay, Schultz zeroes in on what may be the single most important passage in Lovecraft's letters for understanding Lovecraft. In an epistle to Harold S. Farnese of September 1932:

> In my own efforts to crystallize spaceward outreaching, I try to utilize as many as possible of the elements which have, under earlier mental and emotional conditions, given man a symbolic feeling of the unreal, the ethereal, & the mystical—choosing those least attacked by the realistic mental and emotional conditions of the present.   Darkness—sunset—dreams—mists—fever—madness—the tomb—the hills—the sea—the sky—the wind—all these, & many other things have seemed to me to retain a certain imaginative potency despite our actual scientific analyses of them. Accordingly I have tried to weave them into a kind of shadowy phantasmagoria which may have the same sort of vague coherence as a cycle of traditional myth or legend—with nebulous backgrounds of Elder Forces & trans-galactic entities which lurk about this infinitesimal planet, (& others of course as well), establishing outposts thereon, & occasionally brushing aside other accidental forms of life (like human beings) in order to take up full habitation. (*SL* 4.70)

The *phantasmagoria* was a form of theatre which used magic lanterns to project successive images onto walls, smoke, or semi-transparent screens (see Marina Warner's *Phantasmagoria: Spirit Visions, Metaphors, and Media into the Twenty-first Century* (Oxford University Press, 2000). FFY is the distilled essence of the elements of Lovecraft's imagination, as conveyed across the totality of his work. As Schultz remarks: "*Fungi from Yuggoth* is an encapsulation in 504 lines not only of the whole of Lovecraft's life up to the time of its composition, as expressed mostly in his letters and fiction, but also the essence of his later writings."

FFY has had a complicated publication history, best understood by reading Schultz's lucid exposition of the twists and turns. It involves 75 poorly-typed and incomplete copies circulated through the Fantasy Amateur Press Association in 1943; the work's first appearance in complete form in *Beyond the Wall of Sleep* (Arkham House, 1943); misprinting in *Collected Poems* (Arkham House, 1963); and ossification in *Fungi from Yuggoth and Other Poems* (Ballantine, 1973).

It is something of a relief at this late date finally to have this admirable standalone hardcover of the work; the stage is set for critics to examine in detail the merits of FFY. Lovecraft's poetry has long been the least controversial aspect of his work—nearly everyone agrees that it is bad. But now that FFY has been given the textual, critical, and aesthetic treatment it deserves, how does it stand up as poetry?

The sonnet cycle itself, after the first three poems, is a loose arrangement of unrelated sonnets modulating in mood (i.e., as a phantasmagoria). The sequence concludes with chiefly abstract items. The overall quality of the individual pieces is first-rate, and the sequence makes for an enthralling read.

It terms of aesthetic merit, the poems tend to fall into several groups. Some are effective but workmanlike: "Night-Gaunts" (XX), "Nyarlathotep" (XXI), and "Azathoth" (XXII). The bizarre quasi-Gnostic closing couplet of the latter ("I am His Messenger", the daemon said, / As in contempt he struck his Master's head.") is a highlight. Some seem to be rather mechanical program pieces, or intermediaries dutifully written up to sit among their flanking sonnets: "The Lamp" (VI), "Zaman's Hill" (VII), "The Howler" (XII), "The Dweller" (XXXI), and "St. Toad's" (XXV). There is real poetic fire and atmosphere in gems such as "Hesperia" (XIII),

"Star-Winds" (XIV), "Mirage" (XXIII), "Alienation" (XXXII), and "Evening Star" (XXXV). Many have real Lovecraftian savor, including "The Bells" (XIX), "The Well" (XI), "Antarktos" (XV), "The Familiars" (XXVI), and the eerie and distinctive "Elder Pharos" (XXVII), this latter inspired by the Industrial Trust Building in downtown Providence. The very finest go directly to the heart of Lovecraft's psyche: "Expectancy" (XXVIII), "Background" (XXX), and "Continuity" (XXXVI).

Misfires include "Recognition" (IV), "Homecoming" (V), "A Memory" (XVII), "Nostalgia" (XXIX), and a couple of others. These and certain others are marred by exclamation points, and italics, metrical infelicities, coined names, awkward rhymes, and filler words (e.g., some, that, yet). There is repetitiveness in the first words of many lines: "And" and "But." Lovecraft, despite his immense vocabulary, sometimes reaches for the most convenient monosyllabic adjective—black, dark, great, old, strange, vast, mad, and he ubiquitous "half-" modifier—to make the line. But as a whole, FFY hangs together well and is a superb artistic accomplishment in the weird, a fitting success to sit with "The Colour out of Space" (1926), "The Shadow over Innsmouth" (1930), and the rest of the classic tales.

One thing that jumps out in this edition is the centrality of Lovecraft's experience in New York City during the period 1923–1926. Schultz cites several excerpts from Lovecraft's NYC correspondence that echo in FFY. Strangely, some of the most compelling items here are *urban* horror: "Harbour Whistles" (XXXIII), "The Pigeon-Flyers" (X) and "The Courtyard" (IX), the latter based on a note in the *Commonplace Book* circa 1928: "Evil alley or enclosed court in ancient city—Union or Milligan Pl." Union Court was a rectangular space (now demolished) set diagonally in the interior of the block bounded by University Place, Broadway, 11th and 12th Streets with an outlet on University Place just south of 12th St. As with all the poems, links regarding this imaginative *topos* can be traced from the FFY through the prose —in this example, "The Shadow over Innsmouth," "He" (1925), "The Music of Erich Zann" (1923)—and ultimately to the raw material of the *Commonplace Book.*

I can imagine no one better to illustrate this work than Jason C. Eckhardt. Since his start with *H. P. Lovecraft in "The Eyrie"*

(Necronomicon Press, 1979), Eckhardt has done nearly 100 book covers, and illustrated dozens of books in varied genres. His work has appeared in publications from Dell, Arkham House, Hippocampus Press, Centipede Press, and others. Eckhardt is a five-time winner of the Best Editorial Cartoon of the Year award from the New England Press and Newspaper Association. He is also an author of both non-fiction (mostly literary criticism) and fiction, most recently "And the Sea Gave Up the Dead" (2012) in *Black Wings of Cthulhu, Volume 2* (Titan, 2012).

The main thing about Eckhardt, aside from his prodigious technical skill, is an aesthetic sensibility very much in tune with his fellow New Englander, H. P. Lovecraft. Certainly, Eckhardt is to Lovecraft as Harry Clark is to Poe. Here he adopts a subtle, nuanced approach well-matched to the work's mood. The title illustration is a charming two-page spread with an understated image of some strange flora. Tentacles and ichor are nowhere to be seen—here or elsewhere. The dust jacket illustration is somehow evocative, but not imitative of, the drawing by Clark Ashton Smith that R. H. Barlow chose for the cover of his stillborn edition of the poem.

The artist does his work in pen and ink, but his illustrations have the entrancing detail of a woodcut or etching. "Homecoming" is complemented by a simple embellished tondo of a breaking wave. "Zaman's Hill" has an evocative drawing of a New England village with steepled church overarched by a towering mountain, reminiscent of the great Joseph Mugnaini.

Eckhardt treats space in a manner that recalls Hiroshige, and resembles that Japanese ukiyo-e master in his handling of the background and middle distance of landscape; the composition is often forced by the use of some conspicuous object placed in the foreground. Depth is heightened or distorted by fixing the nearest object to the picture plan itself, and using it to frame objects represented as a considerable distance away. At times, perspective seems to be almost isometric: objects do not appear larger or smaller as they extend closer to or farther away from the viewer, and depth and altitude are ambiguous and somehow uncanny.

"The Port," for example, depicts an ocean horizon with a village foreshortened in the foreground. The surfaces are again enlivened and unified by broken pen work, with strokes and stippling that do not obscure the forms, but rather emphasize their shapes and contours. "Hesperia" features a row of sphinxes like those connecting the temples of Karnak and Luxor, leading to a distant palace worthy of Sidney Sime. In the illustration for "The Familiars," a farmer in the center is framed by what might be alien limbs. He is facing away but has turned his head directly to the viewer, evoking a powerful sense of menace. "Antarktos" shows merely a Cyclopean rock cornice above an ice sheet, with a setting sun in the background. It is chilling in every way. "Background" has a human figure in the center of an abstract cosmic radiance, á la Finlay. For "Continuity" the artist simply renders the cornice of a New England dwelling, foregrounding an enigmatic mountain and sky.

Turning from the many merits of this edition, I conclude with the two most important points about FFY relative to H. P. Lovecraft as an artist: it shows that 1) he made a mindful choice regarding his approach to the weird and 2) he had both the sense and the skill to alter an approach that did not work.

Lovecraft had control over the manner in which he wrote. That is, he consciously chose to write in what we now call the Lovecraftian style, because it best achieved his goal of atmosphere. To say that Lovecraft did not have the skill to write concise, "normal" prose is like saying Picasso had problems modelling the human figure.

Two examples of Lovecraft the poet, before and after. First example:

"A Garden" (1917):

As I walk, and wait, and listen, I will often seek to find
When it was I knew that garden in an age long left behind;
I will oft conjure a vision of a day that is no more,
As I gaze upon the grey, grey scenes I feel I knew before.
Then a sadness settles o'er me, and a tremor seems to start:
For I know the flow'rs are shrivell'd hopes—the garden is
    my heart!

"The Gardens of Yin" (XVIII):

All would be there, for had not old dreams flung
Open the gate to that stone-lanterned maze

Where drowsy streams spin out their winding ways,
Trailed by green vines from bending branches hung?
I hurried—but when the wall rose, grim and great,
I found there was no longer any gate.

Second example:

"Astrophobos" (1917):

Crimson burn'd the star of sadness
As behind the beams I peer'd;
All was woe that seem'd but gladness
Ere my gaze with truth was sear'd;
 Cacodaemons, mir'd with madness,
Thro' the fever'd flick'ring leer'd.

"Evening Star" (XXXV):

It shone through all the sunset's glories—thin
At first, but with a slowly-brightening face.
Night came, and that lone beacon, amber-hued,
Beat on my sight as never it did of old;
The evening star—but grown a thousandfold
More haunting in this hush and solitude.

Lovecraft initially was one type of poet, decided that his practice wasn't working, and thus became another type of poet.

In the introduction to *H. P. Lovecraft: Art, Artifact, and Reality*, I wrote that "a dwindling number of uninformed Internet pundits still parrot the received wisdom that Lovecraft was not a good writer." Three years later, from website book reviewers to semi-literate or ill-informed bloggers, it's clear that the majority of people simply don't "get" Lovecraft. So let me repeat: Lovecraft was fully aware of, and fully in control of, what he did. A large component of what he did is theatrical and ludic. He could have done it a different way if he wished. FFY demonstrates this: as an artist Lovecraft had both the awareness and the proficiency to completely discard one approach for another that was more successful. He did so in FFY, and he pulled it off brilliantly.

CHARLOTTE MONTAGUE. *H. P. Lovecraft: The Mysterious Man Behind the Darkness.* New York: Chartwell Books, 2015. 192 pp. Hardcover; "bargain priced" $9.98. Reviewed by Darrell Schweitzer.

It's probably a sign of H. P. Lovecraft's continued posthumous triumph that, after my co-anthologist John Ashmead and I finished taping a television interview about Lovecraft and popular culture for a local PBS station, I wandered into Philadelphia's main Barnes & Noble and found *yet another* new book about Old Gent.

Given the "bargain priced" label and no other price printed on the jacket, it's obvious this one is intended for the "instant remainder" trade. At first glance it might look like a superficial rehash, with lots of pictures, sections, and sidebars arranged like snippets in *People* magazine—Lovecraft for readers with limited attention spans.

But a closer reading makes one more sympathetic. Actually this book is pretty good. It is indeed arranged into quickie bits of a few hundred words each, so it can be easily skimmed, particularly if you skip the synoptic sidebars for each of the major stories. The author's skill is as much in the selection of what she chooses to emphasize as in her actual writing. For the beginner, this will provide an adequate introduction, something to provide an outline of Lovecraft's life and work before tackling Joshi's *I Am Providence*, which is definitely *not* designed to be skimmed through quickly. For the experienced Lovecraftian, the interest may be more in reading *through* the text to see how much Ms. Montague actually knows, what she gets right, and what she doesn't. For all her "Further Reading" list at the end is very scanty, it is reassuring that she knows Joshi's work and the importance of Joshi-edited texts. She also cites Michael Houellebecq. Allusions in the course of the book make it clear she is familiar with much else, from Migliore and Strysik's *The Lurker in the Lobby* to the writings of Robert M. Price. There isn't a whole lot here the long-time Lovecraft reader doesn't already know, although I will admit I don't think I have ever seen a photo of a fat Lovecraft before, and there is one, on page 91, taken in 1924, showing the usually gaunt Lovecraft looking very contented and perhaps about to explode from Sonia's good cooking.

Given that the main research on Lovecraft's life has been done by Joshi, it will be impossible to supplant *I Am Providence* for quite some time. What is left for subsequent biographers is, indeed, what we see here: condensations, and perhaps shifts in emphasis or interpretation. It is inevitable that new writers are going to depart from the perspective of what we might now call the classical generation of Lovecraft scholarship (Joshi/Mosig/Price/Cannon, etc.). Probably influenced by Houellebecq and China Miéville, Ms. Montague puts a bit more emphasis on Lovecraft's racism as an underlying theme in the overall oeuvre, and this leads her to even more questionable conclusions, e.g., that "his views did not mellow with age," when of course they did. We know that Lovecraft's racism was never "cured," but certainly his later letters show him taking the view that such matters are less important.

In any case, it is to Montague's credit that she does not dismiss Lovecraft as either a writer or a (flawed) human being on this basis. (Of course if she did, she wouldn't have a book to write. A volume like this, for the instant-remainder market, is surely aimed at Lovecraft's fans, not people who want to be told why they *shouldn't* be reading him.) She is in more dubious territory when she repeats the claim that Lovecraft had Asperger's Syndrome, an idea I first encountered in Paul Roland's simply awful *The Curious Case of H. P. Lovecraft* (2014). This may be gaining some traction and have to be refuted definitively by someone more expert than myself. My immediate objection is simply this: If Lovecraft had Asperger's in his youth, why did it apparently go away later in his life? His various anxieties, breakdowns, and health problems can be explained by other means. Occam's Razor suggests we leave Asperger's out unless there is some positive evidence.

There is only one case where Montague is seriously wrong about something. Never mind the small stuff, e.g., that the *Weird Tales* cover on page 55 does not actually illustrate a Lovecraft story, or that Ubbo-Sathla is more properly an entity, not a "race." But on page 34 she unequivocally tells us that: "In 1918, Lovecraft sold a story for the first time when *The National Magazine* purchased 'The Marshes of Ipswich.'"

I found myself at a loss over that one. Of course, even the beginning Lovecraft reader knows there is no such *story*. Furthermore, the title itself cannot be found in the Joshi bibliography.

But if we press on a little further, the mystery begins to unravel. In the de Camp *Lovecraft: A Biography* we are told that it's a poem and this was "the first money he is known to have earned in his life." If we then search the index of *I Am Providence* for the *National Magazine* we learn that several of Lovecraft's poems were reprinted in this journal, a professional publication (which presumably paid), although they were all reprints from amateur magazines. Now, back to *H. P. Lovecraft: An Annotated Bibliography*. An index search there reveals a total of *seven* poems published in the *National Magazine*, one of which was "On Receiving a Picture of the Marshes at Ipswich," in the January 1917 issue. This was not the first "sale," since it was preceded by "Brotherhood" in the December 1916 issue. De Camp had the title wrong. The correct title refers to "The Marshes *at* Ipswich," not "of." Joshi tells me that in the *National Magazine* the title was indeed shortened to "The Marshes at Ipswich." The poem in question is on page 275 of *The Ancient Track*, with the longer title. One small mystery remains: the bibliography tells us that that it was published in the *National Magazine* for January 1917 and in something (presumably an amateur publication) called *Merry Minutes* for March 1917. If this is correct, and there is no prior amateur publication missing, does this mean that Lovecraft was sending poems to the *National Magazine* at the same time he was sending them to amateur editors, and by some mishap *Merry Minutes* was delayed and this particular publication wasn't a reprint after all?

Much more interesting than such a bibliographic quibble is the observation (likely true, repeated from several sources) that this was the first money Lovecraft earned in his life, not counting such pennies or nickels he may have gotten from indulgent relatives for the "publications" of his childhood. *This* tells us something about the man and his psychology. He was hopelessly spoiled as a child, indulged in a kind of post-adolescent "invalidism" until his mother died, and so reached his later twenties without acquiring many basic adult social skills. Montague later writes, regarding Lovecraft's failed marriage, "One has to question whether Lovecraft was actually mature enough to enjoy a proper loving relationship with a woman, a situation probably arising from his upbringing." She may be on to something there. Lovecraft married Sonia on the rebound from the death of his mother. Was he looking for a strong woman to protect and control him the way his mother had? We note that even when he was with Sonia in New York, sometimes for the first time in a long while after she had been away on business trips, he spent more time out with "the boys" than he did with his wife. Was the reason that he accepted the collapse of his marriage with so little resistance was that he was looking for an excuse to go back to being a pampered post-adolescent? If he couldn't find a substitute for his mother, he learned to make do with his aunts. Maybe it's because Montague is the first female biographer of Lovecraft; she does seem to write insightfully about his marriage.

Sometimes her scrapbook-like abridgments do get her into trouble, though. On page 105, she tells of Lovecraft at the end of his New York exile, ". . . how he had been 'screaming in a sheer desperation and pounding the walls and floor.'" This could lead to new myths about a half-mad Lovecraft disturbing the neighbors. In truth it is a misquotation due to lack of context. In *Letters from New York* we find the surrounding text, as Lovecraft is explaining his need to cling to the furniture, pictures, etc. that he has retained from his old family home: "When they go, I shall go, for they are what make it possible for me to open my eyes in the morning or look forward to another day of consciousness without screaming in sheer desperate & pounding the walls & floor in a frenzied clamour to be waked up out of the nightmare of 'reality' & my own room in Providence." This may be the rhetoric of desperation, but he wasn't actually pounding on the walls.

Likewise on page 44, the famous "Dunsany is myself" comment is made to seem a bit pompous and silly, when, as Lovecraft readers know, it was not. It wasn't that Lovecraft claimed to be an elegant Anglo-Irish aristocrat and literary genius. In the letter to Frank Belknap Long of June 3, 1923, he rapidly adds, "plus an art and cultivation infinitely greater." The full context makes it clear that he saw Dunsany as an ideal of what he might have aspired to be, but far superior to what he actually was.

Overall, this is a sound short biography. It will not lead the beginner seriously astray. There is even a brief but accurate description of how, subsequent to Lovecraft's death, August Derleth seriously distorted Lovecraft's mythos and critical perception of his thought. There isn't a lot of philosophy here, but Montague makes it clear that Lovecraft was a scientific materialist, influenced by Nietzsche and Ernst Haeckel. She doesn't go completely crazy the way Paul Roland did, suggesting that Lovecraft was or should have been an occultist. If she has her own philosophical biases, I haven't spotted them. Certainly she has not tried to impose them on Lovecraft. There is also some discussion of Lovecraft's subsequent influence, as much as can be accomplished in this format, in a few pages with much space taken up by movie stills and posters.

We can even be grateful for a page of Haeckel's color illustrations of sea creatures, which really might have inspired some of Lovecraft's monsters. This is a handsome volume overall, though with the curious limitation that we never see any of the covers of early *Weird Tales*, the Baird issues that were so important to Lovecraft's early career. Yes, original copies of these cost hundreds or even thousands of dollars, so conceivably neither Ms. Montague nor whoever designed the book had copies, but this also tells us they were unaware of the Girasol facsimile reprints, which are very good and not particularly expensive. Given that this is to some extent a picture book, it would have been useful, for example, to show the reader what the "Imprisoned with the Pharaohs" issue looked like.

VICTOR LAVALLE. *The Ballad of Black Tom*. New York: Tor, 2016. 149 pp. $12.95 tpb. Reviewed by S. T. Joshi.

I think it is safe to say that "The Horror at Red Hook" is close to the nadir of Lovecraft's fictional output. This is not merely, or chiefly, because of its openly racist substructure; "The Shadow over Innsmouth" is also founded, at least indirectly on racist presuppositions (the evils of miscegenation), and yet it remains a towering masterpiece of regional decay and cosmic horror. The weakness of "Red Hook" lies in the disappointing unimaginativeness of its horrific scenario—conventional Satanism, with many details taken directly from the *Encyclopaedia Britannica*—and an uncharacteristic confusion as to what actually happens in the story. Its poor prose style doesn't help. I recall pleading with the Library of America to omit this story from its edition of Lovecraft's

Tales (2005)—I couldn't imagine why Peter Straub had chosen it. I told the Library of America editors that, if anything, "Cool Air" was a better example of Lovecraft's "New York stories." The end result was that the volume included both "The Horror at Red Hook" and "Cool Air."

Given the shoddiness of "The Horror at Red Hook," it would not seem difficult for a contemporary writer to refashion the tale in a superior manner. And yet, I am not convinced that Victor LaValle—a young African American writer who has previously written three novels and a short story collection—has done the job in *The Ballad of Black Tom*. This little book is scarcely a novella; by my estimate, its total wordage is about equivalent to that of *At the Mountains of Madness*. And although LaValle has poignantly dedicated the book to "H. P. Lovecraft, with all my conflicted feelings," I find myself regretting the missed opportunity to make something new and vital out of inferior subject-matter.

We are here introduced to Charles Thomas Tester (who generally calls himself Tommy), a twenty-year-old African American living in Harlem. Gradually we learn that the tale takes place in 1924, a year before "The Horror at Red Hook" was written. (Curiously, the exact date of the events in Lovecraft's story is not specified.) Tommy is struggling to make a living as a singer and guitar player when he meets Robert Suydam at the Dutch Reformed Church in Brooklyn. Suydam invites Tommy to play and sing at a party scheduled at his house a few days hence, offering him the fabulous sum of $500 for the gig. The attendees of the party will be suitably heterogeneous, as Suydam explains: "And the guests will be men like you. Negroes from Harlem, Syrians and Spaniards from Red Hook, Chinese and Italians from Five Points, all of them will be here at my invitation."

Not long thereafter, Tommy has an unpleasant encounter with police detective Thomas F. Malone and a private detective (later named Ervin Howard), who, as Suydam explains, are "collecting proof of my mental inferiority." But Suydam himself has bigger fish to fry than merely dealing with hostile relations; he maintains that his ultimate purpose in pursuing his occult researches is nothing less than to establish contact with "a King who sleeps at the bottom of the ocean."

It is not surprising that LaValle draws upon the Cthulhu Mythos in refashioning "The Horror at Red Hook," since the original story's confusing and hackneyed use of standard occultism is imaginatively stultifying. Whether LaValle knows that, less than two weeks after writing "The Horror at Red Hook" on August 1–2, 1925, Lovecraft devised a detailed plot synopsis for "The Call of Cthulhu" is unclear. At any rate, LaValle exercises admirable restraint in not explicitly mentioning Cthulhu until the very end—although it is unlikely that any well-versed reader will have failed to guess who the "Sleeping King" repeatedly cited in the text could be.

The figure of Ervin Howard is of some little interest. He is perhaps a fusion of Robert E. Howard and Lovecraft himself, uttering conventional racist sentiments that are apparently meant to be representative of the period. More dramatically, at one point he and Malone burst into the apartment of Tommy's father, Otis, and Howard shoots him repeatedly in the mistaken belief that Otis was pointing a gun at him; in fact, it was only a guitar. I imagine we are to see this killing both as symbolic of the evil of Lovecraft's racism and as a nod to the distressing number of black men killed by white police officers in our own day. Howard blandly states: "I felt in danger for my life. . . . I emptied my revolver. Then I reloaded and did it again."

The second half of the novella is narrated from Malone's point of view. He becomes alarmed when he hears that Suydam has purchased a block of three tenements at Parker Place in Red Hook and transferred his entire collection of occult books there. He also learns that Suydam's second-in-command is someone named Black Tom—who can be none other than Tommy Tester. Malone rounds up a large police force to raid the tenements. They bring heavy weaponry and begin firing seemingly indiscriminately at the buildings, while Malone has a tense encounter with Tommy and Suydam in the basement. The upshot is that, to Malone's horror, Tommy has sided not only with Suydam (who, in fact, he casually kills by slitting his throat) but with Cthulhu himself: "I'll take Cthulhu over you devils any day." The novella ends with Tommy looking forward to the time, whenever that will be, when Cthulhu will have cleared off humanity from the planet.

On the whole, *The Ballad of Black Tom* seems routine and mechanical. It seems as if LaValle is merely going through the motions—the motions of adapting a Lovecraftian theme, of revisioning Lovecraft's racism through his own perspective as a person of colour, and of expressing Lovecraft's signature theme of cosmicism. None of the characters are well developed, and several (like Ervin Howard) are mere caricatures. The work should have been expanded into a full-length novel. As it is, it gives the impression of hasty and not very engaged composition. There is abundant room for a re-imagining of Lovecraftian motifs from the point of view LaValle has adopted, but he hasn't come through on the task. *The Ballad of Black Tom* is, in its way, scarcely less conventional than the story it seeks to supplant.

Index to *The Lovecraft Annual* 1–10

A. Authors

Abolafia, Michael J.
   Review of *H. P. Lovecraft's Dark Arcadia* by Gavin Callaghan 8:215–21

Adams, Jonathan
   Following "The Ancient Track" 4:31–45

Andersson, Martin
   Of Regner Lodbrog, Hugh Blair, and Mistranslations 6:36–42
   Review of *O Fortunate Floridian: H. P. Lovecraft's Letters to R. H. Barlow* 2:203–8
   Review of *A Means to Freedom: The Letters of H. P. Lovecraft and Robert E. Howard* 4:202–5

Barlow, R. H.
   The Night Ocean 8:60–110

Beherec, Marc A.
   H. P. Lovecraft and the Archaeology of "Roman" Arizona 2:192–

202

B. Books Reviewed

C. Selected Subjects Discussed

i. Works by H. P. Lovecraft

ii. Other Subjects

www.ingramcontent.com/pod-product-compliance
Lightning Source LLC
Chambersburg PA
CBHW051820090426
42736CB00011B/1574